IMAGES
of America

AFRICAN AMERICANS IN BOYLE COUNTY

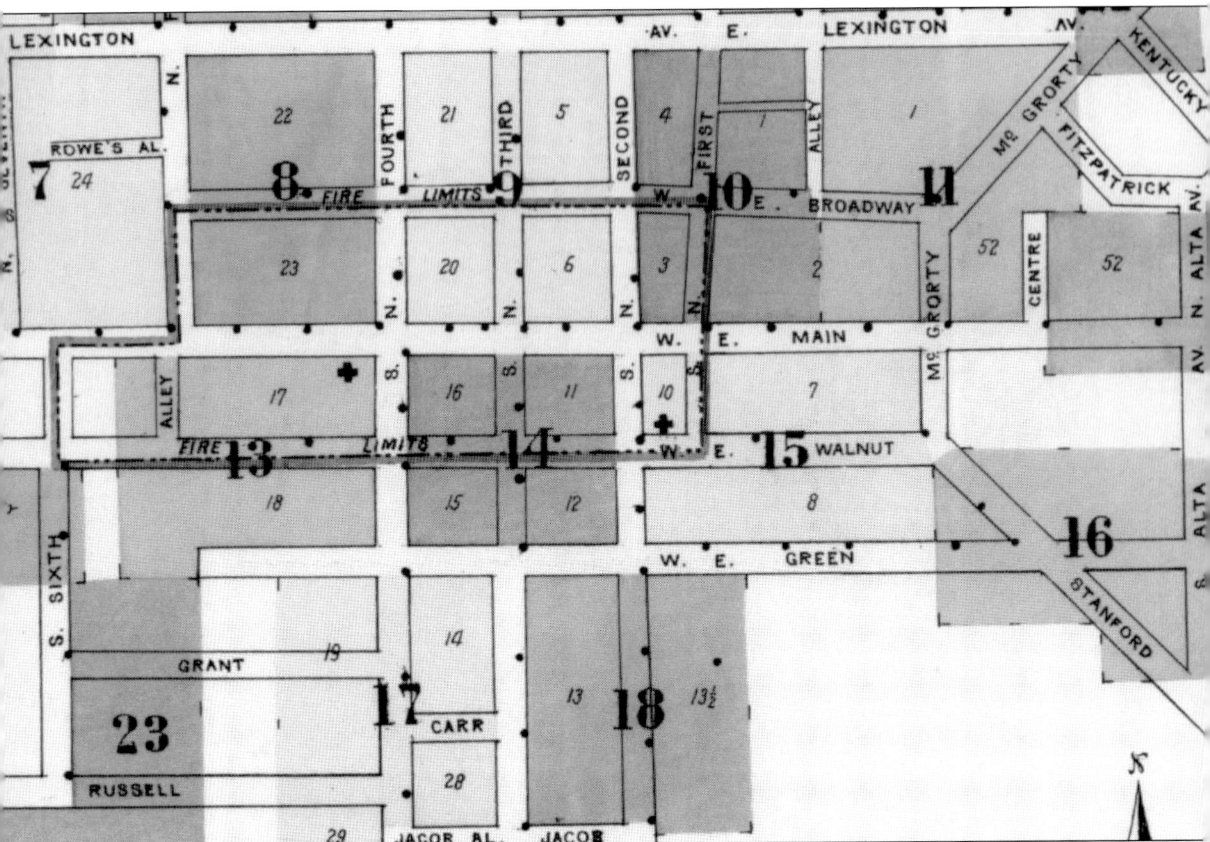

This clip from the Sanborn Fire Insurance Map, 1914, is centered on Main and Second Streets. The area between blocks 14 and 15 was the main African American business district. (Courtesy of the Library of Congress.)

ON THE COVER: Drivers for the Elite Cab Company pose in front of the Doric Lodge and Singleton's Market, first floor. The two-story Elite Pool Room (formerly Green Pastures Restaurant) and Elite Cab Company, in more prosperous days, were owned by Leon and Orestes "Tiny" Richardson. The drivers include, from left to right, George Lee Harlan, William "Buster" Letcher, Calvin Bedinger, and David Robinson. (Courtesy of the Danville Boyle County African American Historical Society.)

IMAGES
of America

AFRICAN AMERICANS IN BOYLE COUNTY

Michael Thomas Hughes and Michael J. Denis
for the Danville Boyle County
African American Historical Society, Inc.

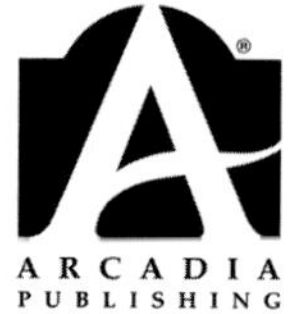

ISBN 978-1-4671-0868-3

Published by Arcadia Publishing
Charleston, South Carolina

Printed in the United States of America

Library of Congress Control Number: 2022934957

For all general information, please contact Arcadia Publishing:
Telephone 843-853-2070
Fax 843-853-0044
E-mail sales@arcadiapublishing.com
For customer service and orders:
Toll-Free 1-888-313-2665

Visit us on the Internet at www.arcadiapublishing.com

This book is dedicated to the African American community of Boyle County, Kentucky, which has lost so much of its history, to see that no more is lost.

Contents

ACKNOWLEDGMENTS

Michael Thomas Hughes has had a fascination with the Black history of Danville and Boyle County, Kentucky, for many years. His first recollections from nearly 70 years ago were of growing up in the African American settlements of Meauxtown, Clifton, and Wilsonville. Several years back, he produced a YouTube video about the history of South Second Street in Danville, the main Black business district in the county.

In 2013, a number of local people joined him to form the Danville Boyle County African American Historical Society (DBCAAHS). Although it seems that Hughes has done everything, he will be the first to admit that he is the lightning rod, attracting Black history in the form of photographs and artifacts, interviews, and news clippings.

Donations coming from all segments of the community have helped the DBCAAHS become an award-winning organization. While Hughes could not have done all this by himself, without him, it is likely it would not have happened at all.

Thanks to those who donated photographs and artifacts, researched the history and genealogies of families, volunteered time to rehabilitate the center's space, donated building materials, the curtain and rod, and furniture, provided us with everything we needed to "OPEN," including a sidewalk sign, and consented to be interviewed by Centre College students.

The Henson family—Eben, Robby, and Heather—has worked with our physical space, and supported us in every endeavor we have started, even producing a play focusing on life on South Second Street, *Good Blues Tonight*, at Pioneer Playhouse.

Thanks to the Boyle County Public Library (BCPL), we have used many photographs in the Charles A. Thomas Collection. The Jacobs Hall Museum at the Kentucky School for the Deaf also contributed photographs.

All images not otherwise credited are either part of the DBCAAHS collection or the society has received permission to use them.

Introduction

Danville, the largest city in and county seat of Boyle County, Kentucky, was incorporated in 1787. It is not the oldest city in Kentucky, but it is arguably the most historic. It was here that 10 constitutional conventions were held, which resulted in Kentucky's becoming a state in 1792. The area that became Boyle County in 1842 also contained the site of the first courthouse in Kentucky (1785), the first US Post Office west of the Alleghenies (1792), the first capital of Kentucky (1785), the first college in the West (1783), the first law school in the West (1799), and the first state-supported school for the deaf (1823). In 1809, Danville's Dr. Ephraim McDowell became the first physician in the world to successfully remove an ovarian tumor from Jane Todd Crawford.

Boyle County also includes the separate cities of Perryville and Junction City (including the former city of Shelby City) and the unincorporated communities of (generally from west to east) Aliceton, Brumfield, Mitchellsburg, Atoka, Wilsonville, Faulconer Station, Persimmon Knob, Worldstown, Clifton, Needmore, Well's Landing, and Stony Point.

Along with white settlers from Virginia, Pennsylvania, Maryland, and other states along the Atlantic coast, Blacks came here, brought by their enslavers. However, by the Civil War, Boyle County had more free Blacks than any other county in Kentucky except for Jefferson (Louisville) and Fayette (Lexington).

Danville was the site of the first Black school in Boyle County, on East Walnut Street, taught by Willis Russell, a teacher listed in the 1840 and 1850 censuses. The first kindergarten for Blacks was established by the City Federation of Women's Clubs. In 1881, John W. Bate established Danville's first public school for Blacks, previous Black schools being freedmen's or church schools.

Outside Danville, Black schools were opened in most communities, and at one time there were more Black children in school in the county than white, though the percentage of Blacks never exceeded 25 percent of the county's population. By the early 20th century, Danville could boast one of the best "colored" schools in Kentucky, the Bate School.

After the Civil War and Emancipation, many formerly enslaved people settled down in various parts of the county, some where they had been enslaved, but others moving away. Several former slaves managed to purchase large quantities of land, which they then sold to other former slaves. Dennis Doram, for example, actually purchased slaves for the purpose of freeing them. He sold land in and around Danville and Clifton to many former slaves. Charlie Wilson used the money he earned as a member of the US Colored Infantry to purchase many tracts of land in what became "Wilsonville," which he then sold to other Black families.

Black communities were of two types. Some were integrated very early, Danville, Shelby City, Aliceton, Mitchellsburg, and Zion Hill for example. Others were settled after emancipation, and for many years were nearly totally African American, namely Clifton, Needmore, Meauxtown, and Sleettown. Over time, most of the outlying communities lost population. As part of the "Great Migration," many men moved north to Chicago, Indianapolis, Detroit, and Cincinnati, among others. The outlying communities were not immune from this migration, though in many cases, the migration was from Clifton and Aliceton to Danville, rather than movement further north. Beginning about 1900, South Second Street became the Black business district for not only Danville, but the entire county. There were some businesses outside Danville, but most of those died out, and Danville grew. The heyday of businesses on South Second Street was between about 1945 and 1960, then a gradual decline began.

As integration allowed blacks to shop anywhere in town, the Black-owned businesses began to suffer economically, and "blight" worsened. As Blacks did not have good-paying jobs, even homes began to deteriorate. Those who did not leave for better jobs were stuck in a downward spiral.

Urban renewal promised blacks that their properties would be "renewed" and repaired, and in general, improved, for the benefit of the entire community. The reality was quite different. Homes on Seventh Street were the first to go. They were torn down, and families living there were given money to buy houses elsewhere. A community and its social links had been destroyed, and a pattern of destruction of Black communities was begun.

Then came South First and South Second streets. Historic Black-owned buildings, such as the Doric Lodge, and the United Brothers of Friendship Hall fell to the wrecking ball and nearly the entire block between South First Street and South Second Street between West Main Street and West Walnut Street became Constitution Square.

After South Second Street was destroyed, urban renewal moved on to West Danville and the Oak Street area, where dozens of homes were destroyed, and replaced by small businesses. Numerous lawsuits resulted, but as few of those were successful, little changed. Many white owners prospered while Black owners lost everything.

Much of the area's African American history is gone, and will never be recovered. But through the efforts of volunteers who want to save what is left, the Danville Boyle County African American Historical Society was organized in December 2013. The DBCAAHS has sponsored several events, including the Soul of Second Street festivals and history conferences, and in 2020, at the height of the COVID pandemic, actually opened a museum/office called the History Center. Members of the DBCAAHS have worked with the Henson family at Pioneer Playhouse to produce a play, *Good Blues Tonight*, which broke all attendance records at the playhouse.

The Central Kentucky African American Cemetery Association (CKAACA) was formed about the same time, with the goal of locating, researching, preserving, and renovating African American cemeteries. The CKAACA has restored the 2.5-acre Shelby City African American Cemetery and the historic half-acre Meadow Lane African American Cemetery and has updated and corrected records for nearly 4,000 burials in Boyle County's largest Black cemetery, Hilldale.

The DBCAAHS and its history center, are preserving what Black history is left, and giving future generations an insight into what was. At the end of *Good Blues Tonight*, the cast calls out as a reminder to the future: "We Were Here!"

One

CHURCHES

For a number of reasons, religion has been, and continues to be, integral to the daily lives of African Americans. For enslaved people, religion was often a way to cope with daily life and death. It also was one way for white owners to control their enslaved people.

At one time, every African American community in Boyle County had its own church, sometimes more than one. A probably incomplete list for Boyle County included Mitchellsburg African American Episcopal Church, Perryville AME Church, First Baptist Church Perryville, Wilson Chapel AME, Needmore Baptist Church, Atoka Baptist Church, Clifton Baptist Church, Mount Zion (Zion Hill) Baptist Church, Stony Point Predestinarian Baptist Church, Junction City Baptist Church, Saint John AME Church in Shelby City, and of course, Danville, which today has several predominantly Black churches, including St. James AME, First Baptist, Second Street Christian Church, Bethel Baptist Church, Vision Church of Holiness, and Christ the Head Missionary Church.

Only the Baptist churches in Perryville, Stony Point, and Clifton, as well as those in Danville, are still active, as people migrated out of the outlying communities to Danville or even Lexington, Cincinnati, and other cities in the north. Even so, Stony Point and Clifton are down to a handful of members, most of whom are elderly.

In both the Methodist and Baptist Churches, African American members were among the early adherents. By the Civil War, however, the churches separated along racial lines, and the current First Baptist Church, the "colored" Methodist Episcopal Church, and St. James African Methodist Church were organized. Interestingly, when First Baptist was organized under that name, the white First Baptist Church insisted that the Black church change its name, but the Black church refused, noting that it was founded originally at the same time as the white church. Thus, Danville today has two "First Baptist" churches.

Other denominations developed rapidly, and tracing their history is confusing due to name changes and splits in membership.

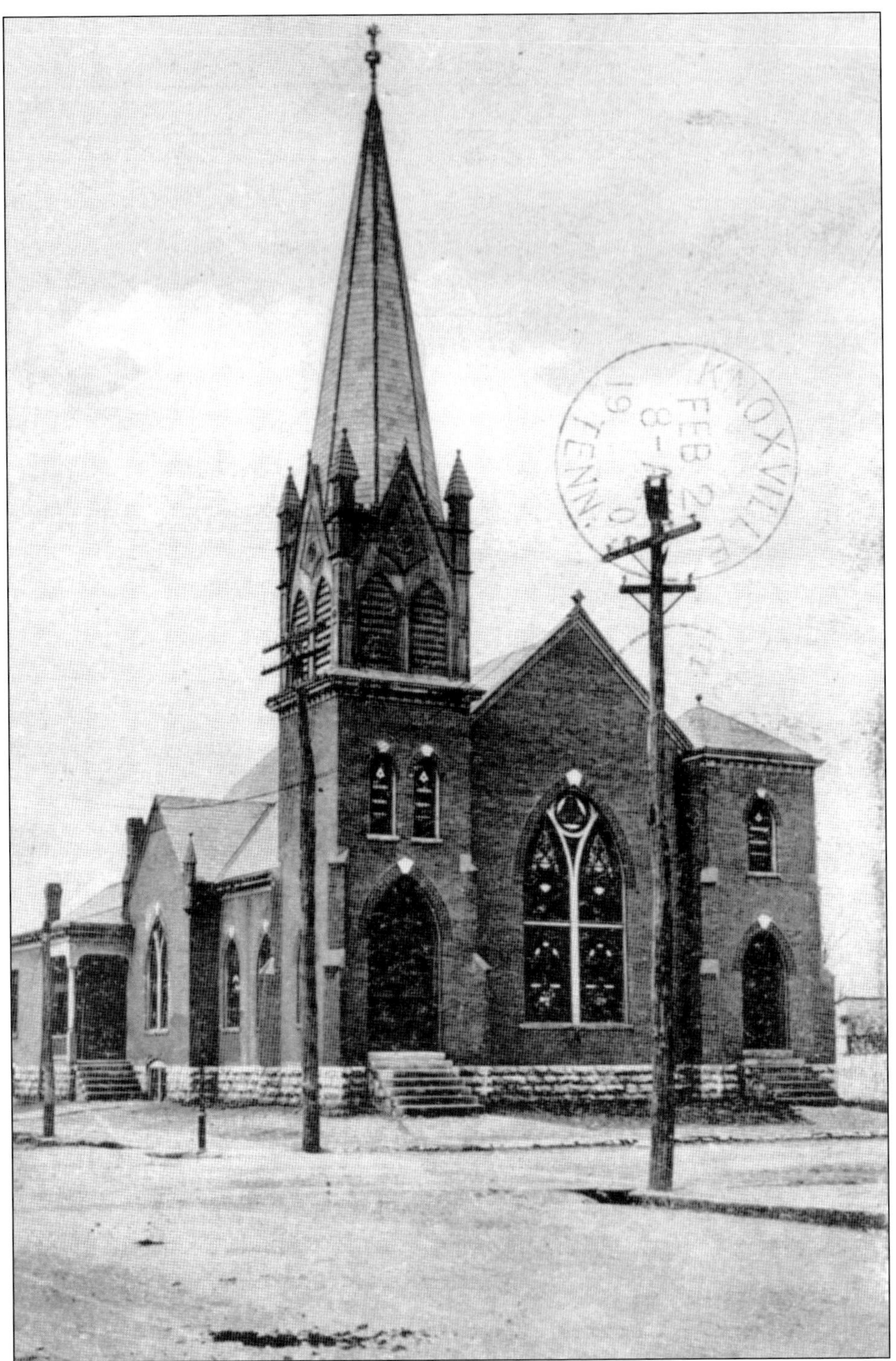

The First Baptist Church, about 1909, was one of the largest Black churches in Kentucky. By 1846, Blacks in the First Baptist Church formed their own church. The church was under the direction of Rev. J.E. Wood from 1898. Rev. Wood oversaw the erection of a new building and the expansion of the church to include over 900 members. (Sharon Stratton.)

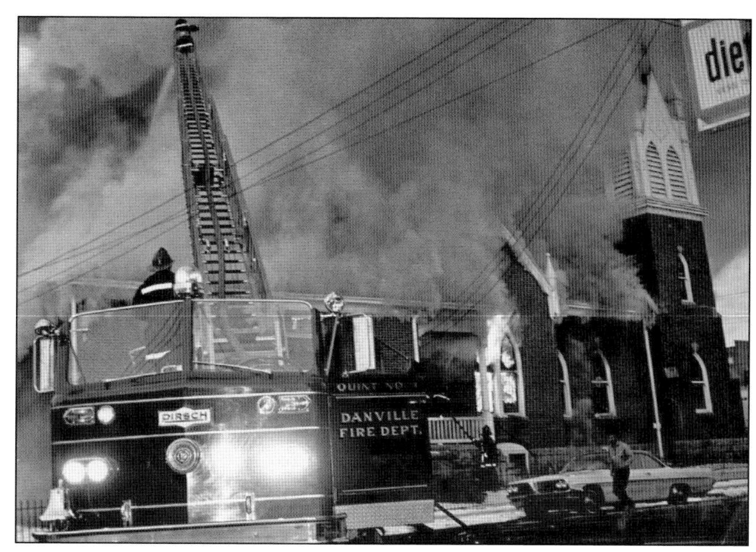

The First Baptist Church burned on December 26, 1966, causing between $300,000 and $400,000 in damages. Fire department reports said the church had been burning and smoldering for some time before the fire was discovered. But by July 1967, plans were underway to rebuild in the same location at an estimated cost of $146,000. (Charles A. Thomas Collection, BCPL.)

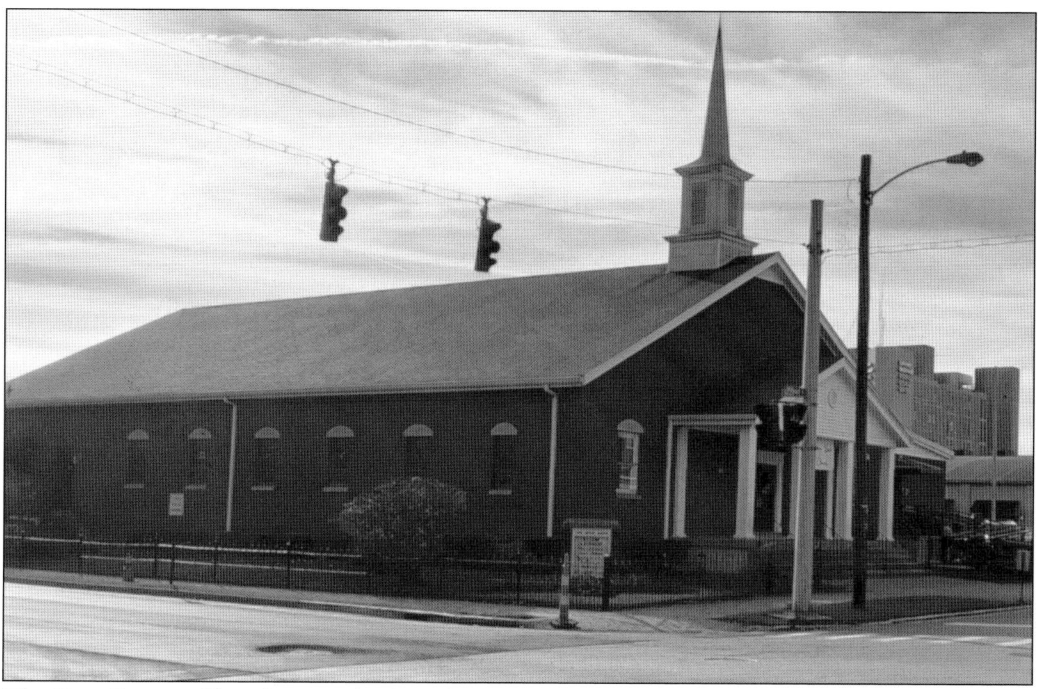

The First Baptist Church was rebuilt and opened for worship on December 24, 1967. The new church had a seating capacity of 450, significantly greater than the church that burned. The 20-year mortgage on the new building was paid off in half the time and was burned on May 22, 1977, with long-time pastor Rev. P.A. Carter being honored by burning the first piece of the mortgage. (Michael Denis.)

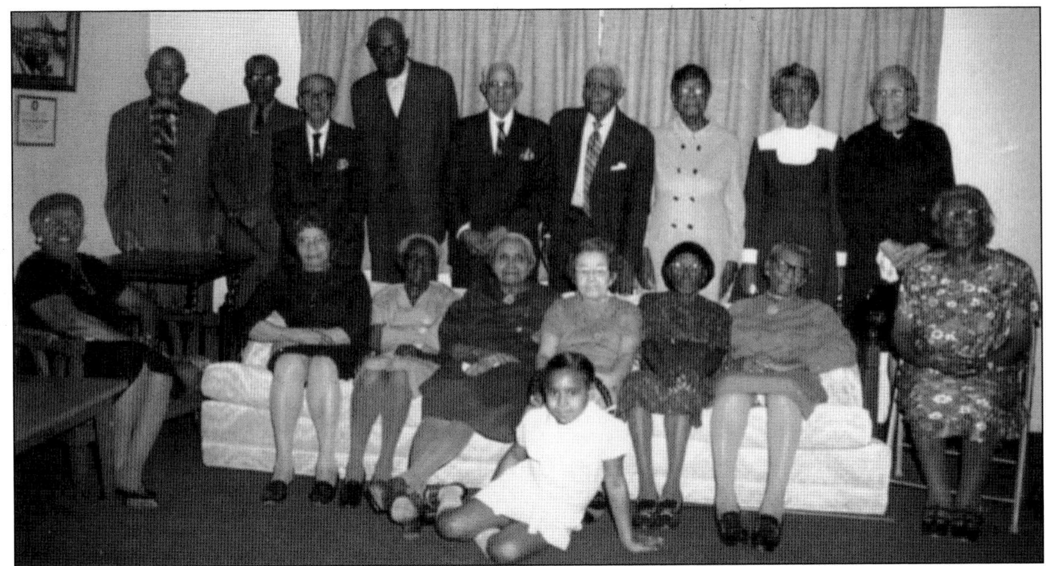

A few members of the First Baptist Church gathered together are Susie Ewing, Levi Tarrance, Cindy Tarrance (the girl sitting in front), Maggie Kinley, and Delia Bell McRoberts. Others are not identified at this time. The Black churches in Danville and Boyle County were often the only social outlets people had.

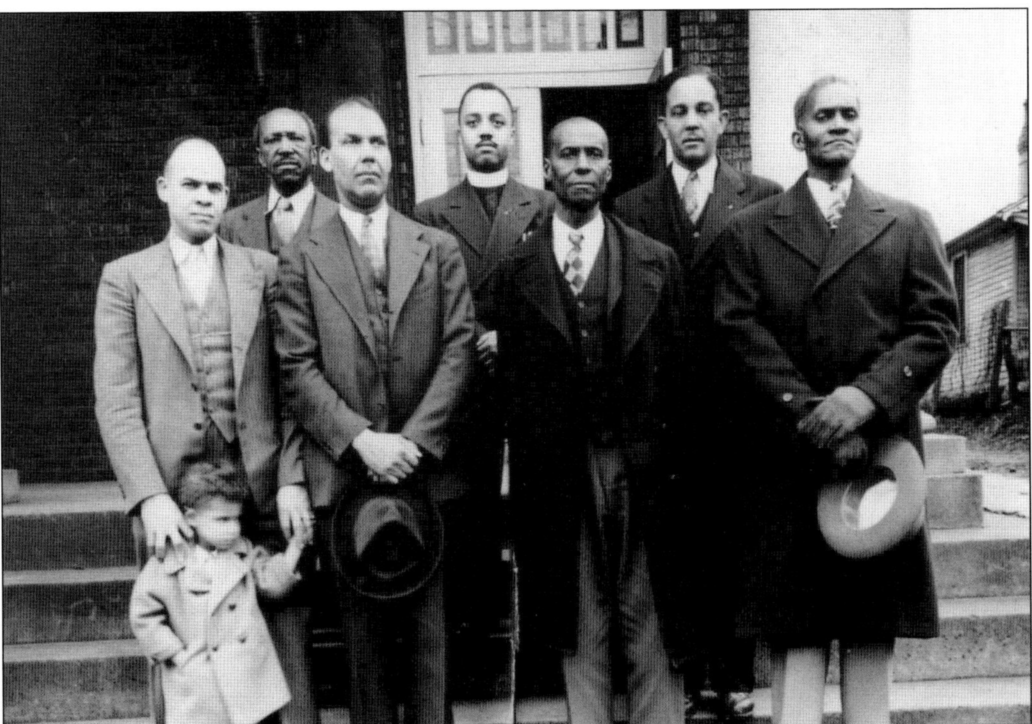

Rev. E.P. Williams, who served from 1945 to 1948, and some church members stand in front of St. James African Methodist Episcopal Church in the late 1940s. On the left is Thomas Revely Junior (1904–1964), and the little boy in front of him is Thomas Revely III (born in 1943). On the right may be blacksmith Rainey Bridgewater. The others are unidentified.

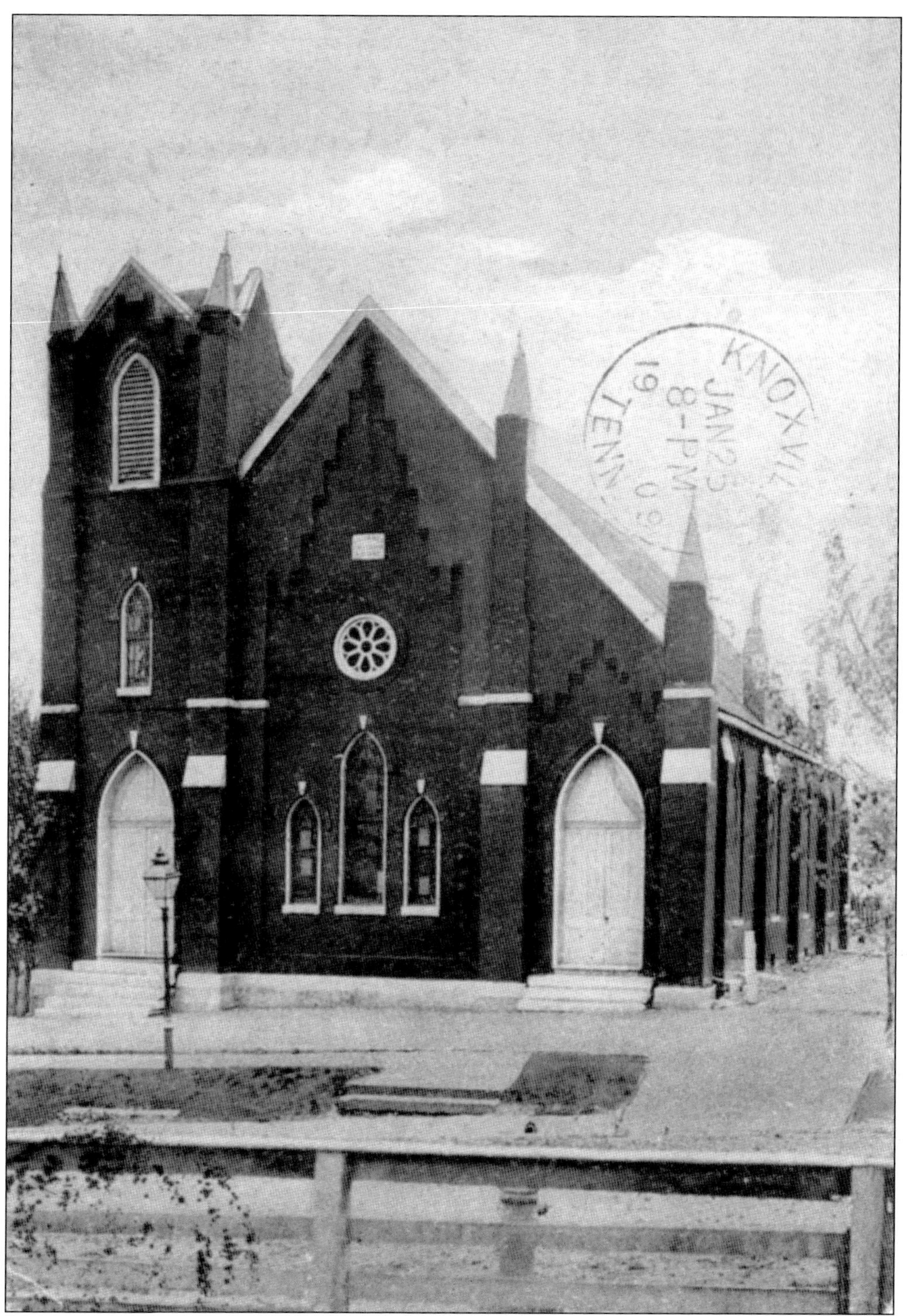

St. James African Methodist Episcopal Church is seen here as it appeared about 1909. Formed as an offshoot of the "Colored Methodist Episcopal Church," this congregation was organized by 1867. St. James AME Church dates from 1867 to 1868, but the Gothic Revival building pictured was constructed in 1882, during the pastorate of Rev. James M. Turner. (Sharon Stratton.)

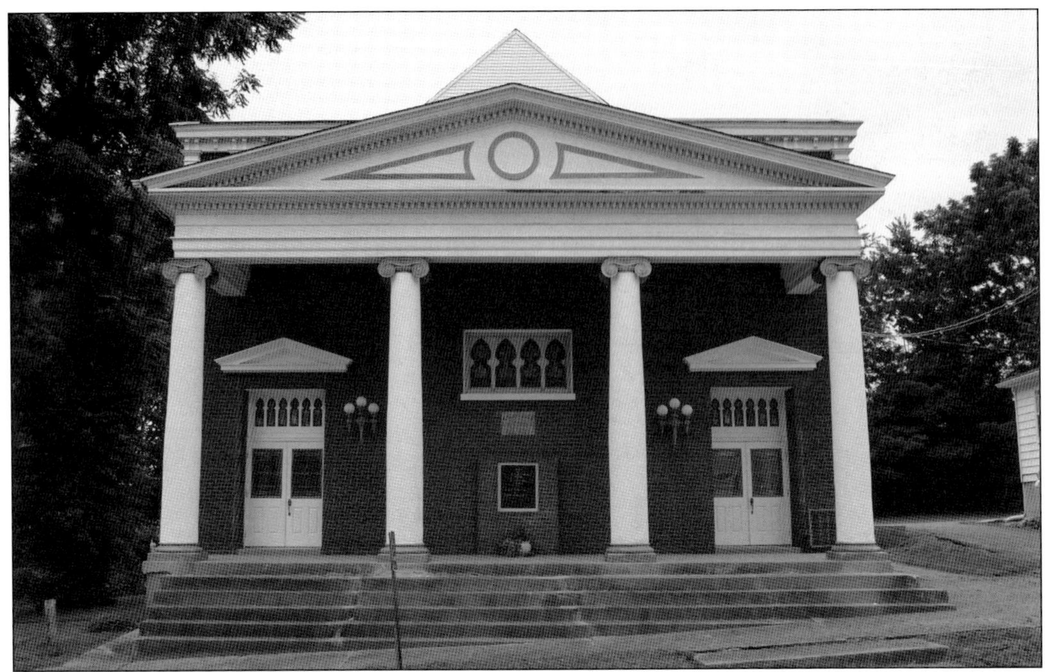

St. James African Methodist Episcopal Church underwent Colonial renovations in the 1920s, which changed its appearance to the point where the original church building would not be recognized. It is rumored that the original three stained-glass windows are still extant, however. It is one of the few "old" churches still in operation. (Michael Denis.)

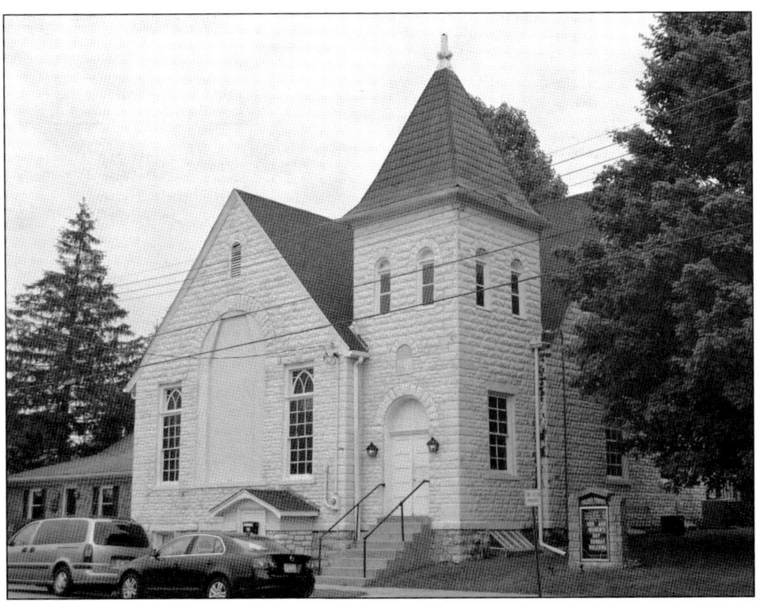

The Second Street Christian Church began as the New Mission Baptist Church in 1892. It was constructed about 1908 when concrete block was coming into fashion as an inexpensive building material. The blocks were made on-site with a Sears machine, which was then used to build other structures in Danville. The building was sold to the Second Street Christian Church in 1927.

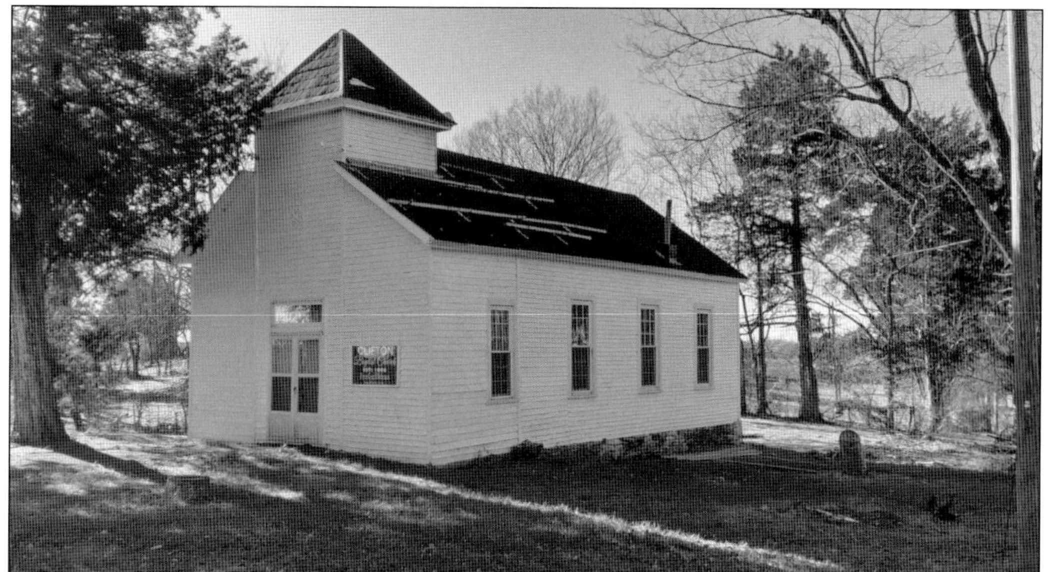

Clifton Baptist Church was founded in 1886 by Rev. Edd Allen, the same year as the Clifton School, where services were held. By 1900, the congregation constructed this building on the school lot. Members included James and Emma Penman, Clay and Malenda Gill, Smith Tarrance, Howard Cowan, Mary Rowe, Andy Woods, Fount Ross, and Mary Pope. (Michael Denis.)

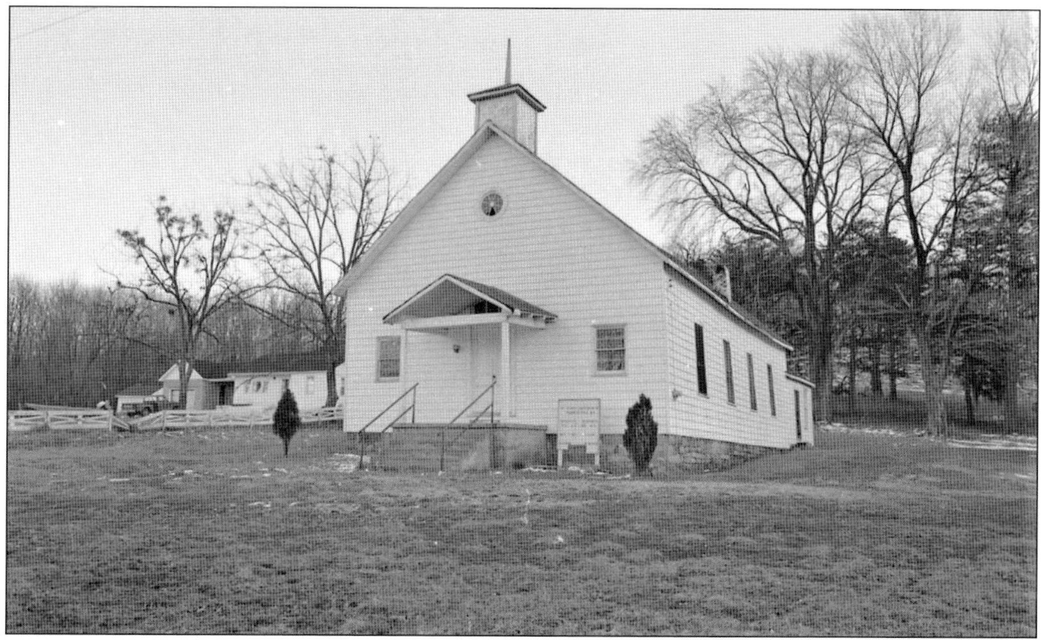

The church at Wilsonville was built in the late 1870s. It was called St. James AME Chapel for many years, but that name was confused with St. James AME Church in Danville, so the name was changed to Wilsonville AME Chapel. The church was quite active in the time period from 1890 to the 2000s. (Charles A. Thomas Collection, BCPL.)

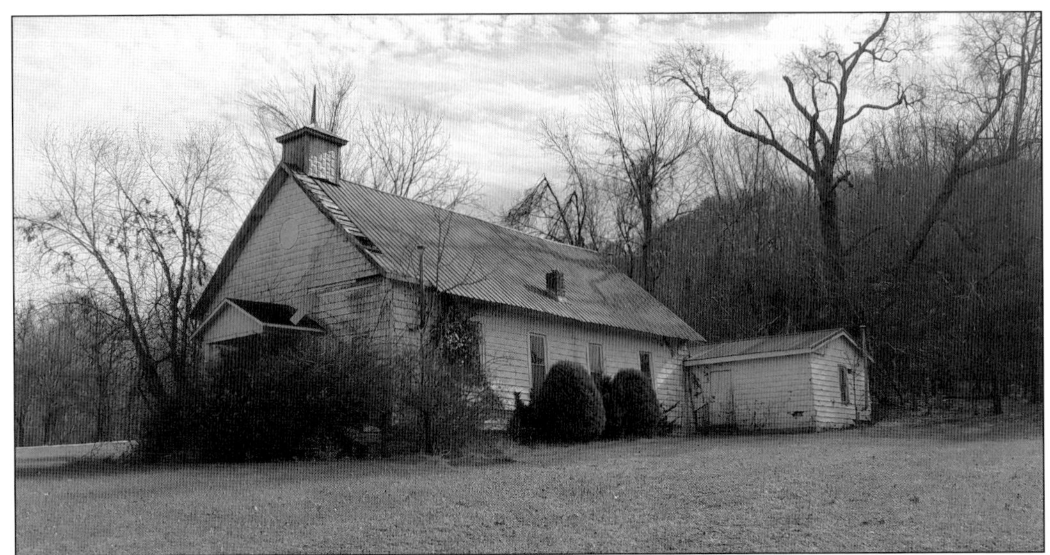

Wilson Chapel today is unused and virtually abandoned. The last events in the chapel took place in September 2012: a homecoming dinner and worship service. Plans are underway to sell both the church and Wilsonville School to a private individual. What will happen to the buildings is uncertain, however. (Michael Denis.)

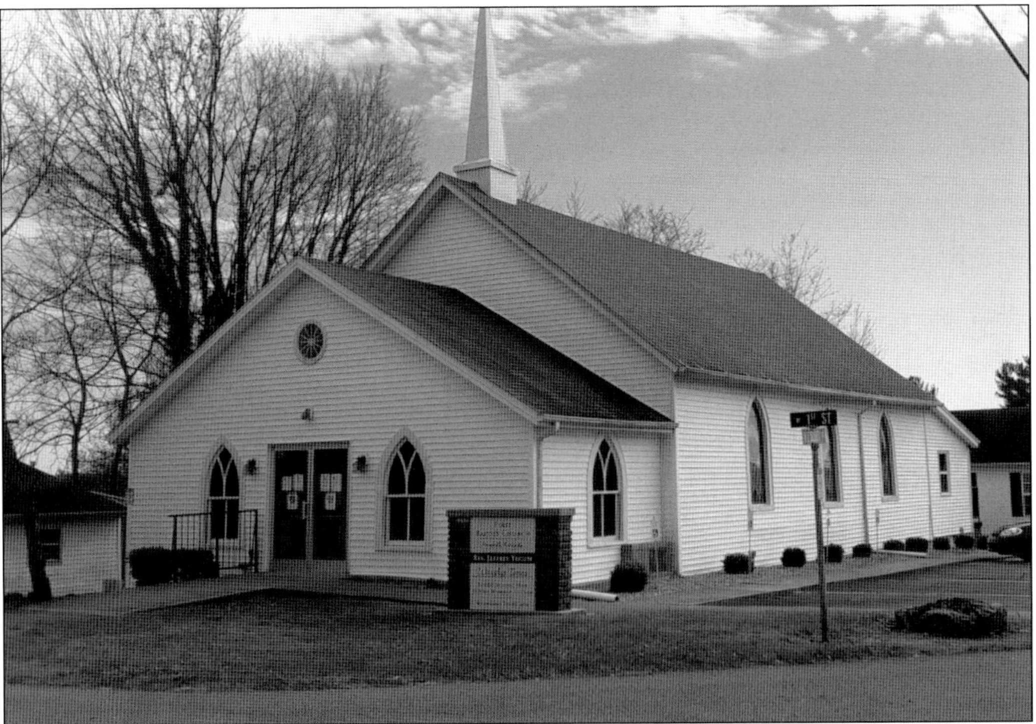

The First Baptist Church Perryville was organized in June 1867, when Black members of the integrated Perryville Baptist Church began to separate. Organizers included Henry Chatham, Nero Grandville, Preston Sleet, S.Q. Goodloe, and Henry Peters. The church building was begun in 1879 under the direction of Rev. Wallace Fisher and completed under Rev. Sam Gill in 1882. (Michael Denis.).

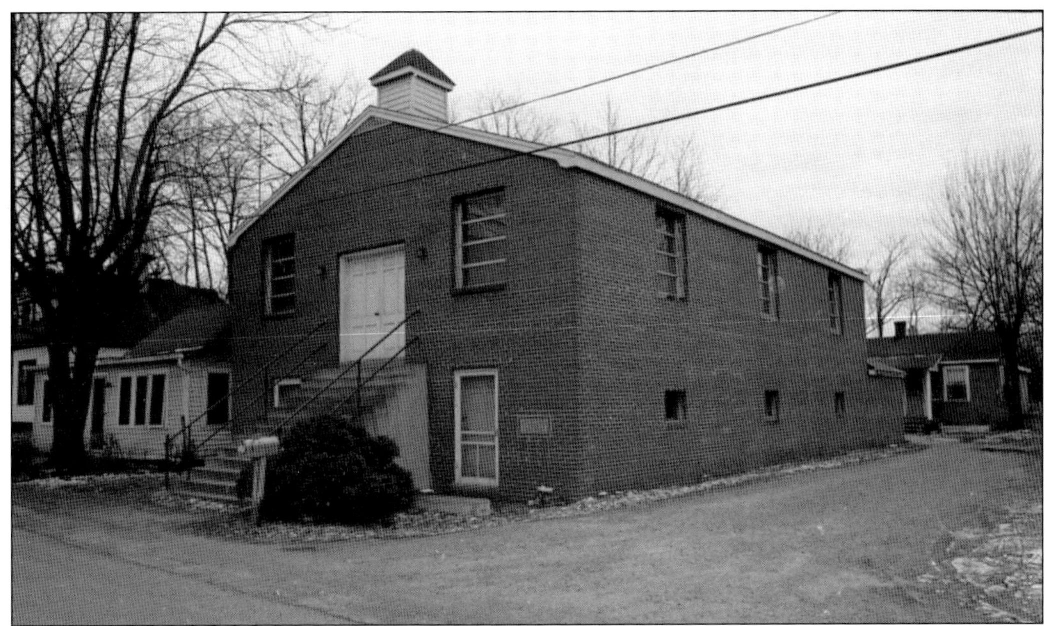

The Bethel Baptist Church, located on Cowan Street in West Danville, was organized by Rev. E. B. Coleman in 1925. This building, "Old Bethel," was built under the pastorate of Rev. Reuben Brantley in 1962. The building was plagued with problems, including bats in the basement, and the congregation decided to build new. (Charles A. Thomas Collection, BCPL.)

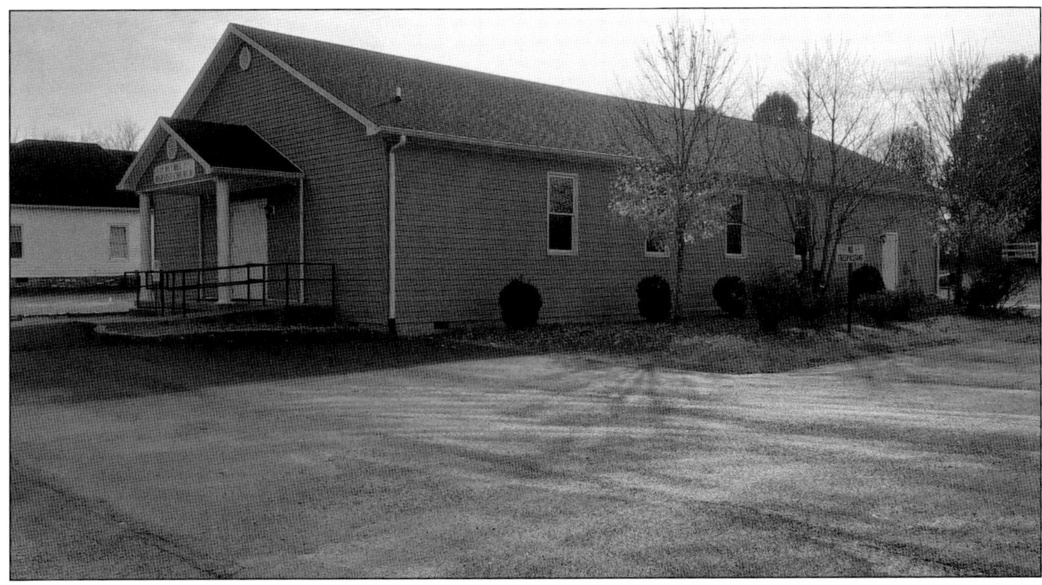

This church, the "new" Bethel Baptist Church, in West Danville, was erected in 2013 in about a week's time due to help from a group of Baptist men and women volunteers from Coleman, Alabama, who spent the week of June 24, 2013, erecting the building. By the end of that week, it was mostly constructed and almost paid for.

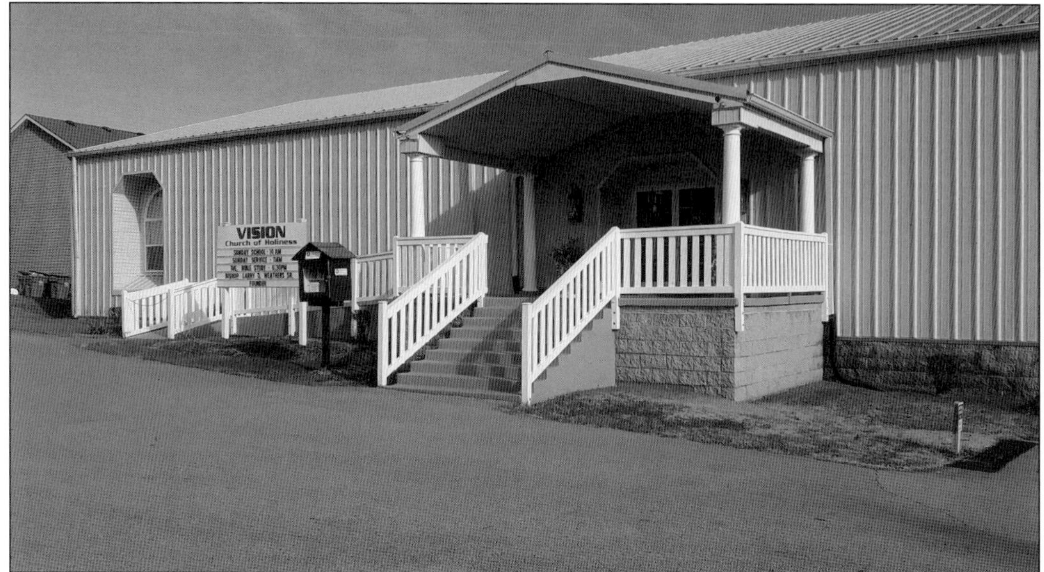

The Vision Church of Holiness was founded on July 16, 2002, by Pastor Larry Weathers, Sr. Groundbreaking for the church building was held July 11, 2004. Weathers's daughter, Melinda, preached her first sermon here on March 10, 2007. In 2013, Reverend Weathers celebrated 40 years in the ministry, but died in January 2021, whereon Melinda assumed the pastorate. (Michael Denis.)

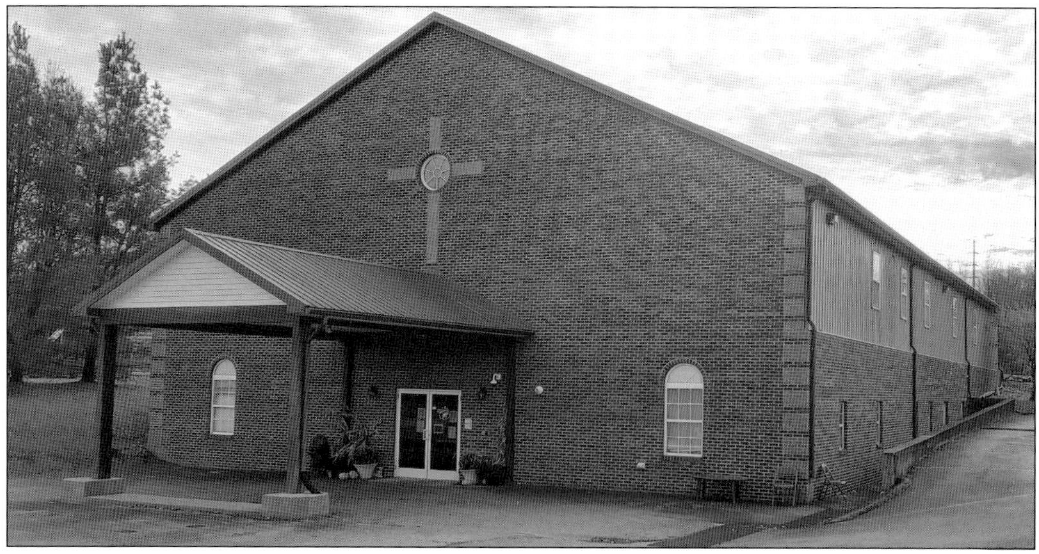

In 1997, Christ the Head Missionary Church was pastored by Rev. Ben Carter. The church was incorporated at 845 East Main Street in early 1999, and it requested permission to build a church in a residential zone in June 1999. The church ran a daycare from the very earliest years but is no longer a primarily Black church. (Michael Denis.)

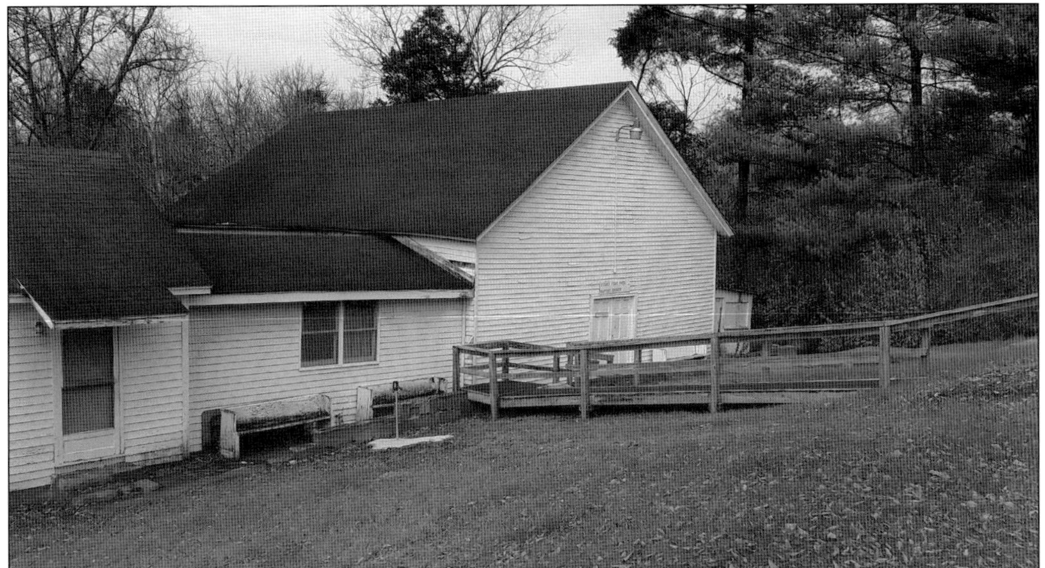

Harry "Poppa" Jackson, born December 25, 1869, had been a member of Stony Point Predestinarian Baptist Church for 75 years and a deacon for over 70 years, when he was the subject of an article in the *Advocate-Messenger*, January 14, 1973. The church purchased the former Stoney Point School (the right side of the building here) in 1945. (Michael Denis.)

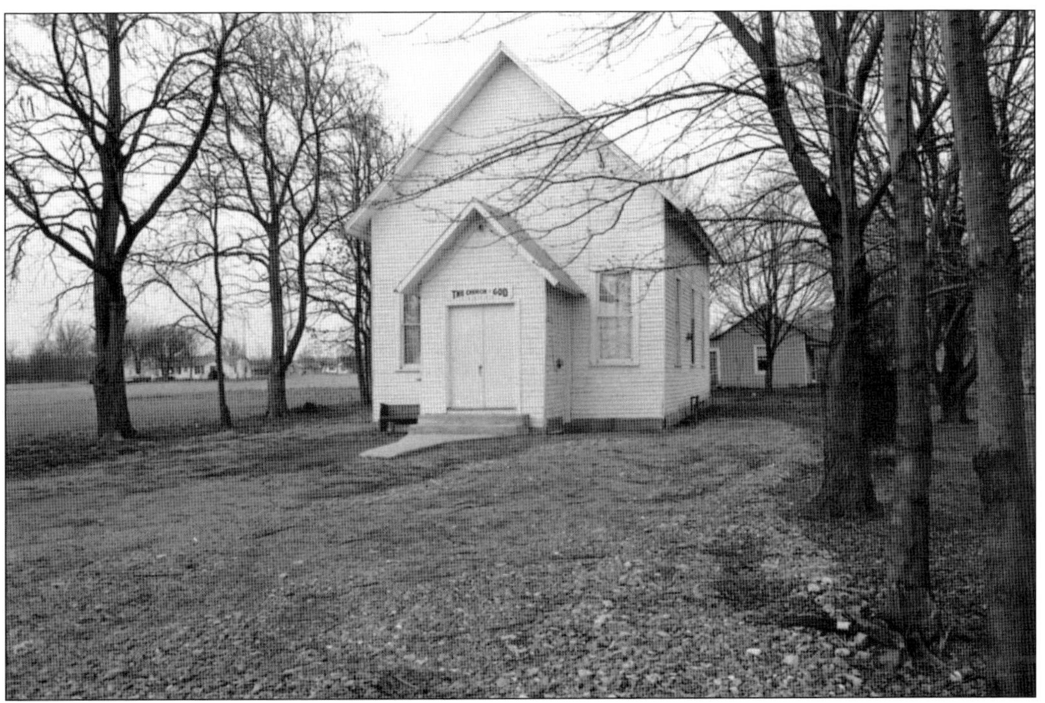

St. John AME Church was located in the Shelby City section of Junction City. This church operated from before 1920 until 1970. It was torn down in the mid-1970s and is now the site of the Junction City Church of God. St. John AME Church is seen here in its later years as the Church of God. (Charles A. Thomas Collection, BCPL.)

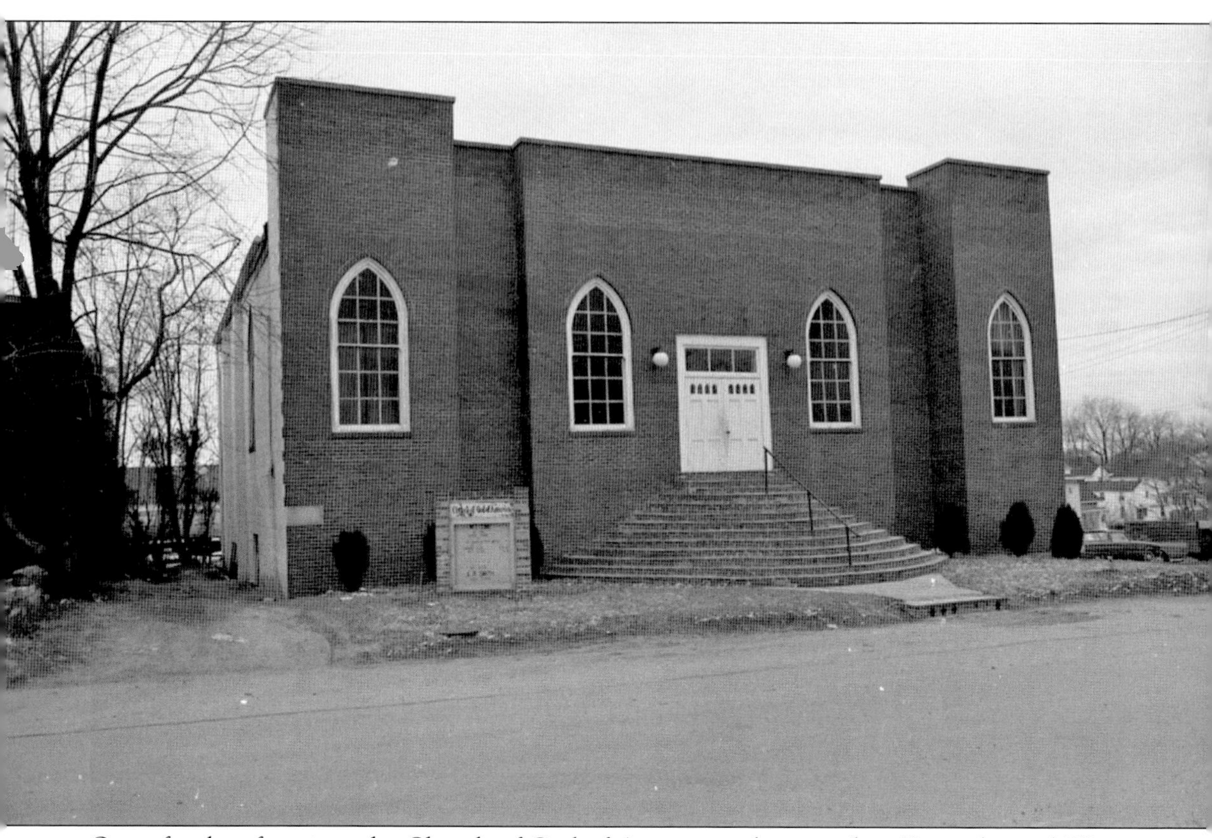

One of only a few sites, the Church of God of America only existed in Kentucky and West Virginia. It was founded in Pulaski County in 1919 by "Mother Brown." After a fire on January 31, 2010, the church on Walnut Street was disbanded, and the location is now used by medical offices. (Charles A. Thomas Collection, BCPL.)

Two

Civic and Social Organizations

Many social and religious organizations were organized among Black residents of Boyle County. Often, these were the only organizations in which African Americans could become members.

The Doric Lodge No. 18 F&AM, Prince Hall Affiliation, was one of the earliest, being organized in 1888 on Main Street, then moving to the United Brethren of Fellowship (UBF) Hall on West Walnut in 1902, and finally, building a three-story lodge hall on South Second Street in 1919.

The UBF built a three-story hall on West Walnut Street in 1900, although they are mentioned as "Maynard No 28," as early as 1897 or possibly earlier. This hall was a three-story building on West Walnut Street where numerous functions were held. The building, at one time, also housed a funeral parlor, a store, and a laundry and was used as a youth center in the 1950s. It was torn down during urban renewal in the late 1960s.

Several of these organizations gave rise to women's groups, such as the Celestine Chapter No. 9, Order of the Eastern Star, and the Sisters of the Mysterious Ten, 1883.

But there were social organizations as well, as many as 40 or more women's clubs, through the lodges and the churches. Black women did not lack social contacts.

The City Federation of Women's Clubs, formed in 1924, was comprised of the Domestic Economy Club and the Busy Sunshine Club. They met in various locations around the city, with one important location being the Goldsmith House, at the corner of South Second and West Walnut Streets. This building was actually saved by urban renewal, but the federation did not survive long afterward.

Two of the most prominent clubs—the Voguettes and the Orchid Girls—formed in 1950 and 1949, respectively, were last mentioned in newspaper briefs in 1959 and 1994, respectively.
Today, most of the social organizations have passed, as the Black community has spread out over central Kentucky, or moved north. Even the venerable Doric Lodge is now gone. The only groups that survive today are church-related organizations, and there are not many of those.

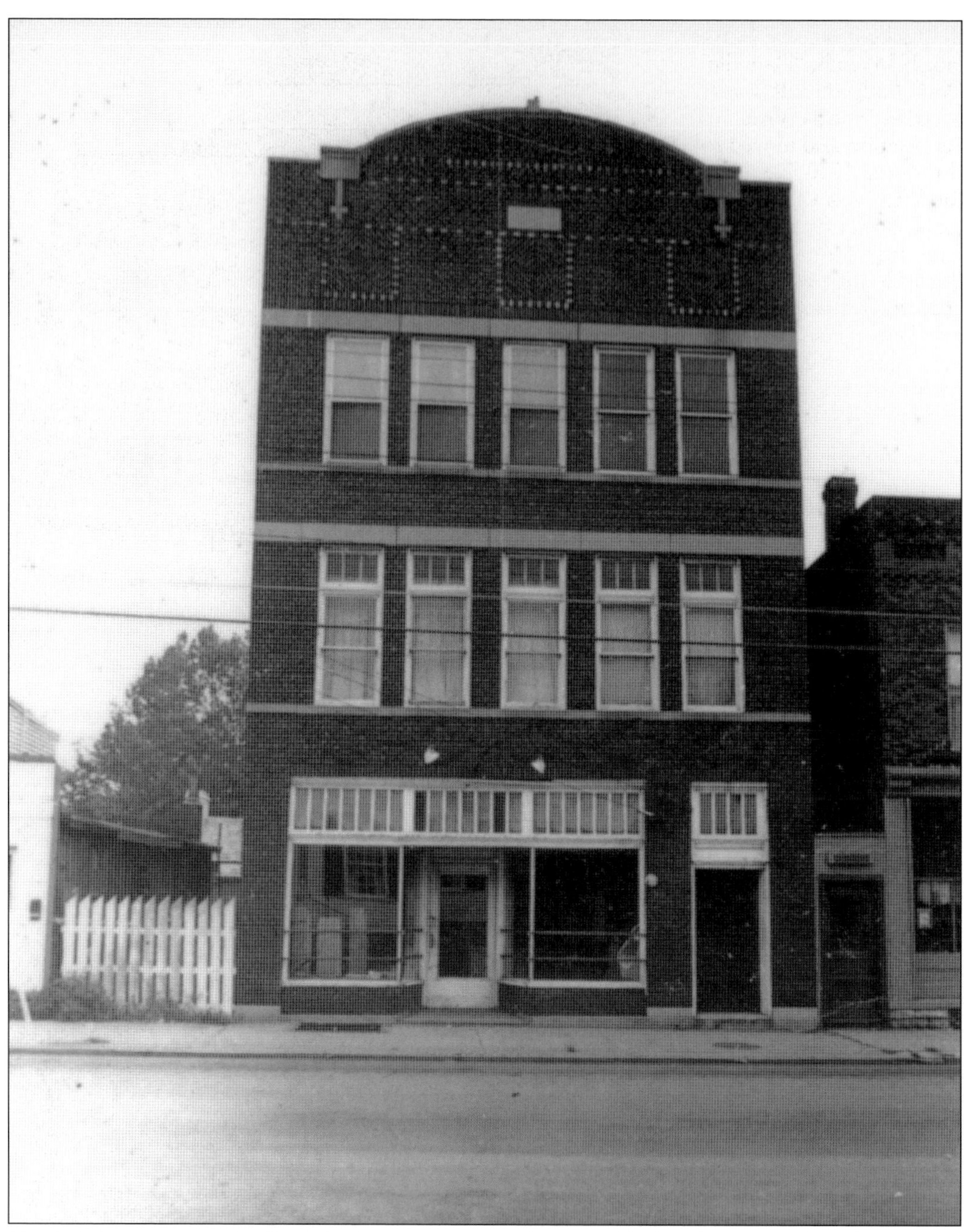

The building housing the Doric Lodge was dedicated in June 1919 and was built by subscription. Ten members of the lodge, which was organized in 1888, pledged $1,000 each to build the building: Ashby Jackson, Nash Rum, J.W. Bate, Charles Stull, V.H. Cheatham, Archibald F. Rochester, Rascal Hudson, Richard Parr, R.B. Hamilton, and James Engleman. At various times, the first and second floors were rented out to local businesses, including beauty shops, barbershops, restaurants, and grocery stores to help defray expenses and to pay the mortgage. The lodge hall was on the third floor. When this building was taken by urban renewal in 1974, the lodge moved to the former IOOF Building on West Walnut Street. (Charles D. Grey.)

Kentucky Historical Marker No. 1958 reads, "Danville's Doric Lodge No. 18 was founded 1888 as Boyle Association and moved to this site in 1920. For 50 years, the lodge was a cultural and social center for the African American community of Boyle County. Donations of $1,000 by each of 10 members of the brotherhood secured a loan enabling the construction of the building in 1920." (Michael Denis.)

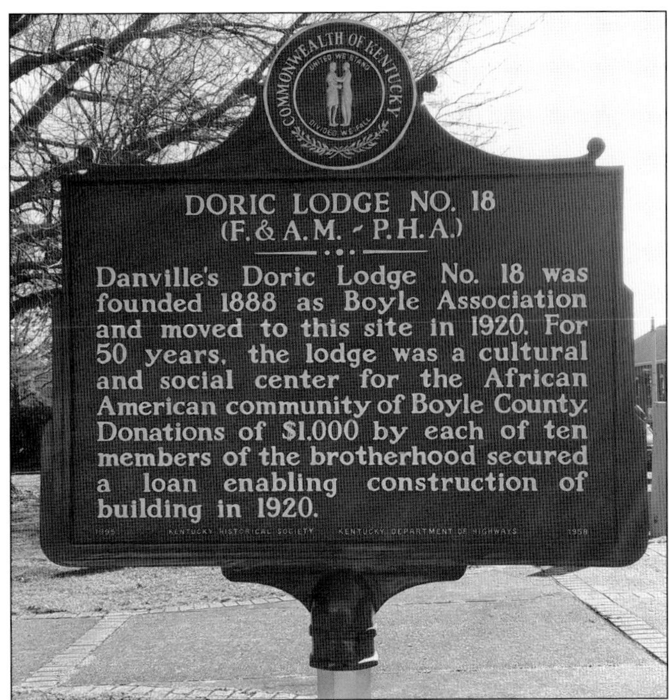

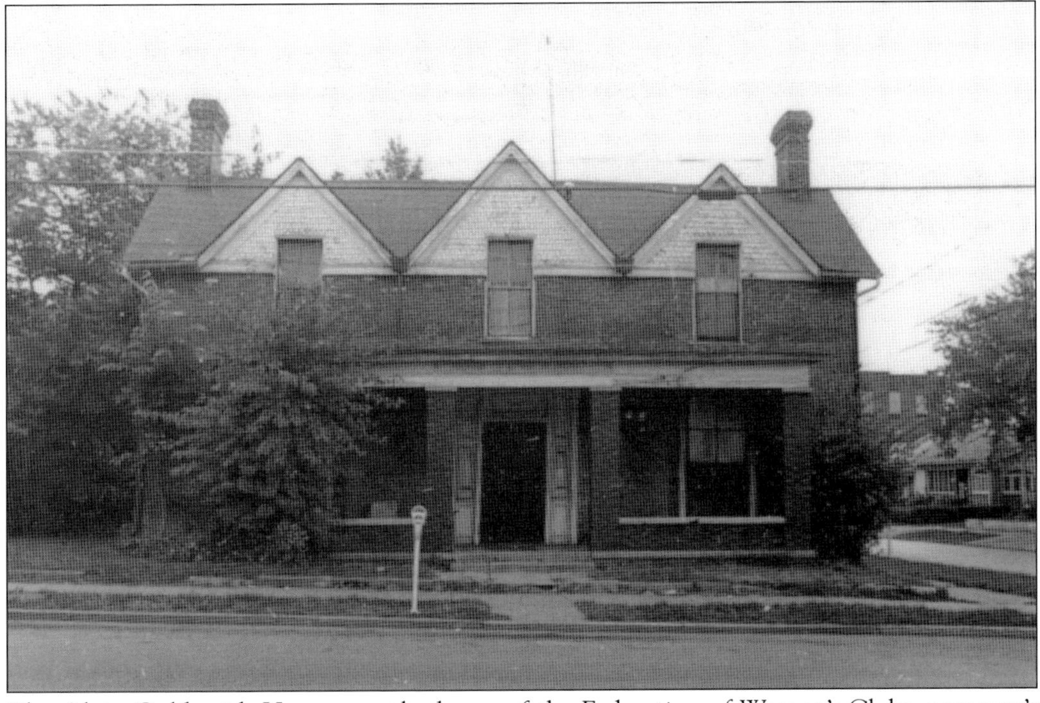

The Alvin Goldsmith House was the home of the Federation of Women's Clubs, a women's organization consisting of the Busy Sunshine Club and the Domestic Economy Club. When urban renewal took this building for rehabilitation, it was nearly the end of the federation, which existed since the early 1900s. The house was built by Alvin Goldsmith, an apprentice to Dr. Ephraim McDowell.

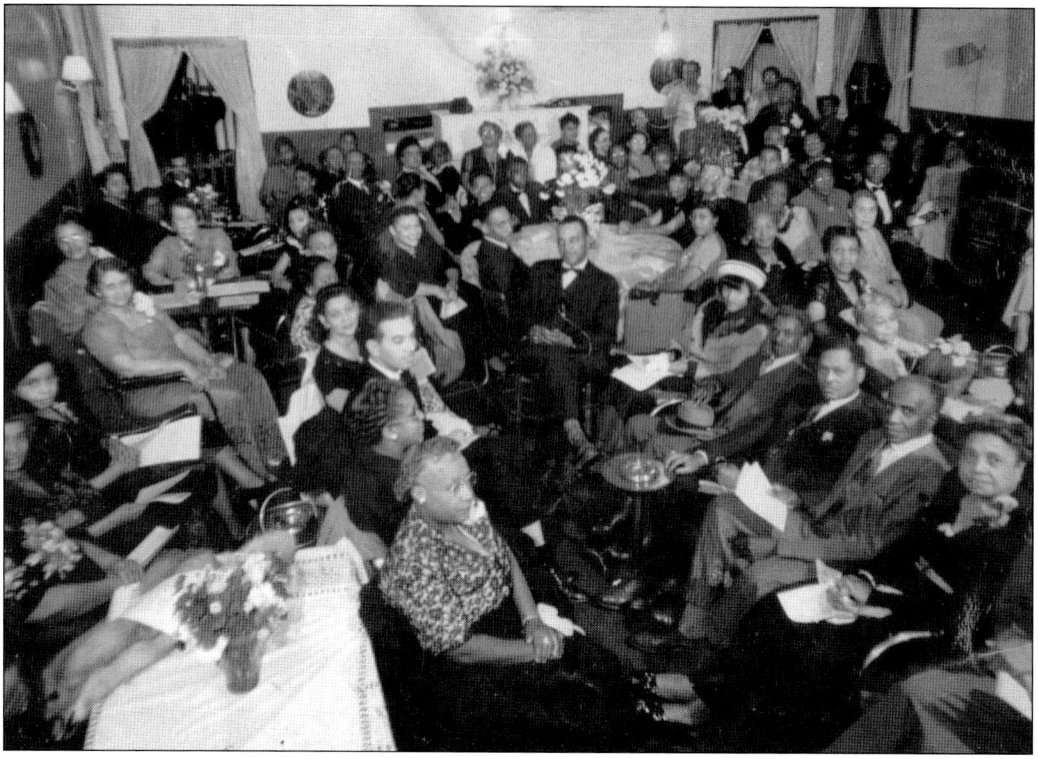

The Domestic Economy Club and the Busy Sunshine Club held an unusual joint meeting at the Masonic lodge. These two organizations and the Doric Lodge No. 18 were among the most important ones in the Black community in Danville. In this photograph are the "movers and shakers" of the African American community in Danville and Boyle County.

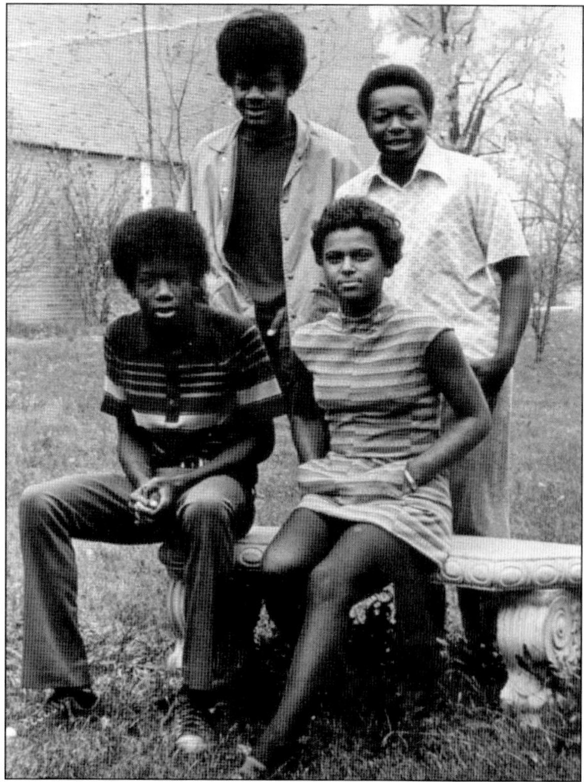

Danville High School students formed a Black Student Union in 1971. Shown from left to right and front to rear are Walter Smith, Cynthia Owsley, Chuck Ford, and Clyde Simpson. Until 1964, when Bate School closed, most African American students attended the all-Black school, but beginning in 1955–1956, some transferred to Danville. Once integrated, the need for a Black student union at the high school became evident.

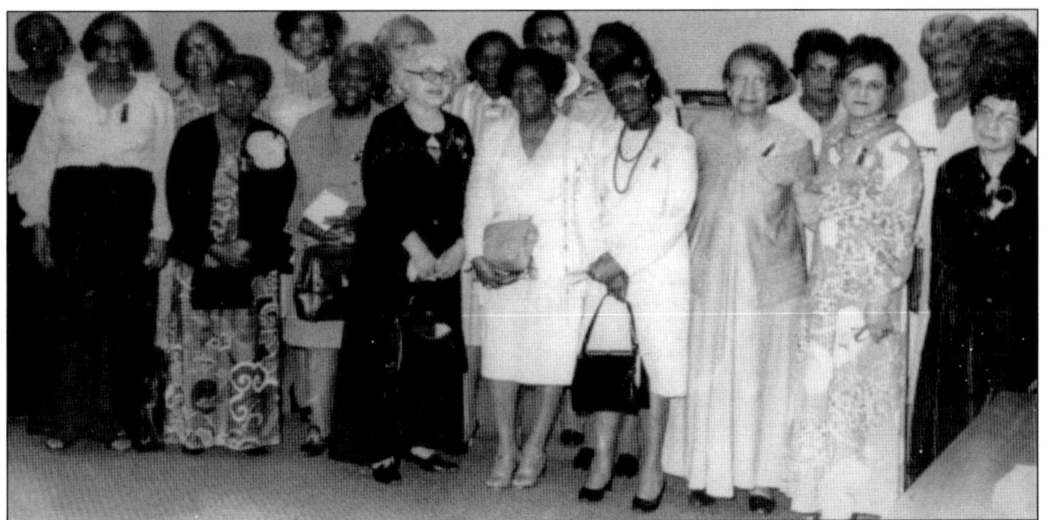

The Busy Sunshine Club was a component of the City Federation of Women's Clubs, the first mention of which was in the *Lexington Herald* on November 16, 1919. Some of the members included (in no particular order) Lettie Bate, Rebecca Bright, Jeanette Cowan, Sophia Craig, Eliza Davis, Georgia Doneghy, Helen Fisher Frye, Alice Goodloe, Florine Ingram, Reeve Jackson, Lillian Jones, Maggie Jones, Annie Lee Moore, Gertrude Sledd, Madeline Summers, and Florence Walker.

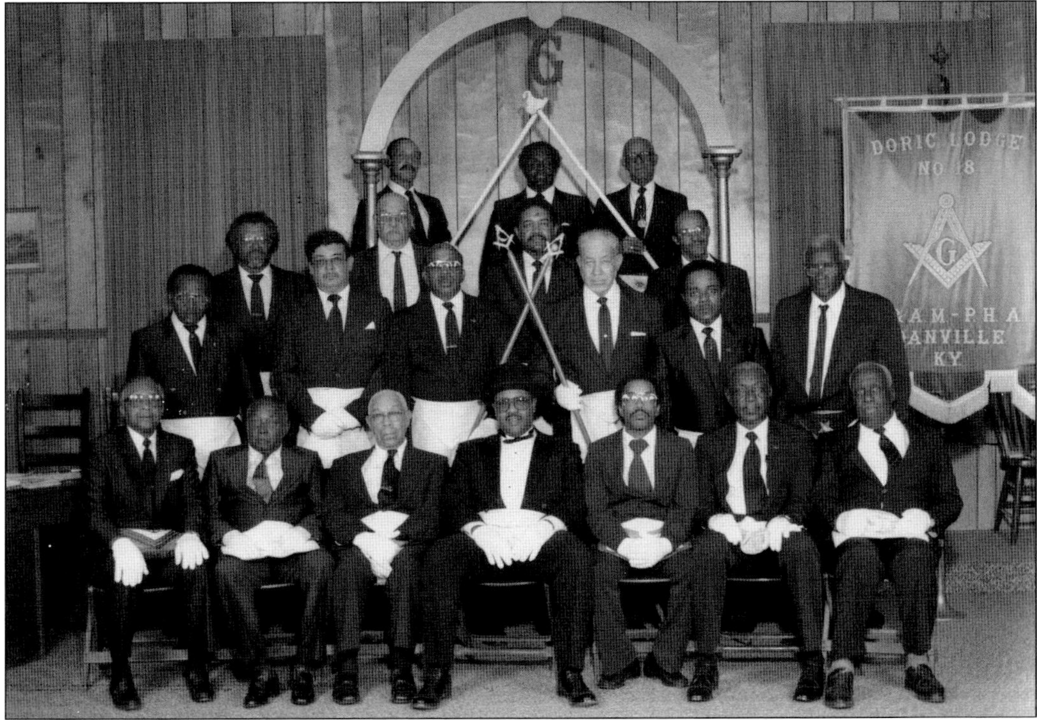

Doric Lodge members seen here, pictured from left to right, are (first row) June Christy, Bentley Lee, Madison Tarrance, Charles Grey, Ralph Boyd Smith, Eugene Harlan, and Allie Gray; (second row) John Marshall, Michael Smith, William Brown, Samuel Miller, Ernest Gooch, and Roy Neal.; (third row) Paul Logan, Ralph Smith, Charles Harvey, and Howard Clark; (fourth row) Eugene Jarman, Earl Segar, and Burchie Logan. (Charles D. Grey.)

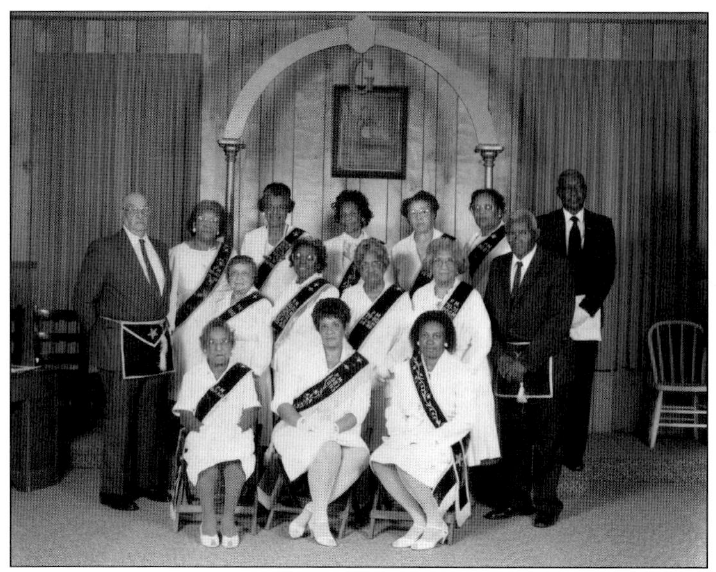

Members of the Celestine No. 9, Order of the Eastern Star Past Matrons and Patrons, pictured here from left to right, include (first row) Naomi Smith, Mary J. Kinley, and Mary M. Whitehead; (second row) Theora Coates, Mabel Letcher, Fannie Thomas, Mabel Tarrence, and Roy Neal; (third row) Ralph Smith, Vernocia Neal, Willa Ball, Opal Harlan, Charles Fields, Viola Young, and Eugene Harlan. (Charles D. Grey.)

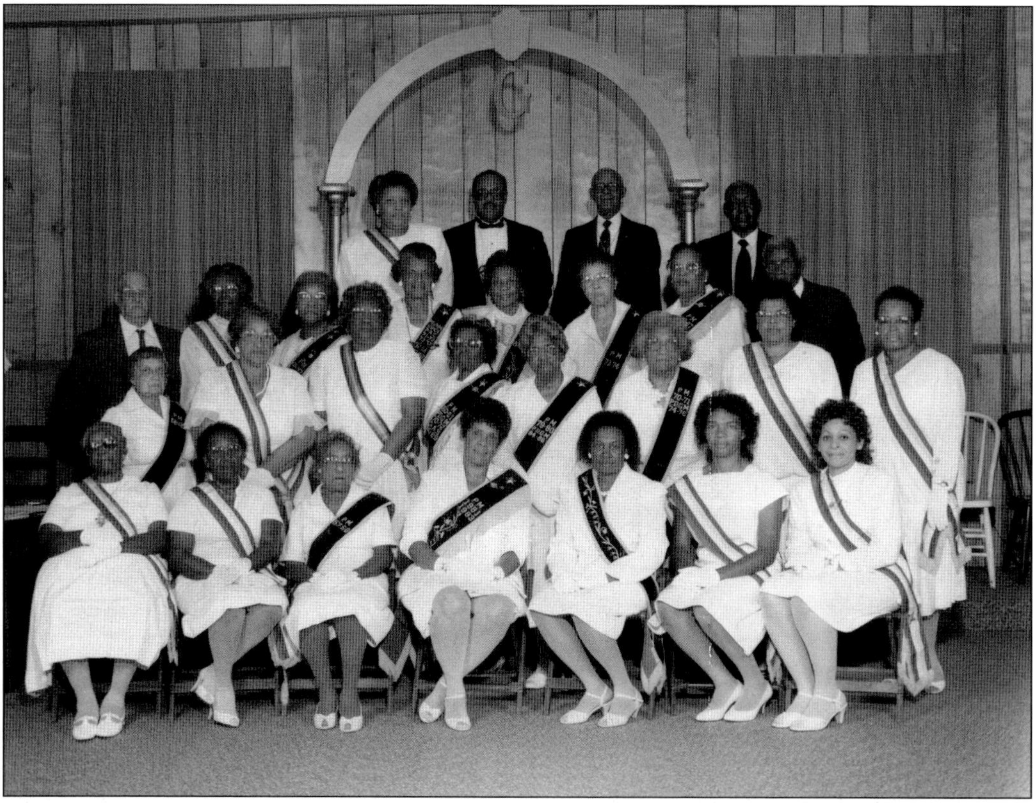

Celestine No. 9, Eastern Star members pictured here include, from left to right, (first row) Mary Woods, Willa Pennix, Naomi Smith, Mary Kinley, Mary Whitehead, Sadie Gambriel, and Audrey Turner; (second row) Theora Coates, Ophelia Jones, Catherine Napier, Mabel Letcher, Fannie Thomas, Mabel Tarrence, June Christy, and Anna Grey; (third row) Ralph Smith, Natalie Harris, Vernocia Neal, Willa Ball, Opal Harlan, Charles Fields, Viola Young, and Roy Neal; (fourth row) Agnes Bartleson, Charles Grey, Burchie Logan, and Eugene Harlan. (Charles D. Grey.)

Three members of the Kentucky Club meet in Danville. From left to right are Rozetta (Jackson) Turner (1914–2008), unidentified, and Theora (Tarrance) Coates (1917–2018). The Kentucky Club had chapters in several other states, made up of people who left Kentucky largely for better job opportunities. A collection of their booklets is in the history center of the DBCAAHS.

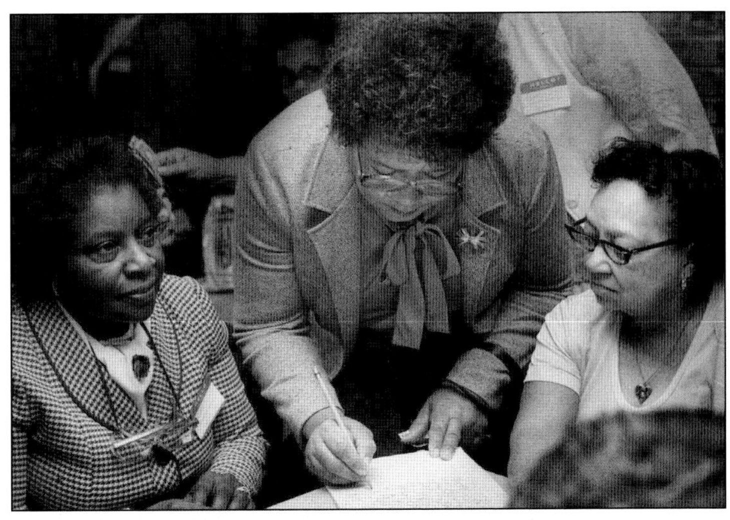

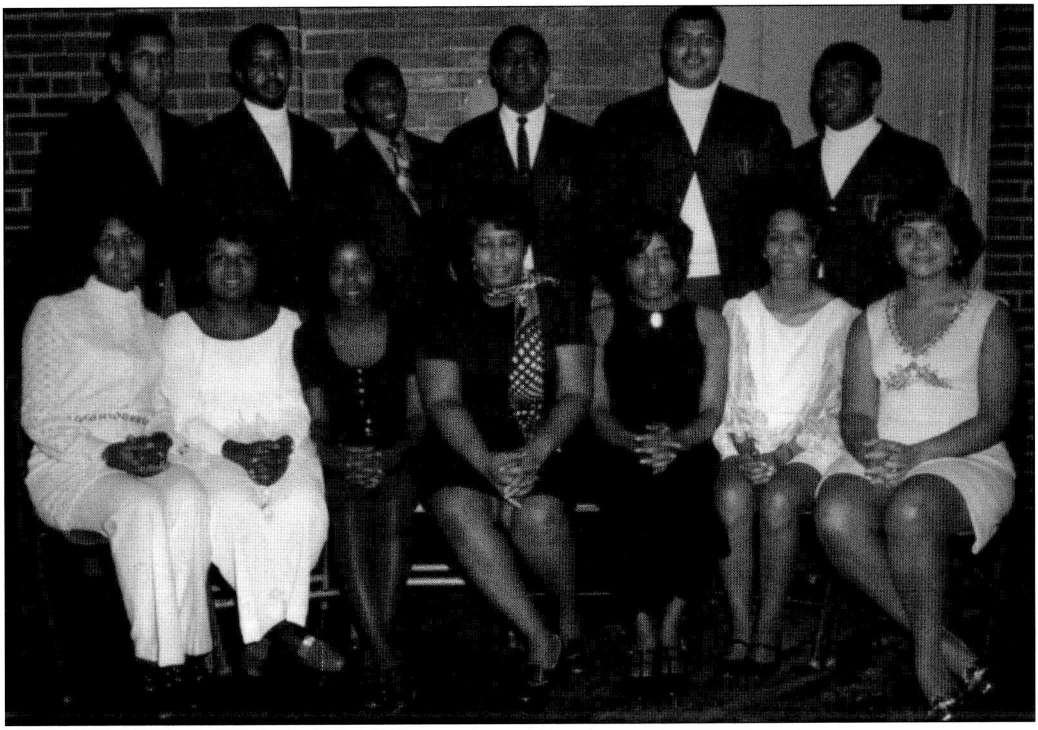

The Jolly Believers Club probably sponsored more dances in Danville than any other club in a comparable time frame. Members are, from left to right (first row) Dorothy (Hunn) Napier, Sharon (Bedinger) McGuire, Anna (Simpson) Brand, Judy (Tresenwriter) Gray, Martha (Leavell) Wilkerson, Nancy (Jones) Grey, and Christine (Singleton) Browning; (second row) Tony Gray, George Brand, Alonzo McGuire, Clifford Napier, Bobby Wilkerson, and Lloyd Browning.

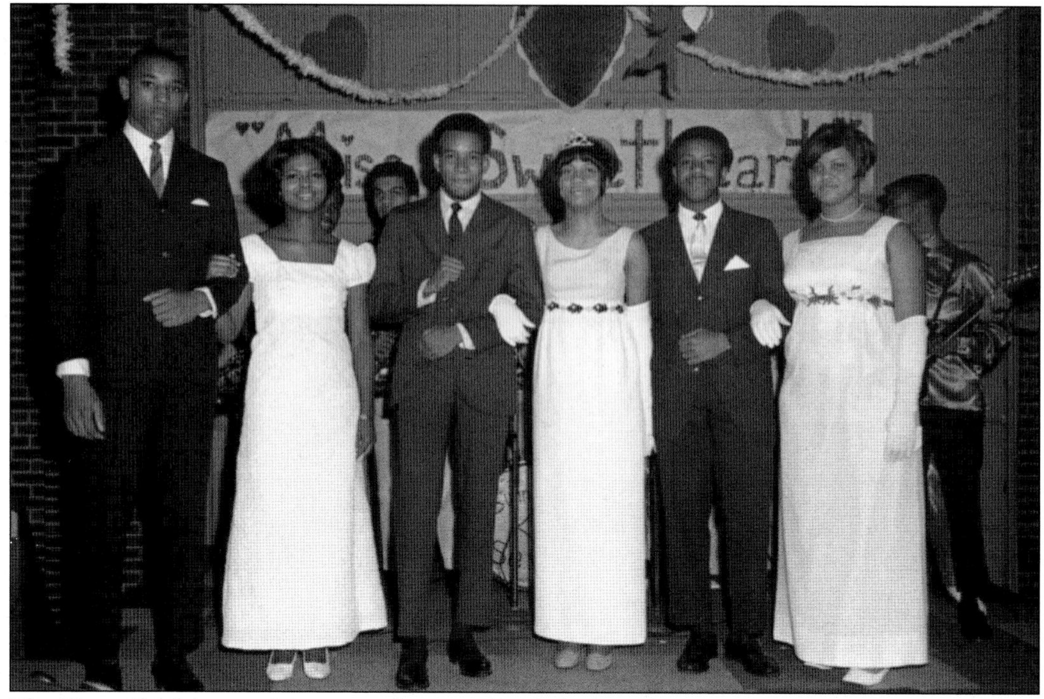

The Danville *Advocate-Messenger* for Monday, February 17, 1969, carried this photograph of "the first dance" of the Jolly Believers Club, February 15, 1969. The "Sweetheart of 1969" event featured 18 girls who entered. Identified from left to right are Rodney Dunn, Jerri Sue Doty of Paint Lick (first runner up), Gary Lockett, Jackie Bowman of Danville (queen), James Simpson Jr., and Deborah Kay McCowan of Danville (second runner-up).

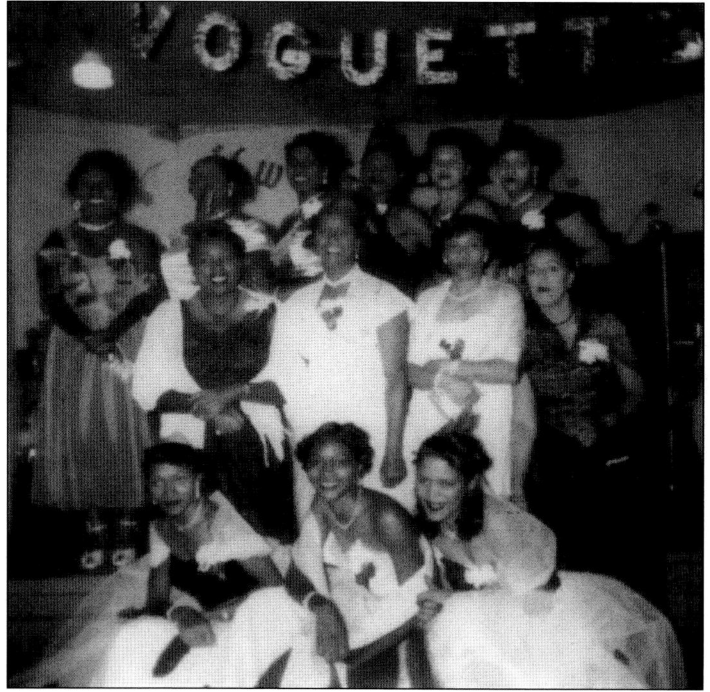

The Voguettes Club was one of over 40 Black women's clubs in Danville. A group of women met in March 1950 at the residence of Mabel Letcher to organize the Voguettes. Officers and members were Mabel Letcher, Florine McPherson, Alma McCowan, Maxine Caldwell, Catherine Faulkner, Marjorie (Wright) Miller, Ann Prewitt, Mary Margaret Crowdus, Ruby Cloud, Venus Miller, Cleo Richardson, and Dorothy Langford.

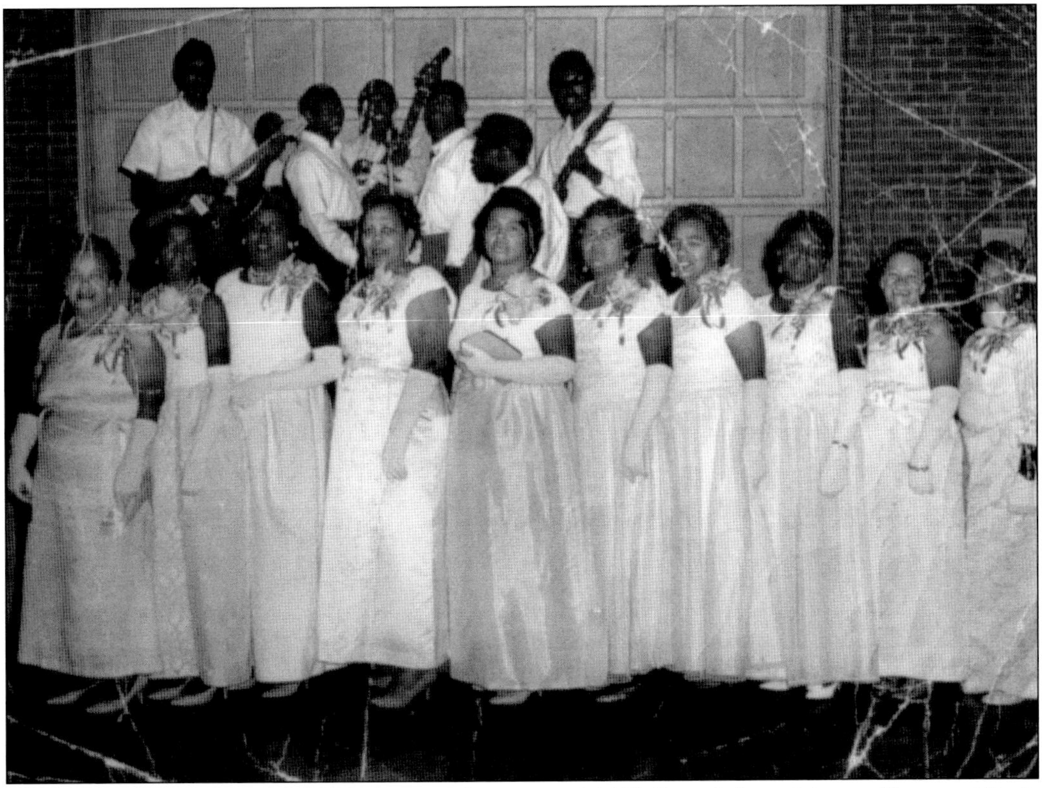

This photograph of the Orchid Girls was taken around 1966. From left to right are (first row) Ruth Griffin, Martha Grey, Mattie Lancaster, Sue Ella Baughman, Alma McCowan, Mattie Hill, Mattie Elliot, Naomi Simpson, Helen Baughman, and Annie Segar; (the band on the stage) Nightowls Band members, Johnny Roy Yocum, (unidentified person hidden by Johnny Roy's guitar), Alonzo McGuire, Dennis Jones, Thomas Ford, Cecil Smith, and Harvey Yocum.

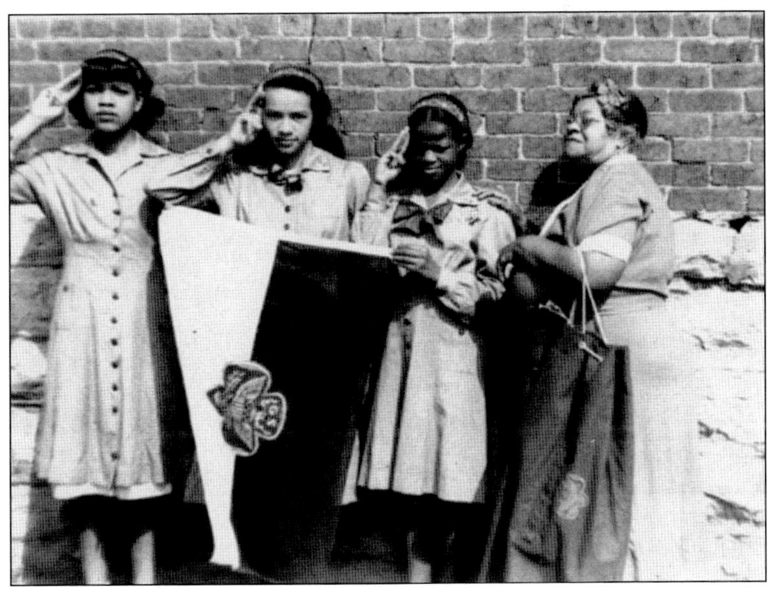

Pictured at Girl Scout Cookie sale time, in 1953 are, from left to right, Ann Carol (Jones) Prince, Viola (Lankford) Pittman, Delores Whitney, and Sadie W. (Jones) Turner (1884–1960). Turner was a longtime teacher in Boyle County, teaching at Junction City, Stony Point, and the Bate School. This image was included in the 1955 chamber of commerce scrapbook.

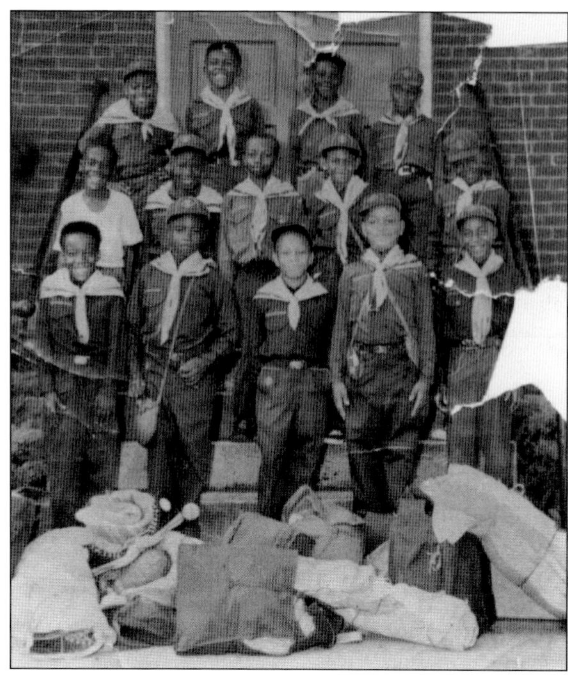

The First Baptist Church Cub Scouts were going camping in the early 1950s. Pictured from left to right are (first row) Roy Neal, William Howard Rice, Walter Trumbo, James Jones, and Charles Ford; (second row) Billy Joe Johnson, June Shavers, James Munford, Larry Burgess, and Ronnie McCowan; (third row) Donald Lee Faulkner, George Gilbert Fields, Horace Ball, and Gary Ford.

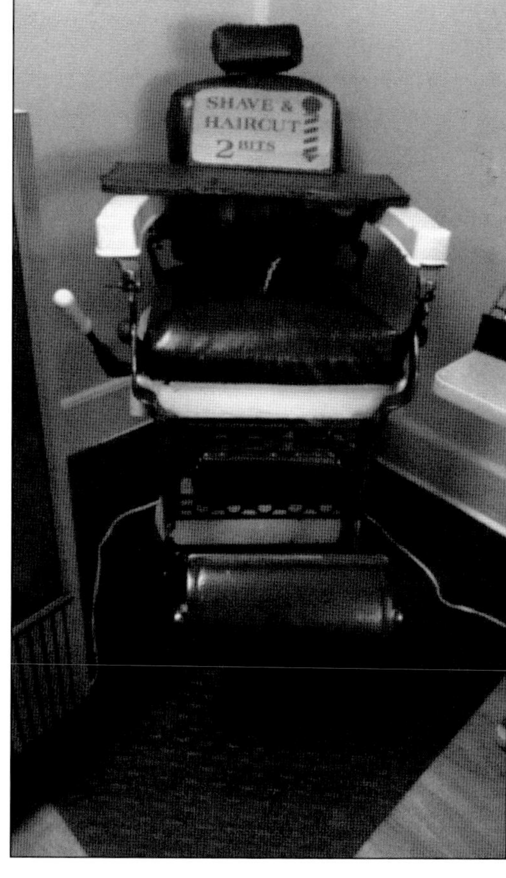

The barber chair at DBCAAHS History Center came from one of the many barbershops, possibly Tibbs', and was used by Eustatia Johnson in her beauty shop. This artifact is a prized loan to the history center, as it epitomizes the importance of barbershops to the Black community— a place to get a haircut, but also a place to socialize. (Michael Denis.)

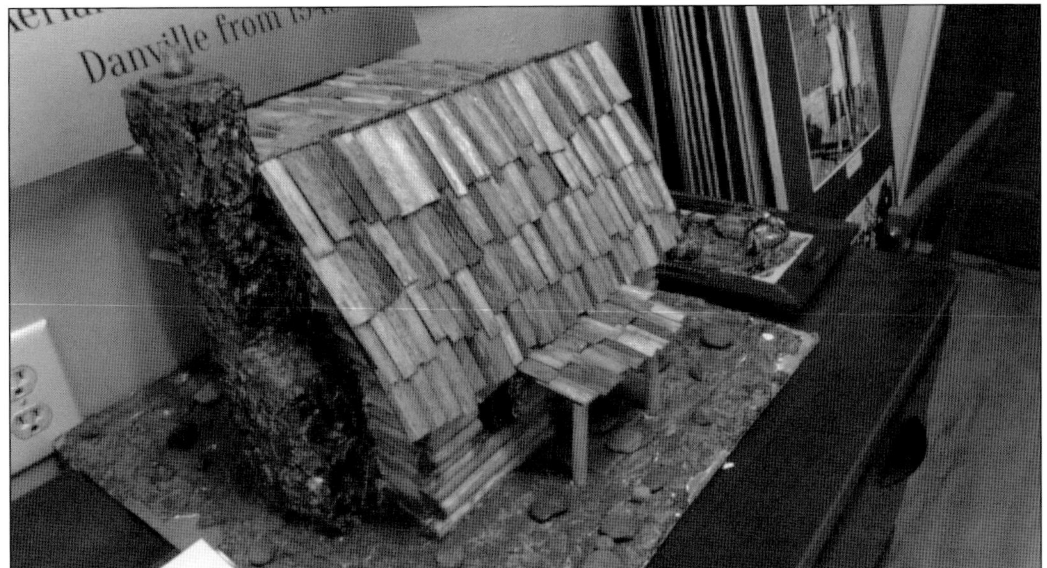

This model by Charles Julian Dawson is at the DBCAAHS History Center. He began making folk art out of natural or recycled materials in the 1980s. After his death in 2005, the Community Arts Center hosted an exhibition of his work which was reported in both the Danville and Lexington newspapers. Each cabin is distinctive, and many of the buildings were multi-story. (Michael Denis.)

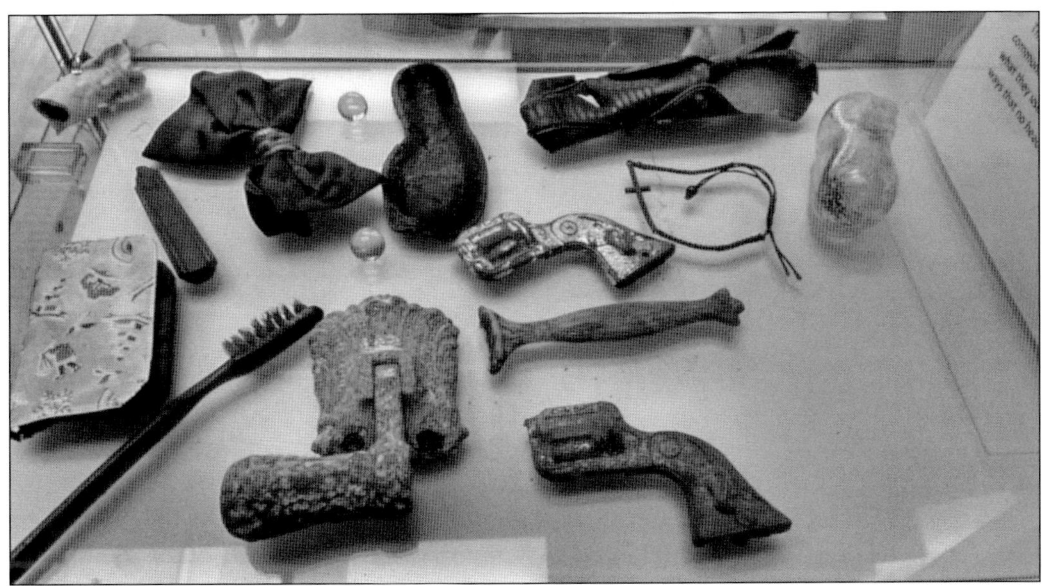

Artifacts from children's graves at the Shelby City African American Cemetery are displayed at the DBCAAHS History Center. It was the custom for family members to leave at the gravesite mementos of the child, such as the toy guns or clothing, like a small shoe sole and bow. The large piece center front was actually a casket handle that had migrated through the soil to the surface. (Michael Denis.)

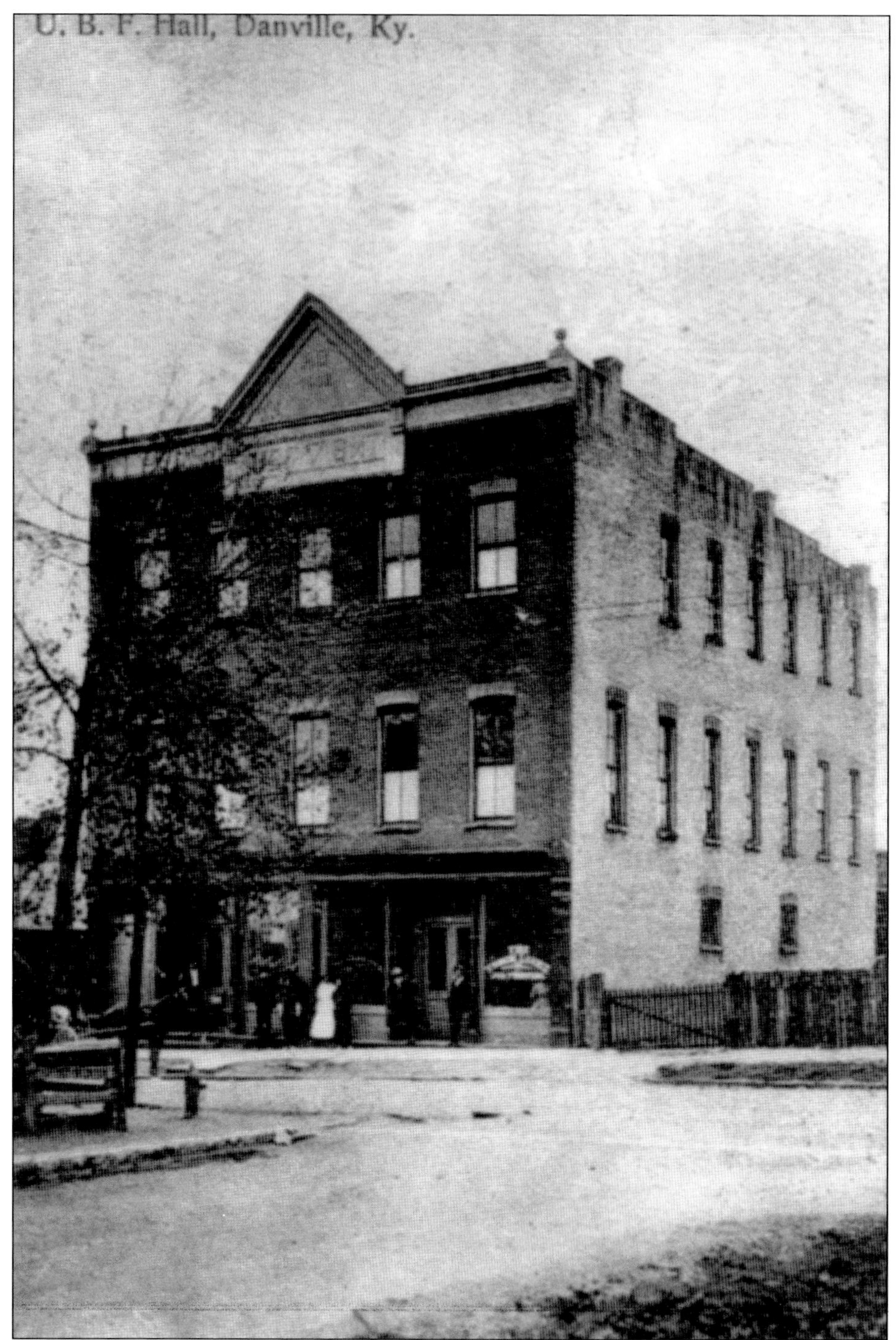

United Brotherhood of Friends Hall, built in 1900, was located on West Walnut Street, opposite South First. The building at times housed a funeral business, a grocery store, a laundry, a shoe store, and others, with the UBF using the third floor for meetings. Doric Lodge No. 18 met here before it built the South Second Street building. By 1954, it housed a youth center where many activities were held.

Three

Businesses

South Second Street, from Main Street to Walnut Street, was the heart of the Danville African American community. It was not the only place in Boyle County that had businesses catering to African Americans, but it was far more extensive here than anywhere else.

Beginning in the late 1800s, businesses blossomed in this block, both on the east and the west sides. Restaurants, grocery stores, barbershops, taxi stands, and pool halls thrived until the 1950s on South Second Street and other streets in the area.

By the 1940s, "blight" began to appear in the neighborhood. The rundown condition of many buildings was beginning to become an embarrassment to the "white" community. So, something had to be done.

As African Americans became more able to shop in formerly integrated stores, they shopped less and less in Black-owned stores, thus contributing to the decay of the Black community. Thus, as African Americans became the beneficiaries of more freedom and equality, their communities began to feel the neglect that shopping in "white" stores would necessarily engender.

By the 1960s, urban renewal began to tear away at the blight. One member of the local chamber of commerce even suggested that removing the Black business district would be good for white businesses and visitors. Thus, urban renewal, as in many other parts of the country, took on a racist tone, as it did in Lexington, Indianapolis, and New York City.

Homes, businesses, and offices began to feel the reality of the wrecking ball. Black-owned businesses often felt the destruction of racism, whereas historically "white" buildings were spared. Not much "renewal" was involved in urban renewal.

Today, there are only a handful of Black-owned businesses, several of which are barbershops. The closest to South Second Street is a shop in the Henson Hotel at the corner of North Second and West Main. Other Black-owned businesses are almost all sole proprietorships. There are no Black-owned restaurants or stores and few, if any, doctors, professional services, or lawyers.

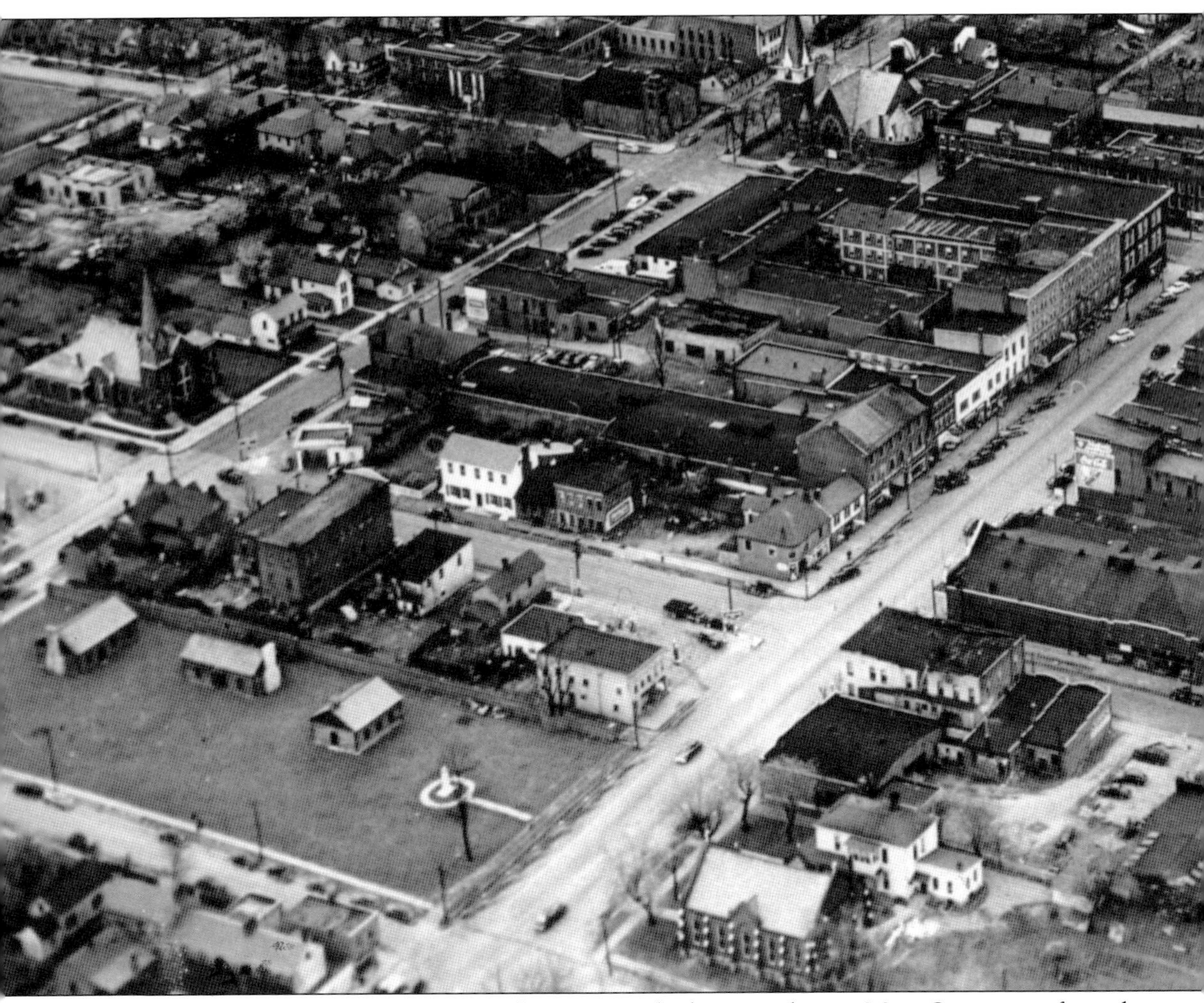

This aerial view of downtown Danville in 1947 is looking southwest. Main Street runs from the bottom center to center-right. South First is the first street on the left running left to right, with South Second being the next one. Constitution Square Historic Site is seen in its infancy, with a wall separating it from the African American business district on South Second Street. The white building in the middle of the far side of South Second is the Ephraim McDowell House, Opposite it is the three-story Doric Lodge. On the corner of South Second and West Walnut is the First Baptist Church, which burned in 1966. (Michael Wiser.)

These men are sitting across from McDowell House in front of Green Pastures Restaurant on 29 May 1939. The dedication of the restored Ephraim McDowell house was not open to Black residents, so these people watched from across the street in front of the Green Pastures restaurant. Beginning fourth from right seated are Herbert Harris (with hat), Leo Pope, and Johnny Johnson (with hat).

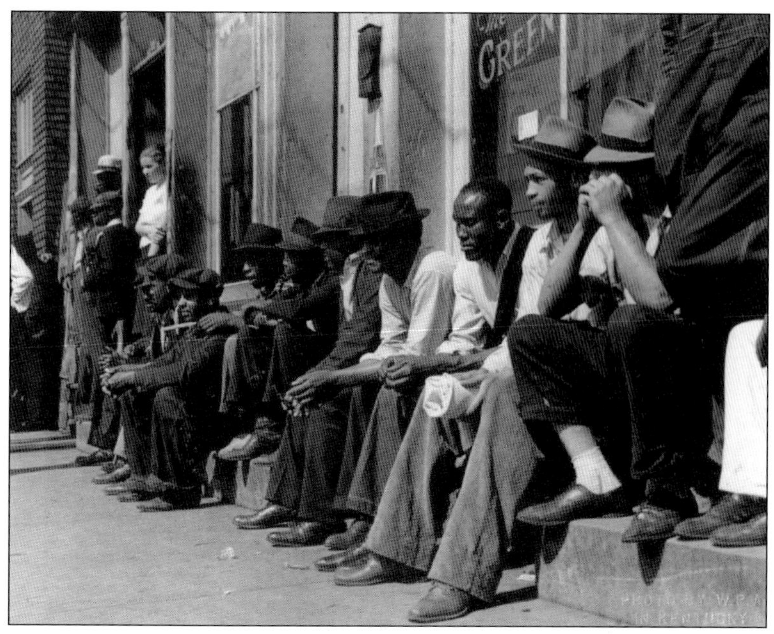

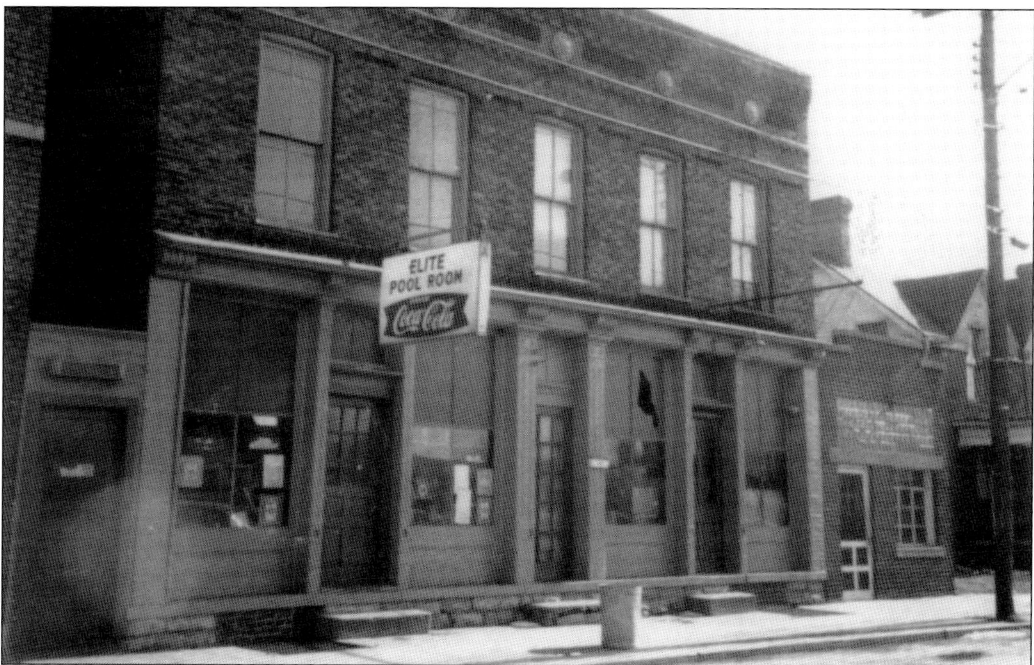

The Elite Pool Room, Elite Cab Company, and the Goldsmith House are seen about 1970. The Goldsmith House was rehabilitated, being used as offices for Constitution Square, the Heart of Danville, and a gift shop. It was last owned by the City Federation of Women's Clubs. The Elite Pool Room and single-story Elite Cab buildings were torn down shortly after this photograph was taken.

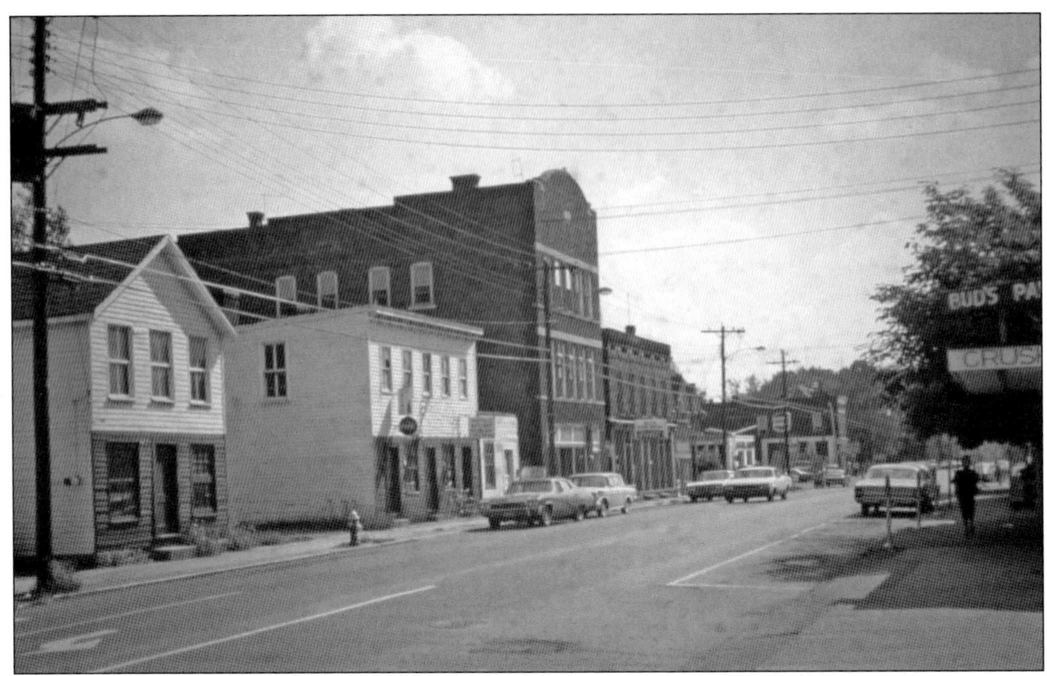

This is the east side of South Second Street looking south. From left to right are Harlan and Ross's Café, Mrs. Obie Clark's restaurant and the Danville Bike Shop, the Doric Lodge; the Elite Pool Room (formerly Green Pastures Restaurant), and the Goldsmith House. By 1971, only the lodge, the Elite Pool Room building, and the Goldsmith House were still standing. (Guy Ingram.)

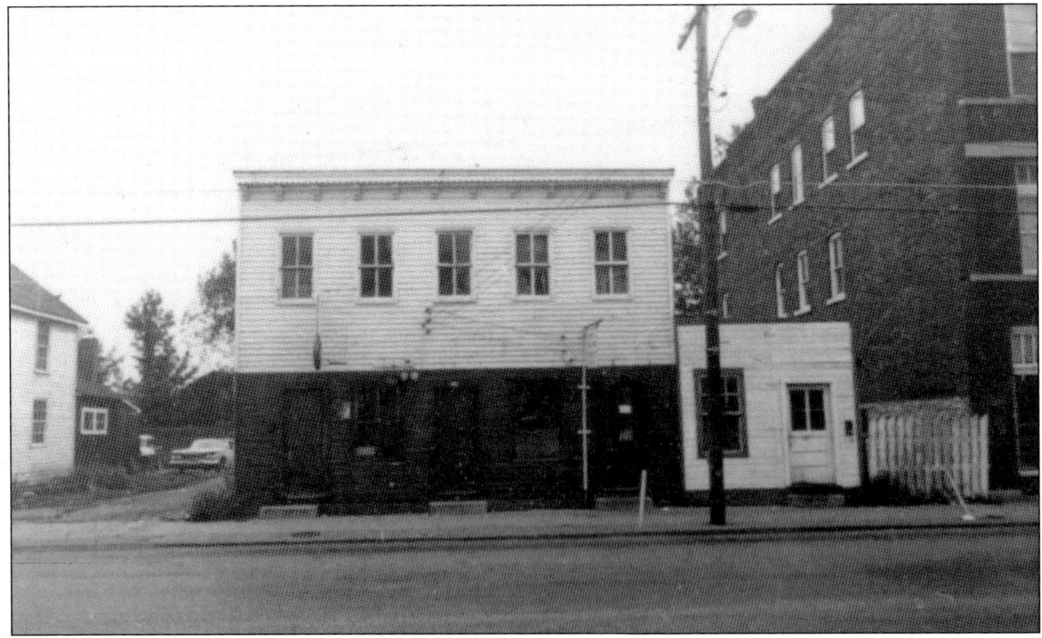

The three-story Doric Lodge is on the right, and Doneghy's Restaurant, later the Danville Bike Shop is the one-story building to the left of the Doric Lodge. The two-story building on the left, so often seen in many of these photographs, housed numerous businesses over time, including Ross's Restaurant and others from the 1920s to the 1960s.

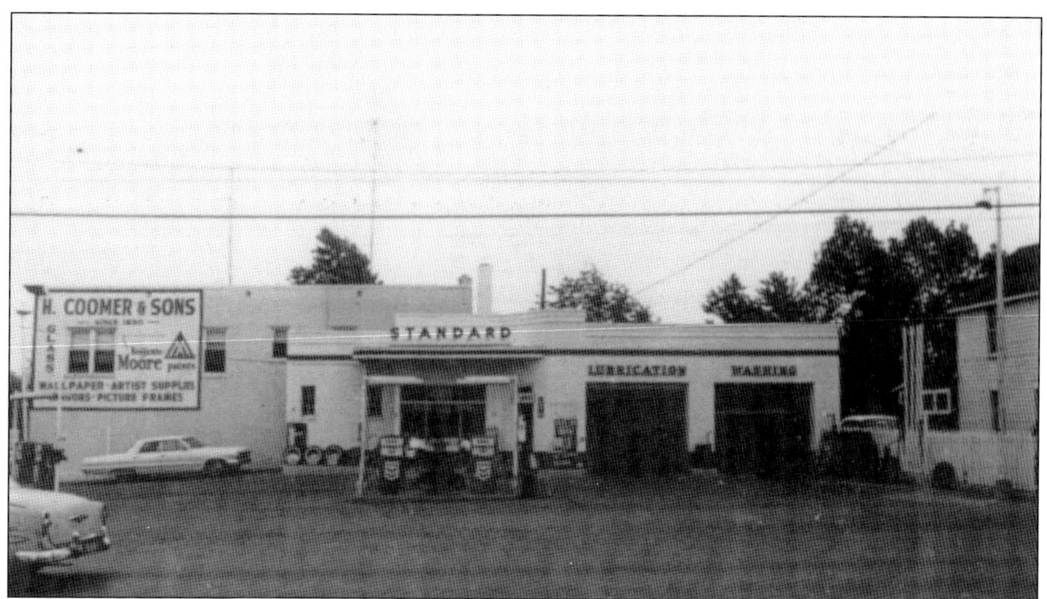

Curd's Service Station (as of 1945) was located on the southeast corner of South Second and West Main Streets. This corner once was owned by Gibeon Doram, where he had a bakery and confectionary patronized by both African Americans and whites. It is now the current northwest corner of Constitution Square, where Governor's Circle is located.

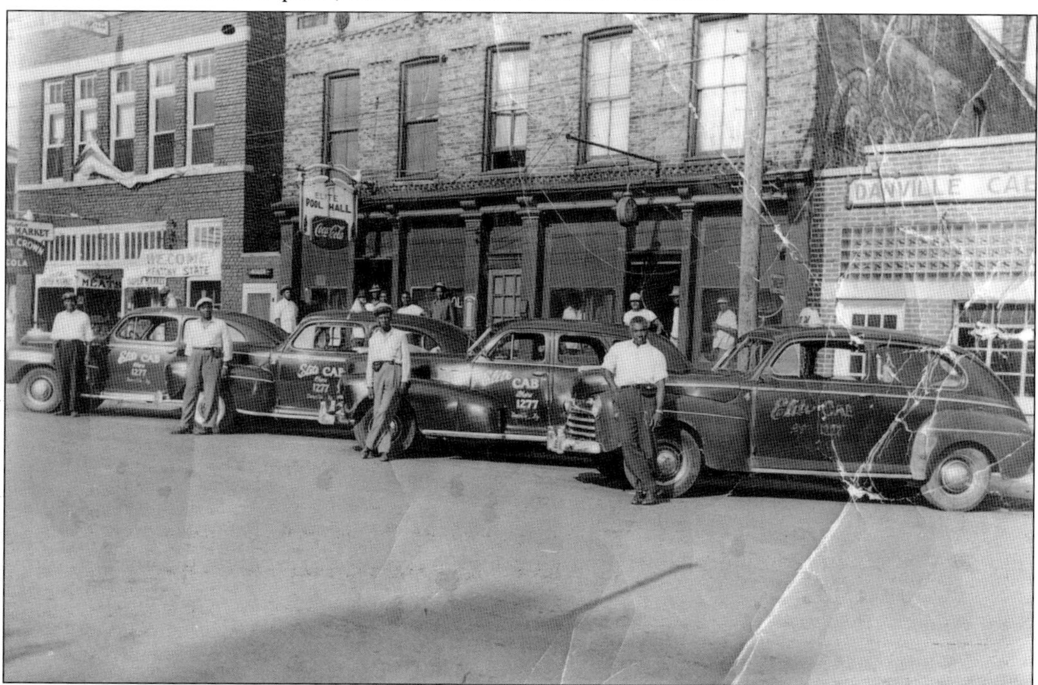

Drivers for the Elite Cab Company pose in front of the Doric Lodge and Singleton's Market, first floor (with the "Welcome Kentucky State" banner). The two-story Elite Pool Room (formerly Green Pastures Restaurant), and, Elite (or Danville) Cab Company are seen in more prosperous days, with owners Leon and Orestes "Tiny" Richardson. The drivers, from left to right, are George Lee Harlan, William "Buster" Letcher, Calvin Bedinger, and David Robinson.

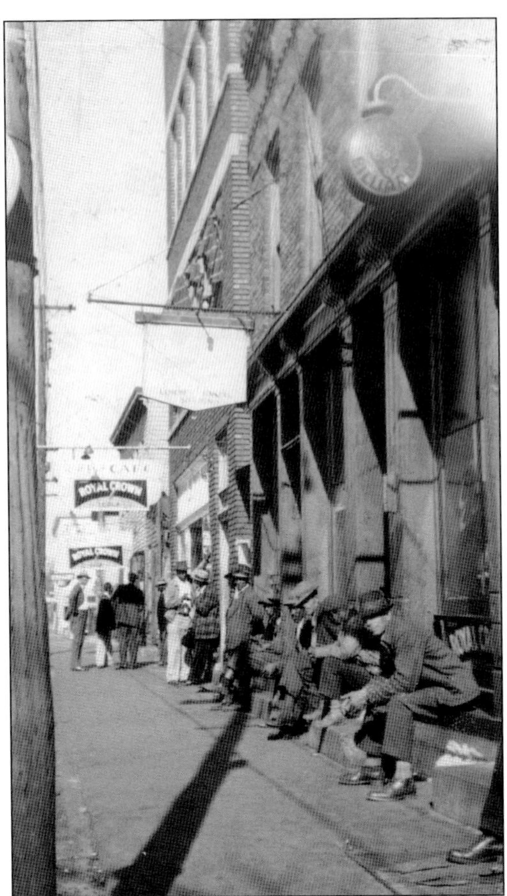

South Second Street was in its heyday in the 1940s when the street was bustling with people and businesses were prospering. Ross's Restaurant was in the white building, far left. There was another restaurant in the Doric Lodge, and people are sitting in front of what became the Elite Pool Room.

The two-story building that housed the Elite Cab Company is seen here, after the small one-story building next to it was demolished. The ads had been painted many years earlier. Royal Crown Cola had a bottling plant in Danville, but one wonders what circus it was that came to town and when.

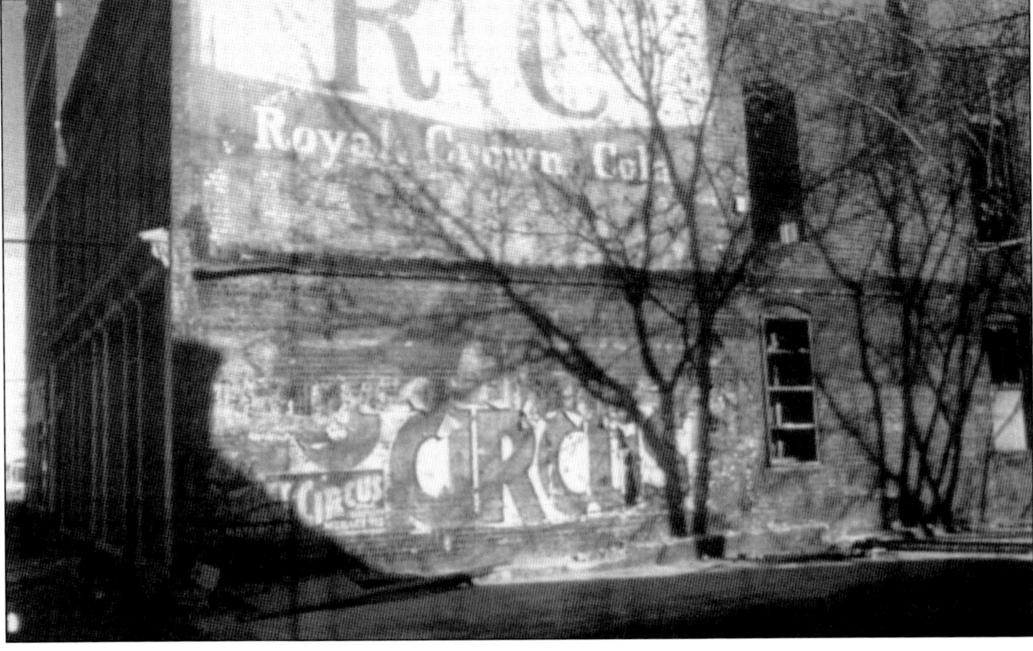

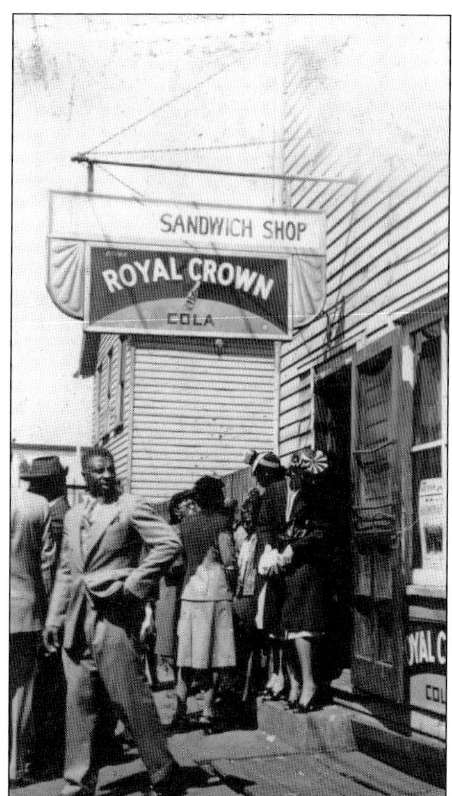

These people are dressed up for Easter Sunday on South Second Street. The white-painted wooden building in front of which these people are standing was north of and separated from the Doric Lodge by a bicycle shop. This two-story building with a sloping roof housed a number of different restaurants on the first floor over the years.

Tibbs Pool Hall, seen here in 1966, was located on the east side of the 200 block of South Second Street and was one of the last buildings to fall to urban renewal. James B. "J.B." Tibbs, son of barber John Tibbs and grandson of barber Benjamin Tibbs, is left, with Terry Bruce, right. Benjamin Tibbs was one of the wealthiest African American men in Kentucky at his death in 1898.

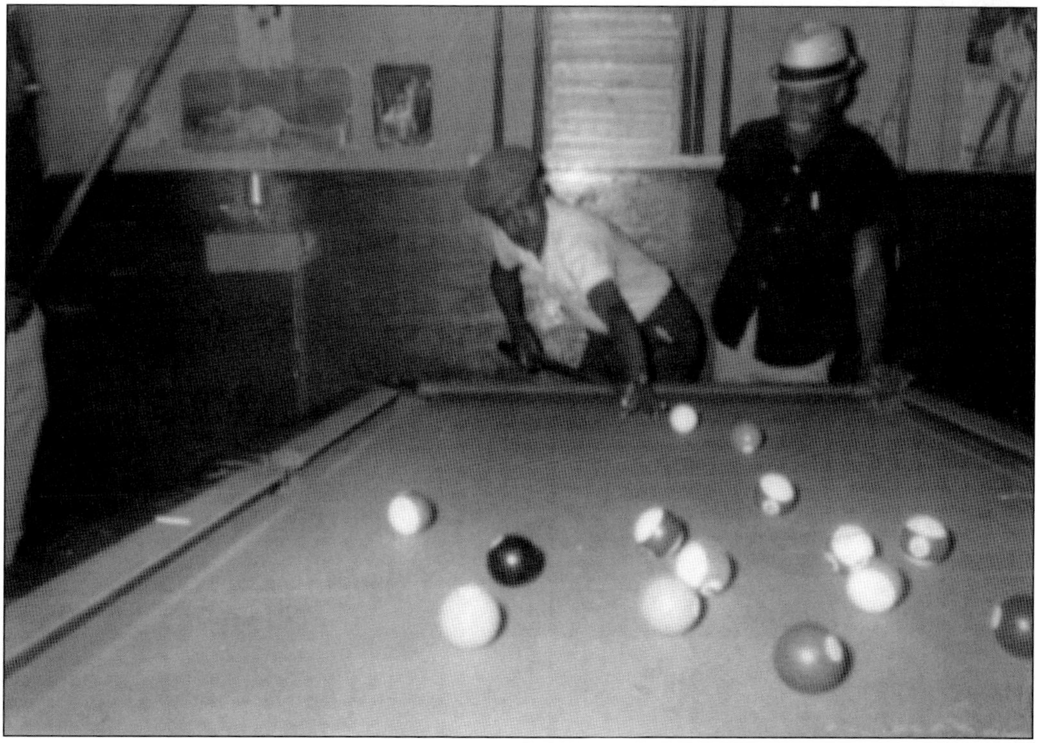

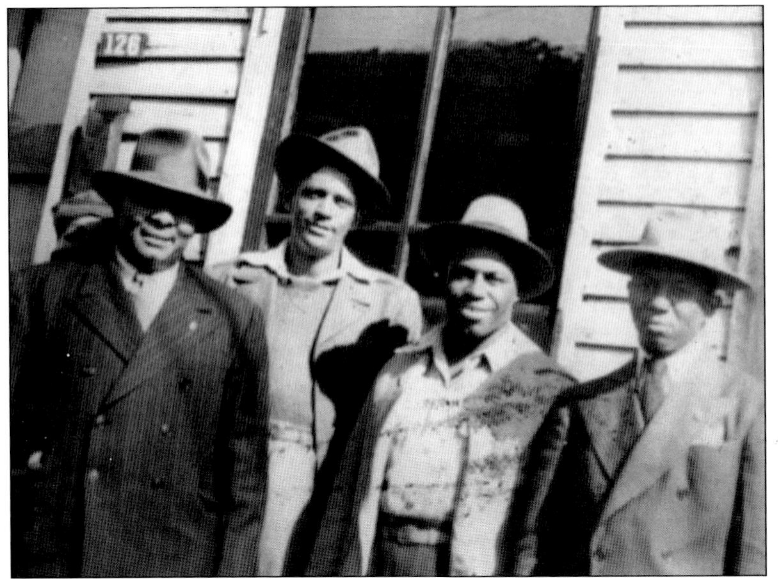

Seen here at 126 South Second Street, where the Doneghy brothers (later Reverend O'Neil's) barbershop was located in 1909, were, from left to right, William "Sinkhole" Harlan, unknown, "Cat" Andrews, James "Jimmy" Coates. At this address as early as 1797 was the market master's house, the public market being on present-day Constitution Square.

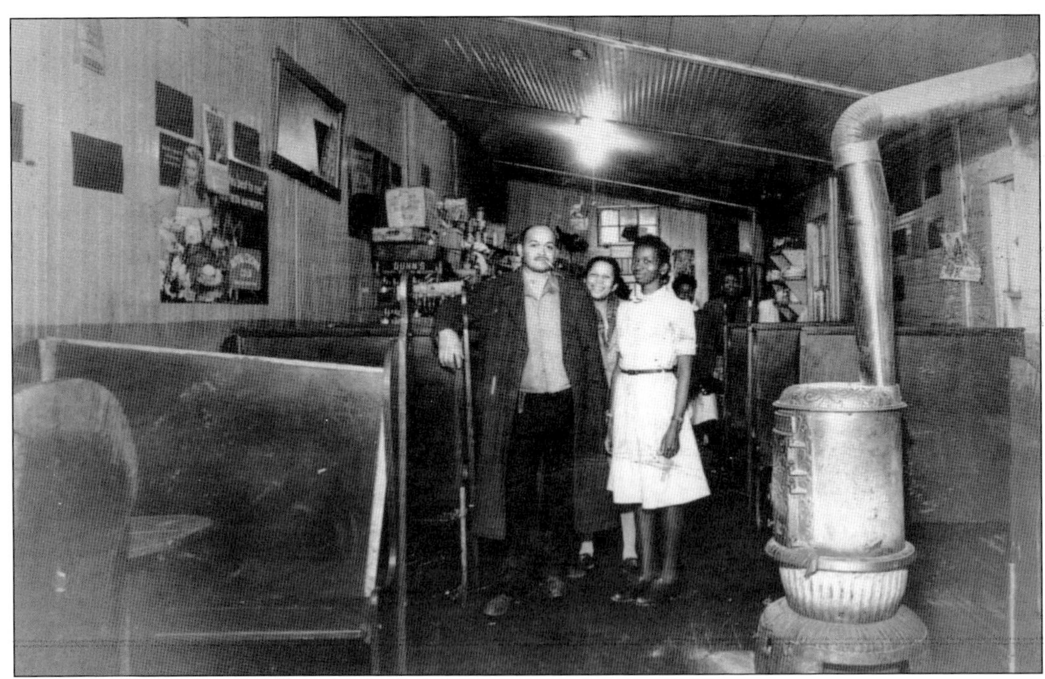

Ross's Restaurant, at 126 1/2 South Second Street, was in business at least from 1942 to 1956. Seen are Horace Ross Sr. (1911–1976), and his wife, Mary Elizabeth (Carpenter) Ross (1918–1994), in white. Owners of other restaurants have included Sam Cook, Carrie McKee, Jacob Warren, Sam Woods, Robert Jones, Paul Griffin, William Wade, George Roach, Harriet Bottoms, Green Pastures, David Hale, Manlius Neal, Samuel Miller, Lloyd Parker, and Emma Turner.

Minnie Lou Hale holds the little boy, Billy Harlan, in front of one of the white wooden buildings north of the Doric Lodge. This view of Second Street, from about 1944, shows above Minnie's head, the White House Restaurant, and the State Theater on West Main Street. Looking at all the cars, one can see that South Second Street was the heart of African American Danville.

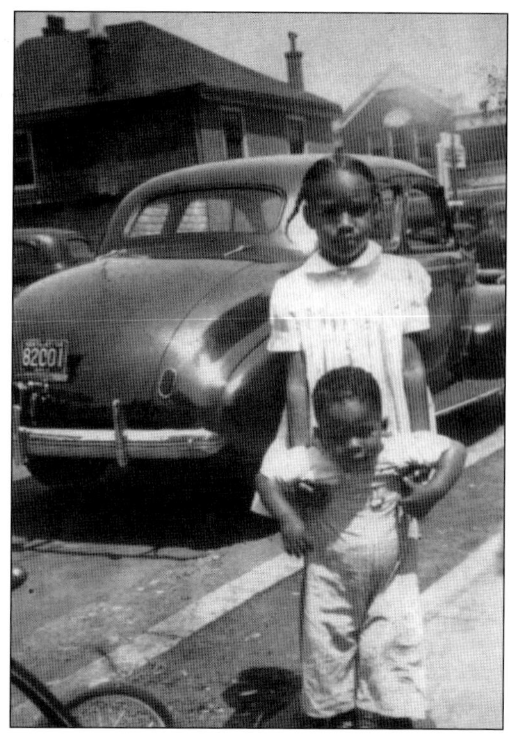

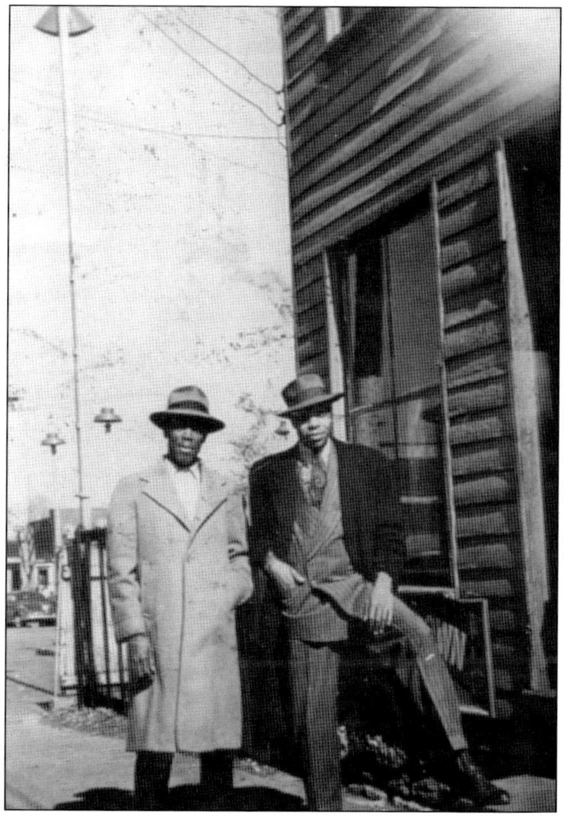

These dapper gentlemen are posing in front of 112 South Second Street. This three-story building is seen in many photographs of the area and hosted numerous businesses over time. Behind the man on the left is a Curd's service station (as of 1945), which was on the corner of West Main and South Second Streets.

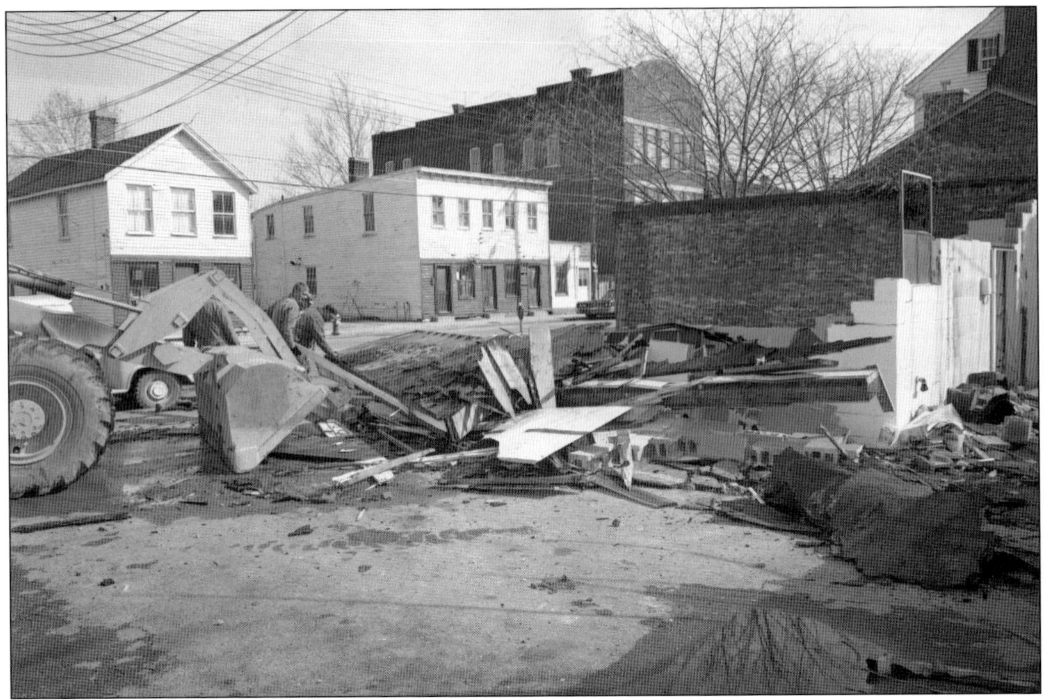

As urban renewal began, the building on the corner of West Main and South Second Streets was cleared. Here are seen three major buildings that were eventually torn down, plus the Ephraim McDowell house on the far right. The brick wall, center right, is still there and now displays a painting of William "Bunny" Davis. (Charles A. Thomas Collection, BCPL.)

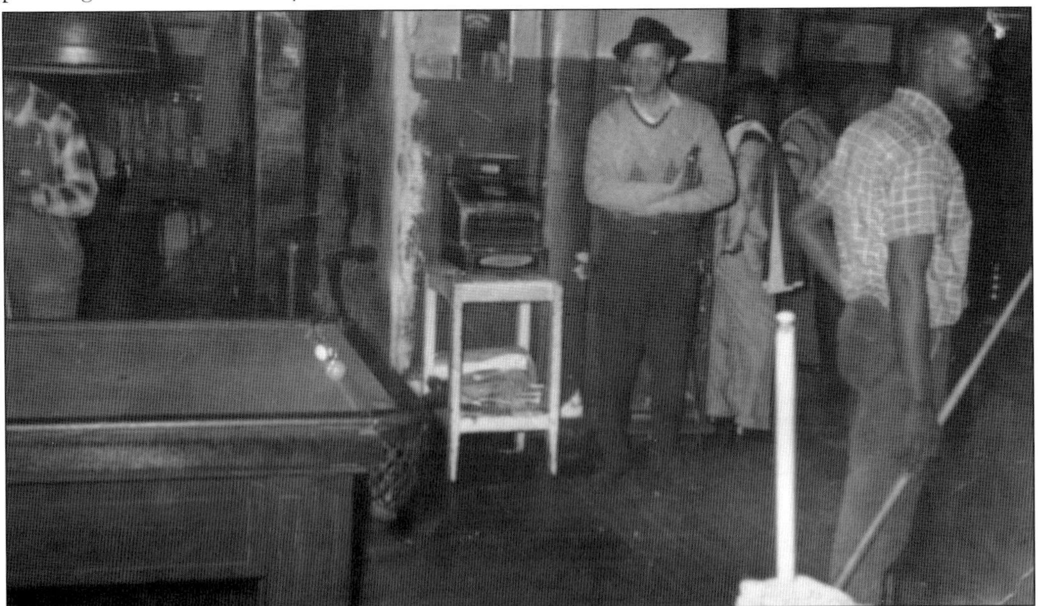

Leon Richardson, with hat and arms folded, and James Stallworth, with the cue, are in Richardson's Elite Pool Room, which was in business by 1945 and for a few more years after. It was owned by Leon's father, barber, and entrepreneur Either One Richardson (not a nickname), who owned a great number of properties in the Black business district by the 1960s.

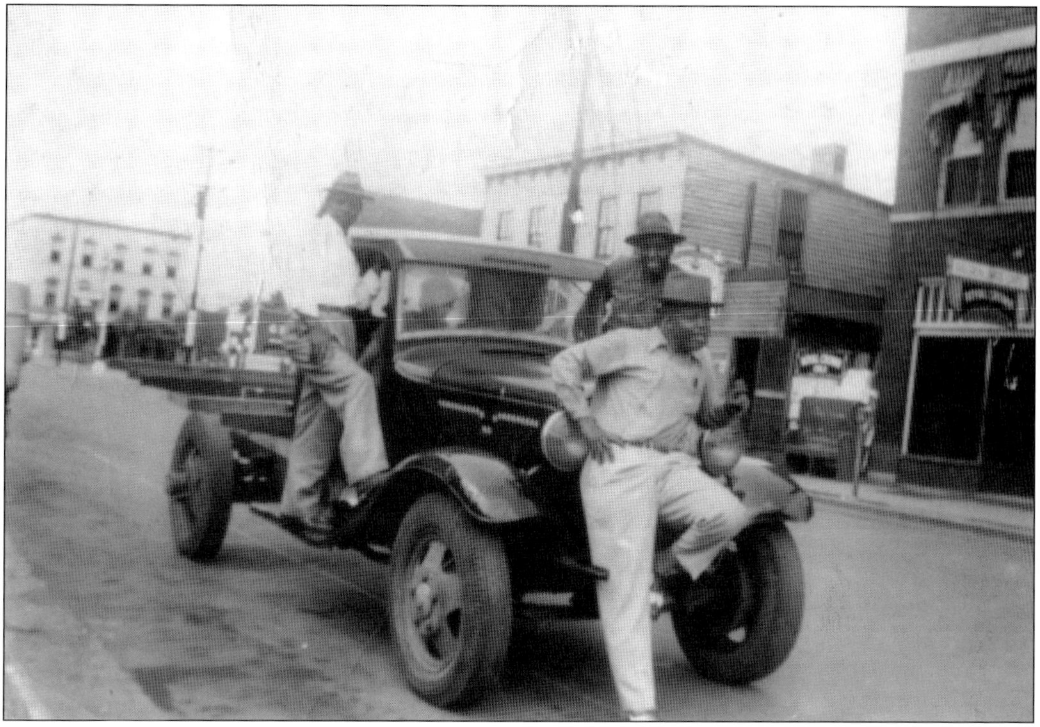

Pictured on South Second Street in front of the Doric Lodge are James "Jim" Singleton and William "Buster" Letcher (standing) and George Fields (front). In the background are the Henson Hotel on West Main Street (present home of the DBCAAHS) and two wooden buildings that housed various businesses over time.

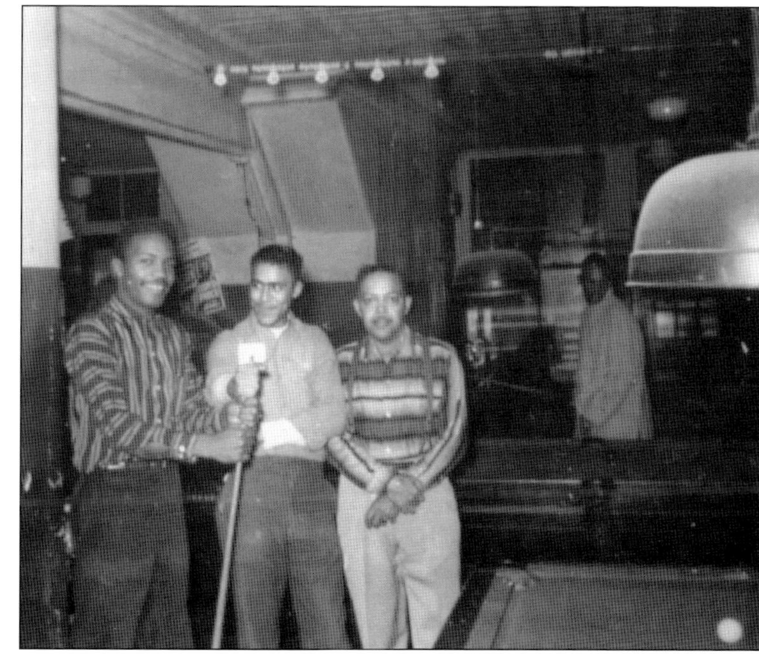

Pictured from left to right at the Elite Pool Room, Kenneth James Prince (1933–1990), Richard Lee Buckner, and Archie Doram (1908–1958) are ready to "rack 'em up." Prince married Ann Carolyn Jones, Bate's homecoming queen in 1949. Buckner was the son of Lucille (Ford) Buckner and lived in San Francisco in 1987. Doram, the son of Octavius and Scottie (Doneghy) Doram, was killed in an automobile accident in Graefensburg, Kentucky.

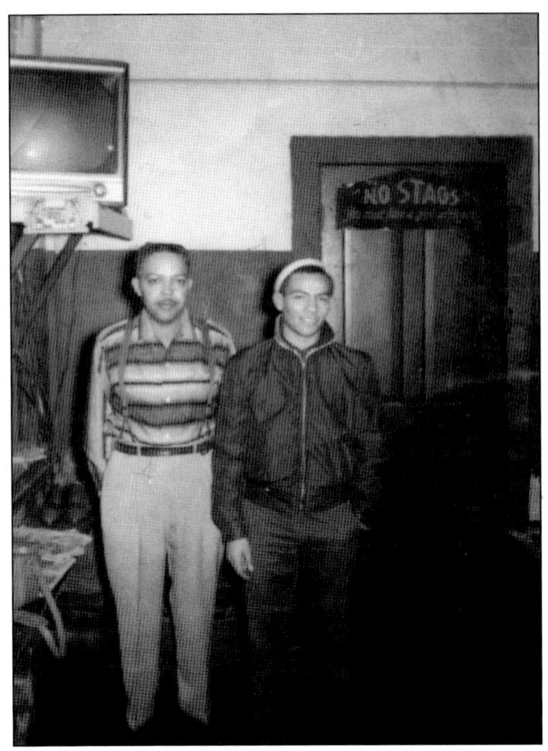

Archie Doram (left) and James Doram Jr. are seen at the Elite Pool Room, probably the same day as the previous photograph. Archie owned a nightclub on South Second Street. The Doram family has a long and compelling history in Boyle County, ranking among the "first families" of the area. They are descended from Dennis and Diademia (Taylor) Doram, pictured at the beginning of Chapter 7.

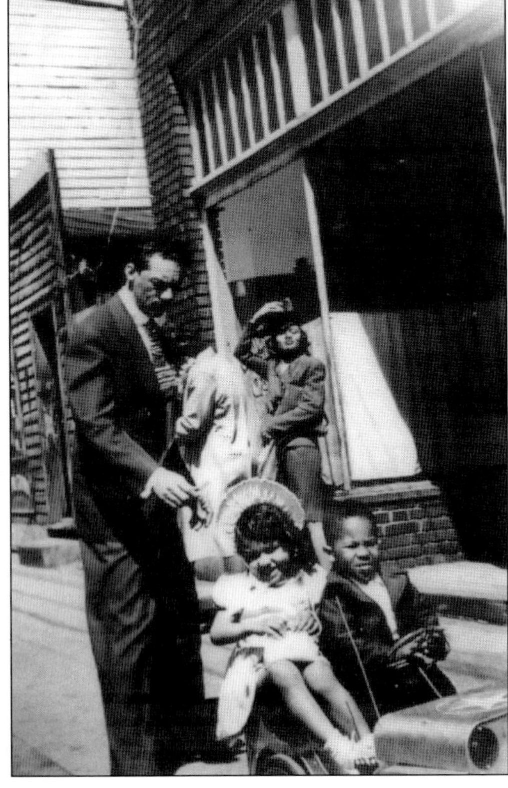

Betty Sue (Caldwell) Griffin, daughter of Allen and Elise (Taylor) Caldwell, is seen in front of the Doric Lodge in about 1945. She graduated from Bate High School and Fisk University, Nashville, doing graduate work at several universities, and has been honored as a Kentucky Colonel, the 1999 National Council of Negro Women's outstanding educator, and a member of the US Office of Civil Rights. The boy may be William Harlan.

The Golden Gate Café was in operation in 1948 at 128 South Second Street. These ladies apparently are dressed up for Easter Sunday, as many similar photographs show similarly dressed-up people. What this image also shows, incidentally, is that African Americans took great pride in their appearance, and the women were often "dressed to kill."

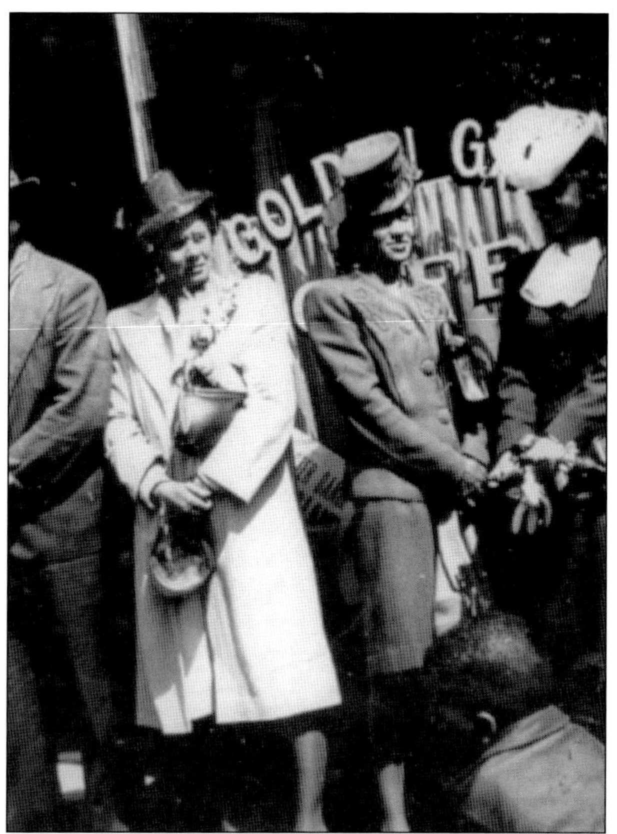

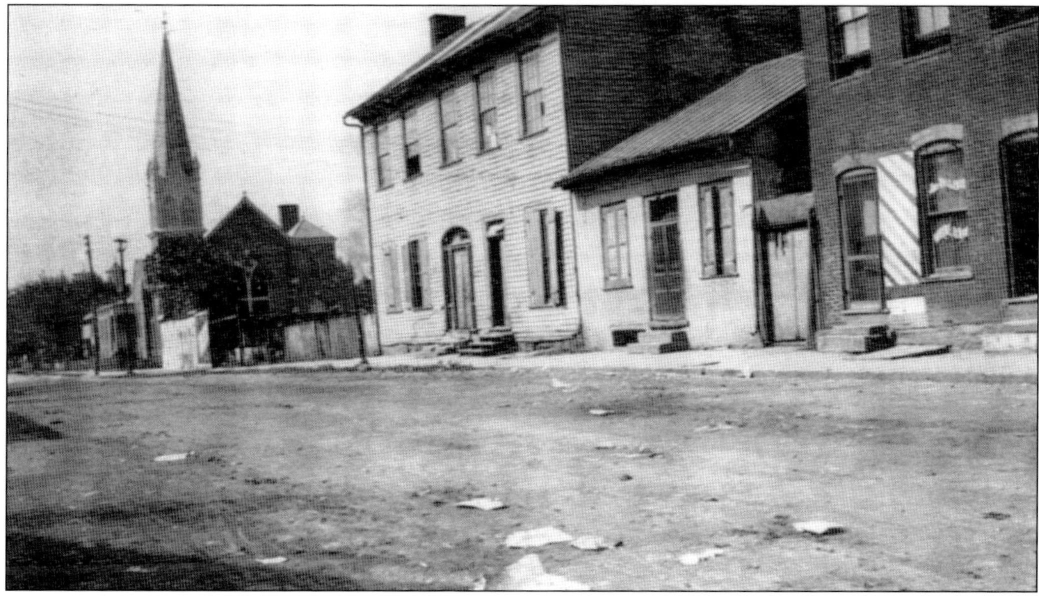

The Ephraim McDowell House and Apothecary Shop are seen about 1910 before renovation. In 1914, the Apothecary Shop was a pool room, according to the Sanborn Fire Insurance maps. The McDowell House and Apothecary Shop are the only buildings remaining though the church was rebuilt after a 1966 fire. The next few photographs show the progression of the renovation.

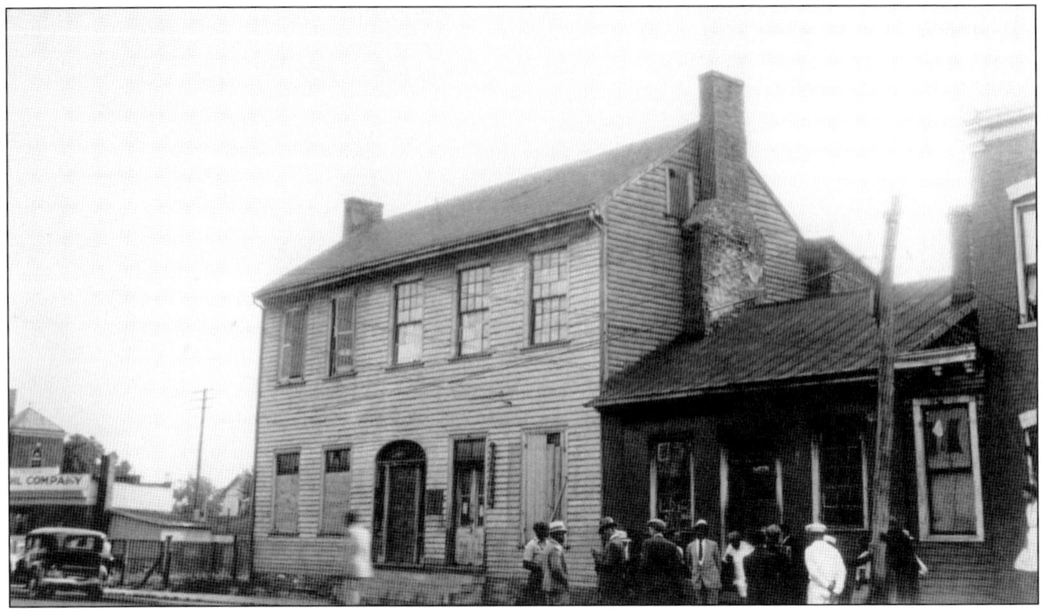

The Ephraim McDowell House and Apothecary are shown in the mid-1930s just before any restoration took place. Both buildings had deteriorated significantly over time and contained numerous small businesses, barbershops, restaurants, and apartments. When the apothecary was a restaurant, it burned, which is notable in this photograph. Note several front doors on the main house and the orientation of the front steps.

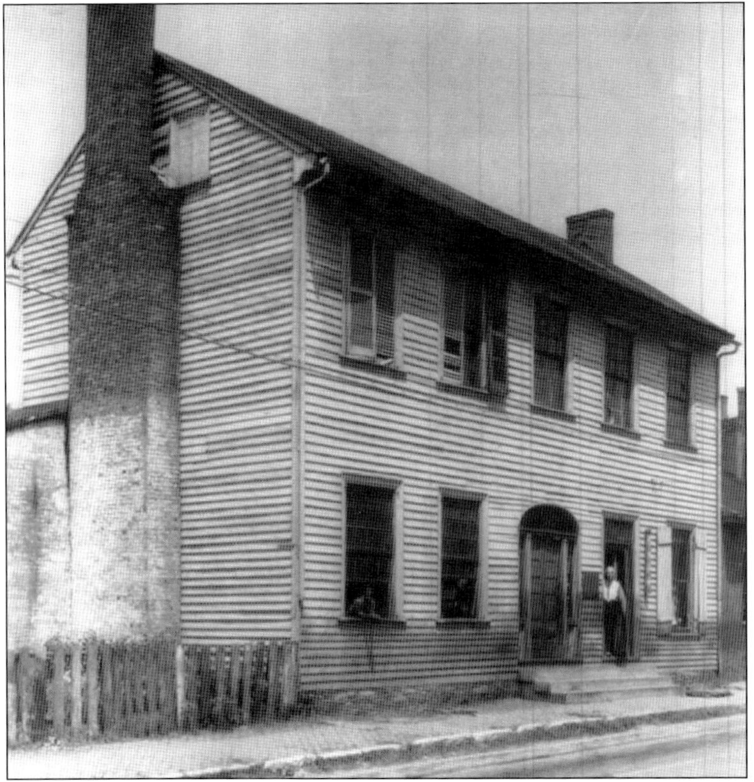

A different view of the McDowell House shows the dilapidated condition it was in before it was renovated. This historic site was the first building in the South Second Street area to be restored. It would be another 25 years before the next effort at restoration was made in the area.

The building in the center is now the Apothecary Shop of the McDowell House It had burned at one time when it was a restaurant, as seen in this photograph. The Chicken Shack, seen on the right in 1957, was on the first floor of Dallas Jones's building. This restaurant, even in this condition, was one of the most popular on South Second Street. (Danville Boyle County Chamber of Commerce.)

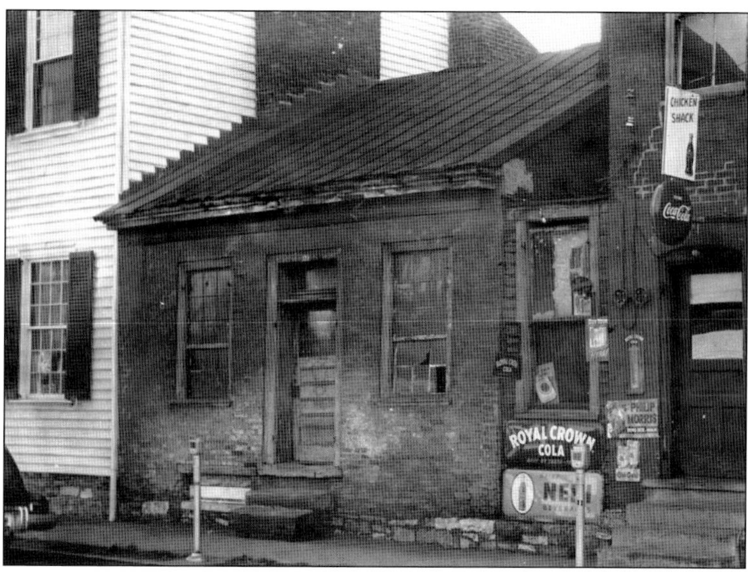

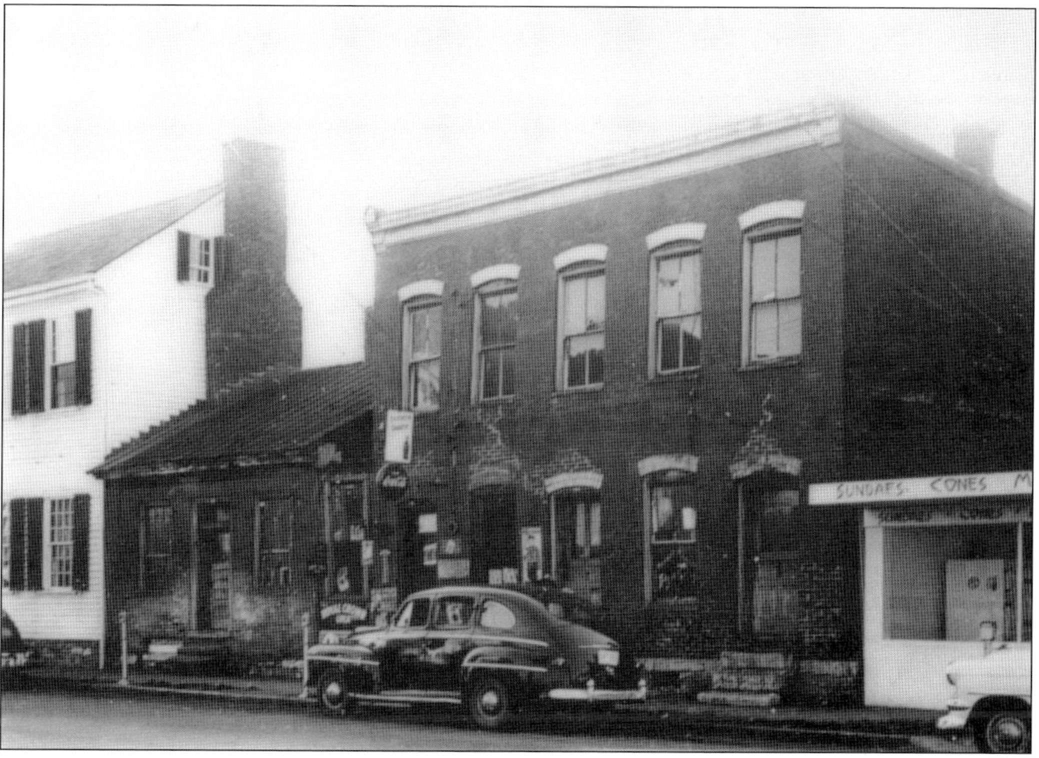

The home of the famous surgeon Ephraim McDowell was restored, and later, the original apothecary shop was also restored. All three buildings housed either Black apartments or businesses prior to 1939. The two-story brick building which held numerous Black businesses was torn down during urban renewal. Dallas Jones had a barbershop upstairs, and the Chicken Shack was on the first floor.

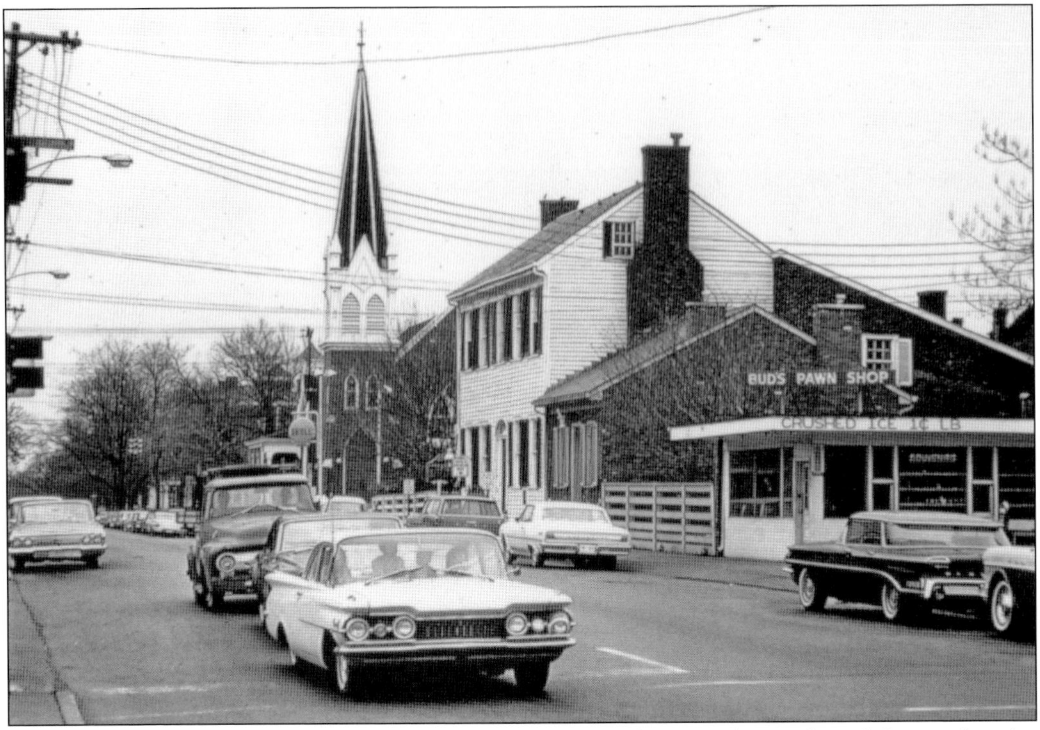

This view looking south on the west side of South Second Street shows, from left to right, the First Baptist Church, which burned in 1966; a Shell gasoline station owned by William "Bunny" Davis; and the McDowell House and its attached apothecary. The fencing where Dallas Jones had his barbershop and several restaurants were located is now part of the apothecary garden.

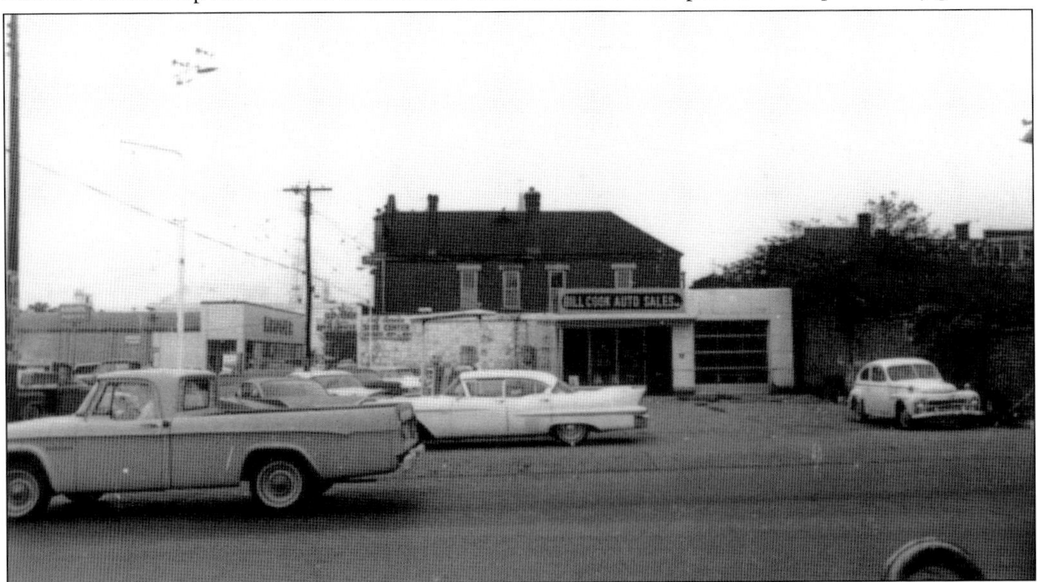

On the northwest corner of South Second and West Walnut streets was a service station owned in the 1950s by Bunny Davis. The brick building in the center was the former Odd Fellows Hall (white), which became the new home of Doric Lodge No. 18 after the building on South Second Street was demolished in the mid-1970s.

Orestes "Tiny" Richardson worked in Bunny Davis's service station. The Richardsons were a large, prominent, and respected family in Danville from the late 1800s on and owned several businesses and a great deal of other property. Orestes's father, Either One, was the chief barber at the City Barber Shop on West Main Street.

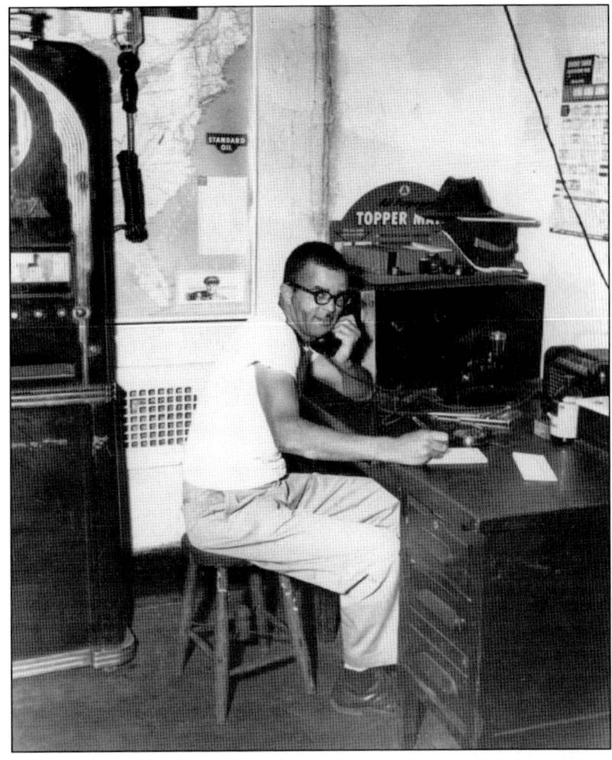

Mable Harlan and Mayme Davis are pictured in the Red Top Club on Duncan Hill, which was, at that time, south of the city limits. The Red Top was in existence as early as March 1939, but after going through several managers, the property was put up for sale in April 1948.

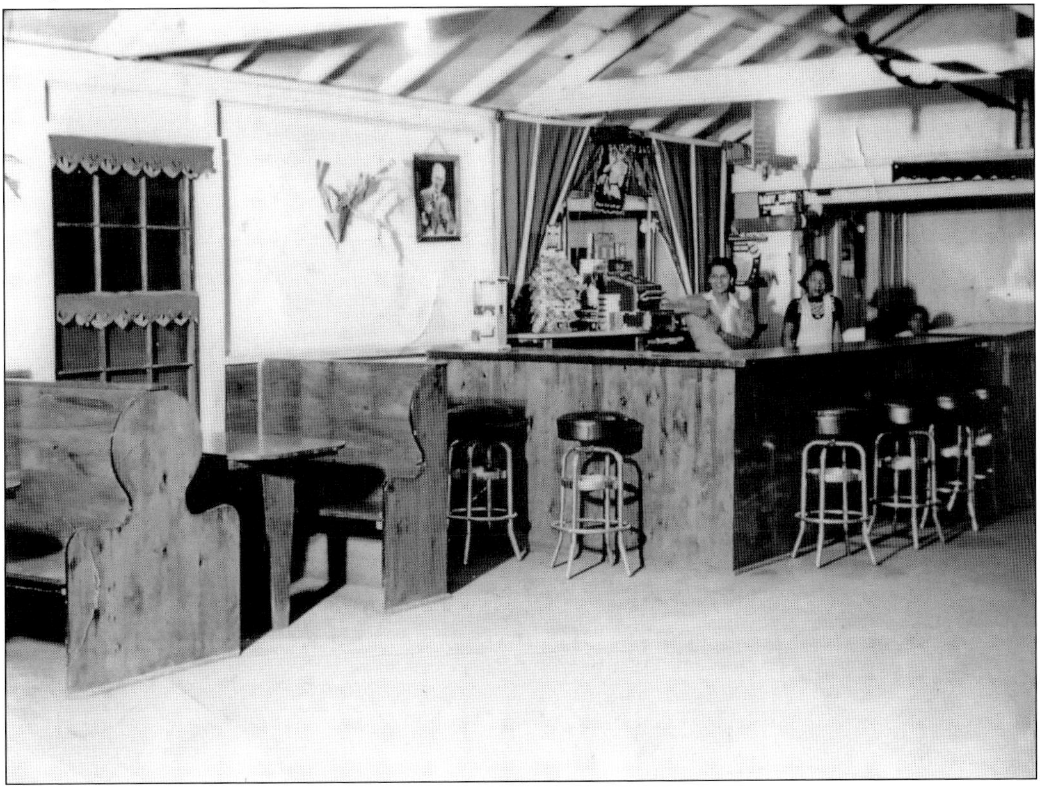

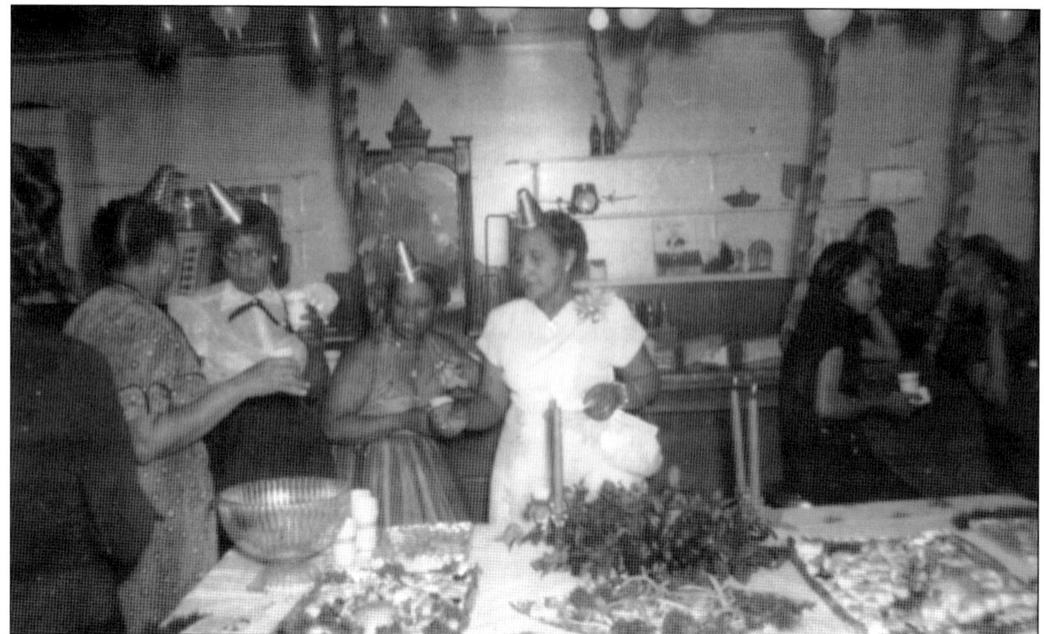

This photograph shows an Orchid Girls party at Club Hollywood, located at the south end of the South Second Street district. This was one of the more popular party venues for the Black community. The lady in white is Annie Segar. Many African Americans complained about unequal enforcement of liquor laws, in that Black establishments were often raided when white ones were spared.

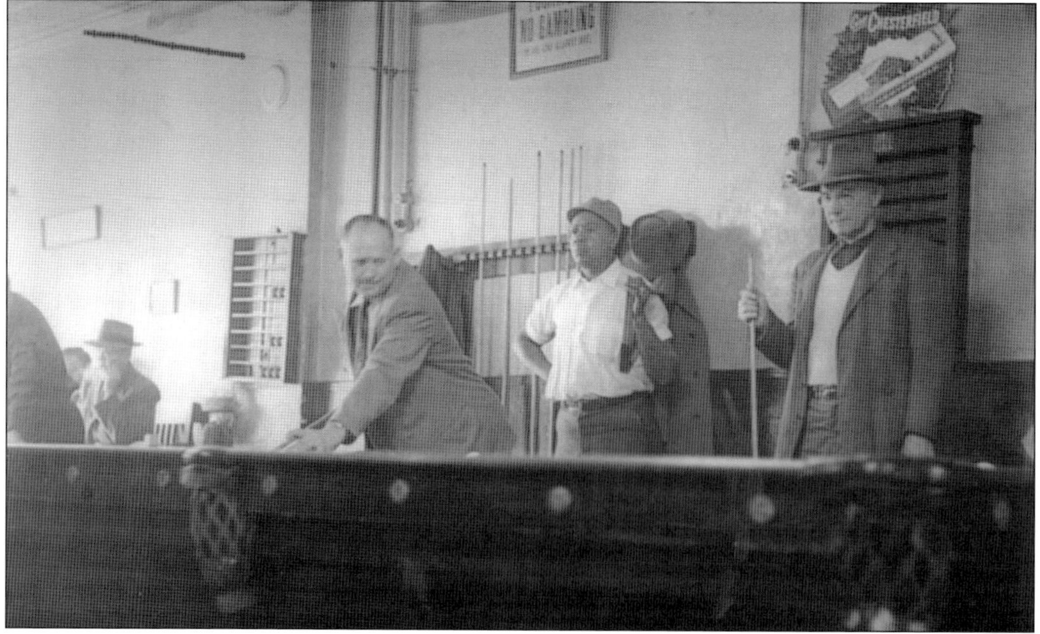

Ace Billiards, 303 West Main Street (now an upscale restaurant), while not part of the African American community, was nonetheless a place of employment for some. John Hayden, the African American in the white shirt is shown in other pictures shining shoes for white customers. This location has hosted several upscale restaurants since the billiard parlor closed.

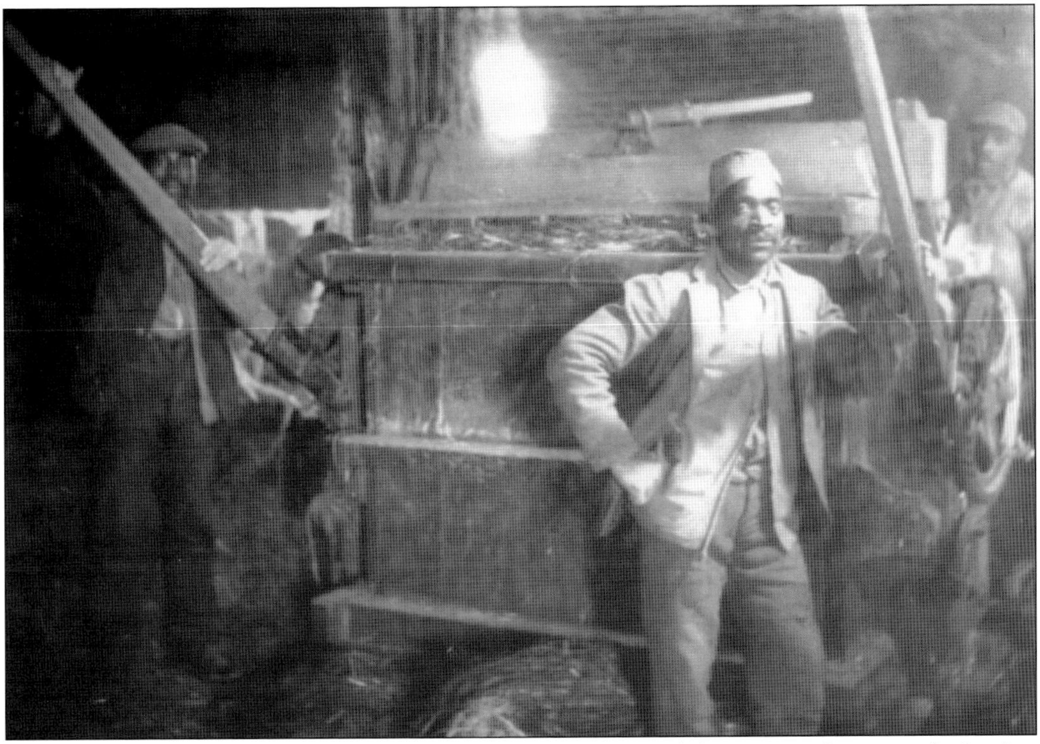

Inside a hemp-processing plant, the work was hard, dirty, and dangerous, the type of jobs that were often relegated to African Americans. Hemp was one of the first crops grown in Kentucky, in Danville, and for many years, Boyle County was a leading hemp producer in the United States. Several buildings downtown even have stone window trimmings showing hemp rope, a tribute to several "rope walks" in the city.

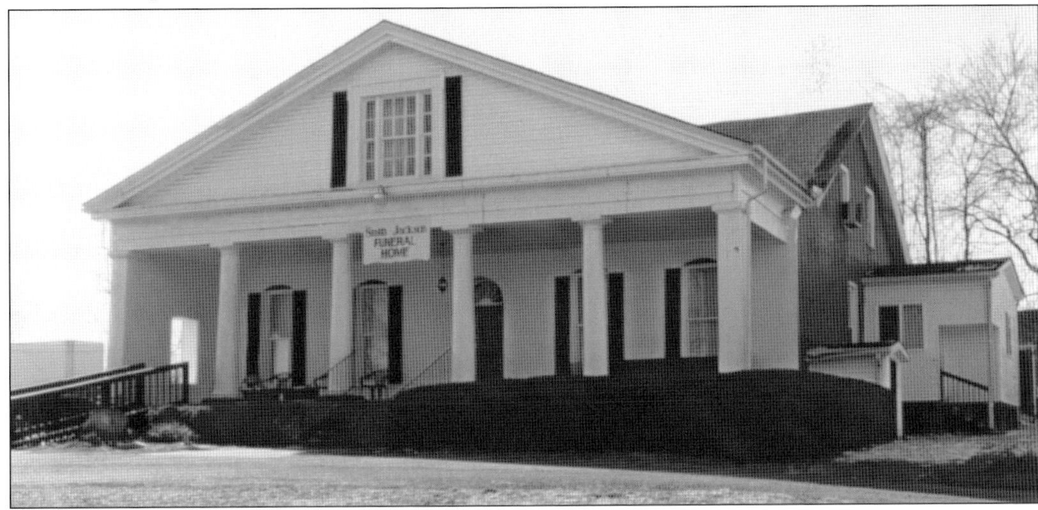

Smith-Jackson Funeral Home was begun by Ashby Jackson at 106 West Walnut Street in the early 1900s. He was joined by John W. Smith (and later by his son Michael) by 1939. When that building was destroyed by fire, this historic building on Bate Street, known as the "Woodcock House" or "Crutchfield House," was purchased. It had been home to several African American organizations prior to that. (Michael Denis.)

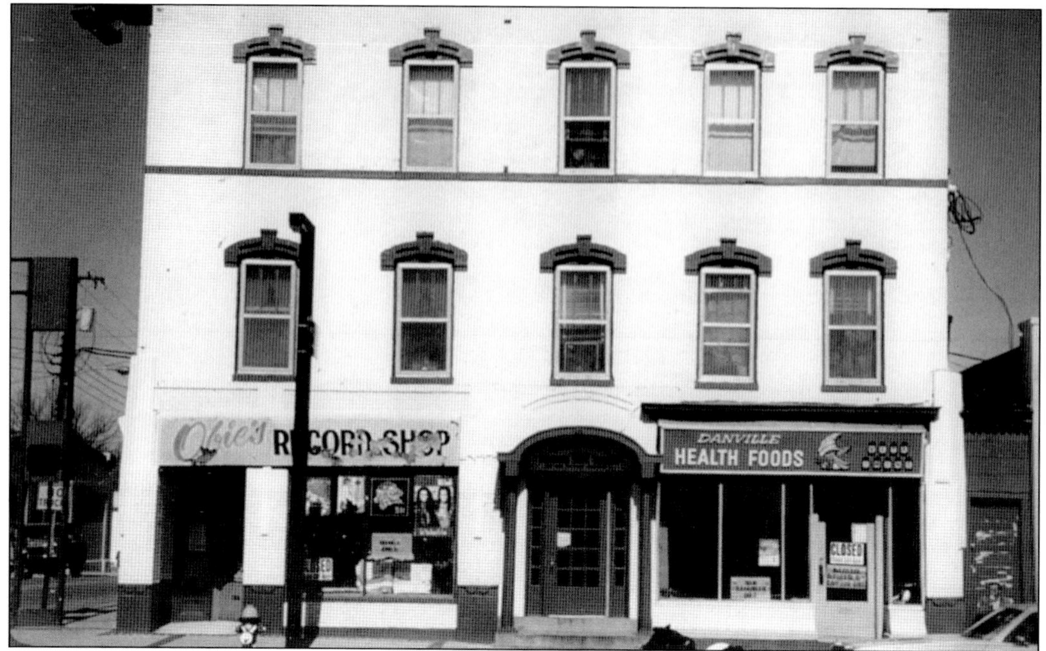

Obie Slater's Record Shop was located in the Henson Hotel on West Main Street. Slater also managed a nightclub in Lebanon, Kentucky, that hosted many of the great Black musicians of the 1950s and 1960s. The Danville Boyle County African American Historical Society's history center is in this building, around the left corner.

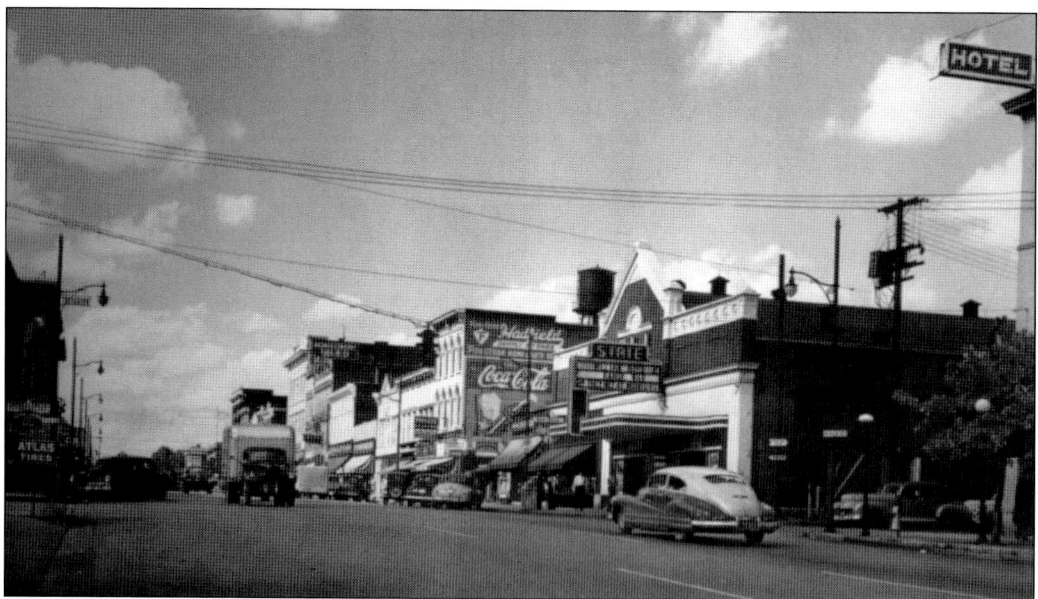

This view is looking west on West Main Street in 1939. Many of the stores shown here accepted African American patrons, but with limitations. Women could shop for clothes but were not allowed to try them on. If Blacks were allowed to attend movie theaters like the Kentucky (they were not allowed to in the state), they had to sit in the balcony and could not use the restrooms or buy food at the concessions.

Four

Schools

When one speaks of the many schools in Boyle County that educated African Americans, arguably the most important of these was Bate School. Beginning in 1881 as a one-room school, and finally serving as the junior high and middle school for the entire city of Danville, Bate for many years after the 1910s was the only Black school in Danville and, in 1921, became the only high school in the county that Black students could attend.

Early on, in the 1830s, there were also numerous other Black schools in Danville, including ones run by Willis Russell and Gib Doram, as well as the freedman's schools, one run by the Concord Presbyterian Church, and the another run by the First Baptist Church. By 1900, there were still several schools that educated African Americans, notably the Danville Polytechnic School which enrolled up to 600 students at one time. About that time, there actually were more Black students attending Boyle County schools than there were white students.

Thus, the focus is in large part on Bate here, because it was so important, but also because so much of the other Black school histories, and even buildings, are gone or soon will be. Other schools in Boyle County at times were located in Aliceton, Wilsonville, Perryville, Faulconer, Atoka, Needmore, Clifton, and Shelby City, with most consolidating or closing before 1964.

By the time city and county schools integrated in 1964, the Wilsonville and Perryville schools, the only schools outside Danville serving African Americans below high school levels, had closed. Bate School became Danville Bate Junior High School, then Danville Bate Middle School, and finally, John W. Bate Middle School.

The Kentucky School for the Deaf (KSD) was founded in 1823. It opened its "colored division" in the 1880s and educated Black students from then on. Five photographs of KSD are presented here through the generous permission of the Jacobs Hall Museum of the Kentucky School for the Deaf.

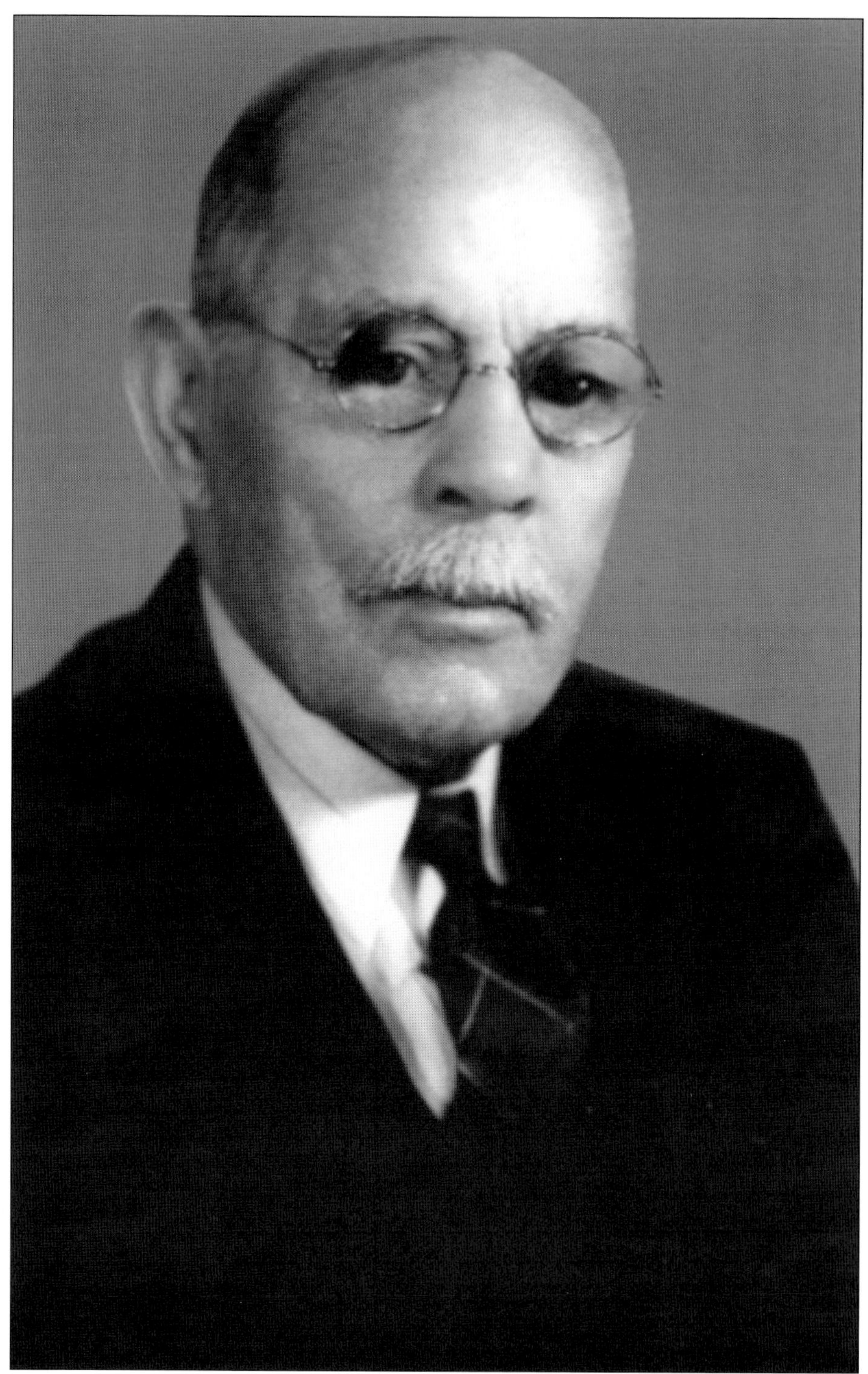

John William Bate (1855–1945) was born enslaved in Louisville but received an AB from Berea College in 1881 and an AM in 1891. He moved to Danville and served as an educational leader for 59 years. Retiring at age 85, Bate noted, "I found a one-room school and I left a building of twenty rooms. . . . I found 6 students and left a school with 600."

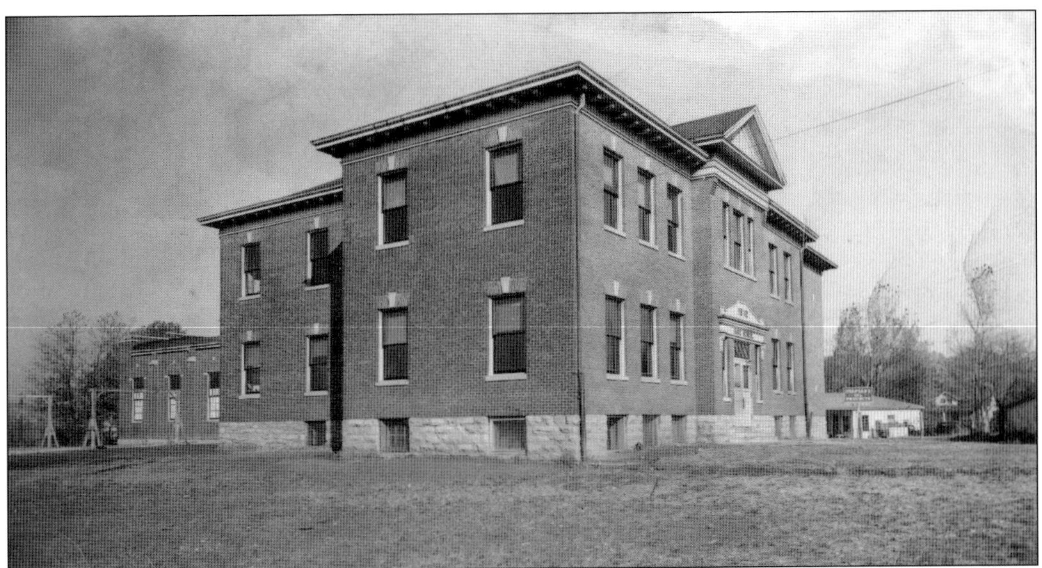

Begun as a one-room school, John William Bate became principal in 1881. He oversaw the construction of a brick building and several additions, which looked like the photograph by the 1920s. Bate housed grades first through eighth until 1915, when high school grades were added. An addition was later built on the left side. Bate was recognized as one of the best "colored" schools in Kentucky.

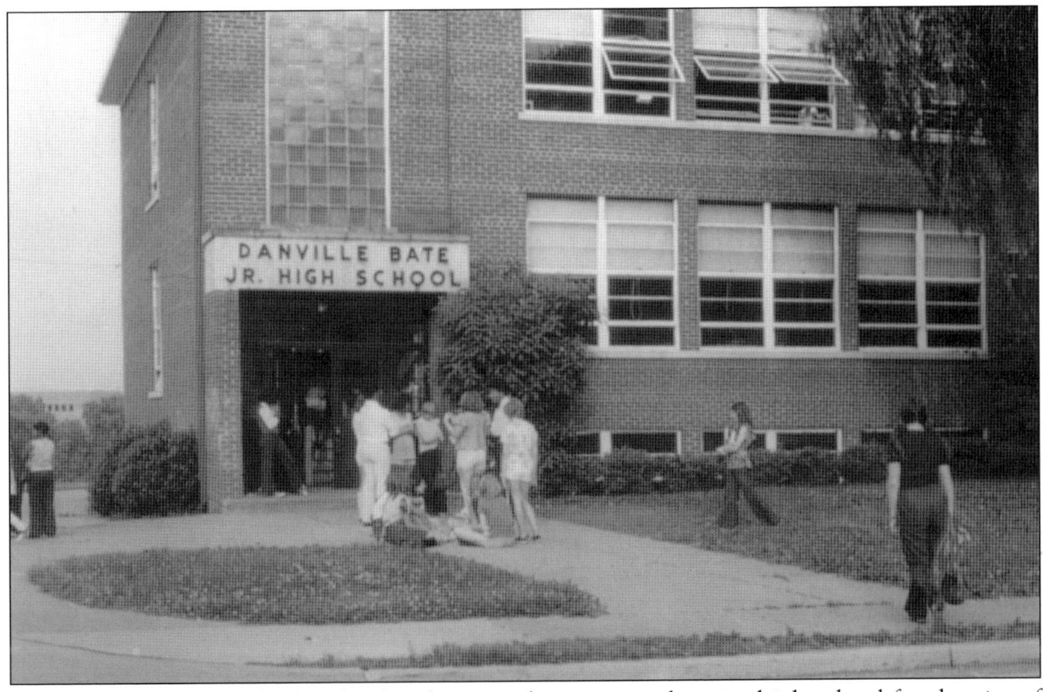

After Bate closed as a high school, it became the integrated junior high school for the city of Danville, called Danville Bate Junior High School, and remained that even after a new building was constructed. Thus, from 1964 until the mid-1970s, when the original building was replaced with the present building, it served the city as a junior high and a middle school.

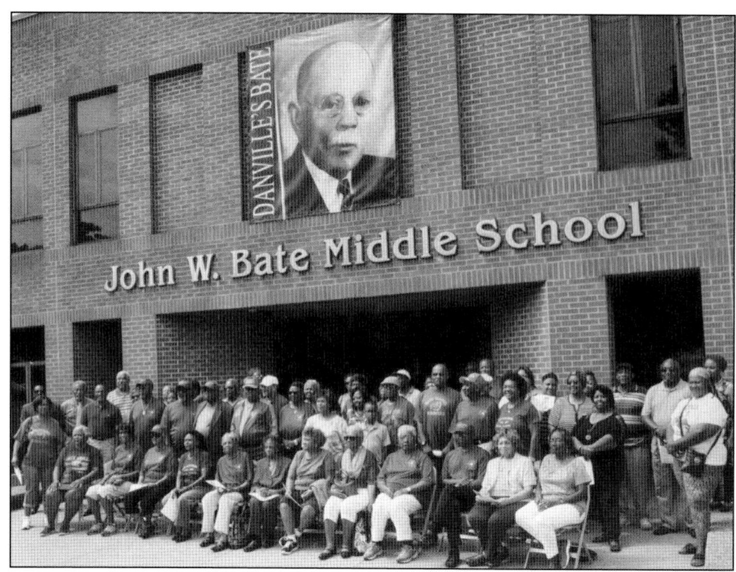

After the Bate School was torn down, the present building was constructed. Danville decided to change all school mascots to "Admirals" and all school colors to blue and white. But Bate alumni and alumnae stood firm in keeping the "Bulldogs" and purple and gold for their beloved Bate school. In the end, the city relented and even changed the name from Danville Bate to John W. Bate Middle School.

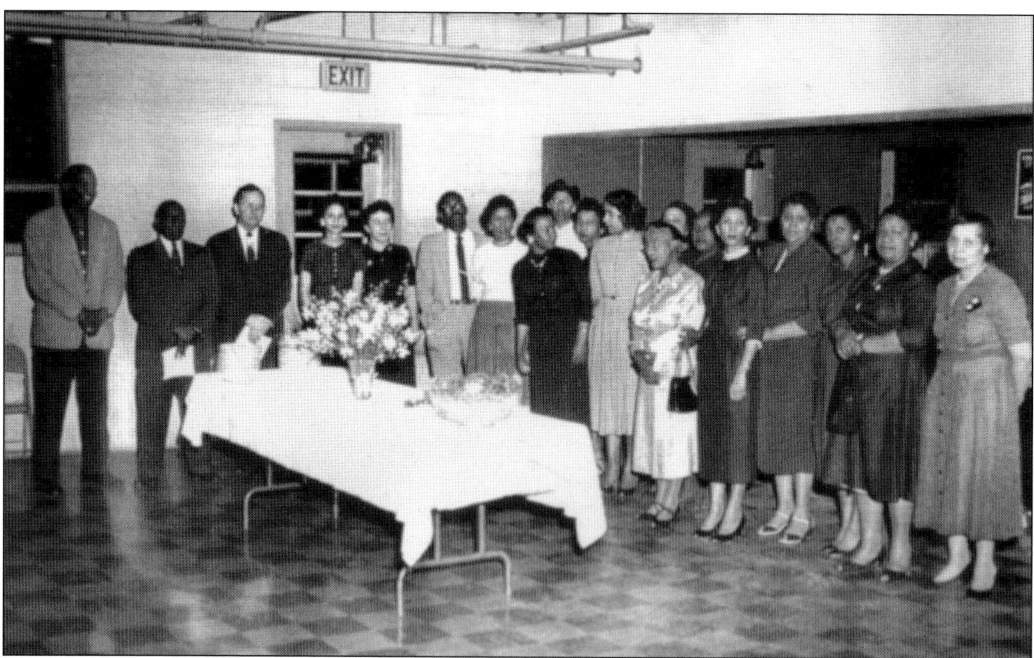

The faculty and administration pictured in May 1955 included, from left to right, coach Ozenia Hawkins, principal William Summers, Supt. John Robinson, Delores Revely, Lindell Parr, William Cherry Jr., Bertha Bowman, Amelia Burton, Helen Fisher, Birdie Edwards, Mary Riffe, Margaret Helm, Ella Pryor, Lillian Jones, Ruby Riffe, Lola Dale, Lucy Stephens, Zula Levingston, and Gertrude Sledd. (Charles D. Grey.)

A general gathering of the "Negro Education Association" was held at Bate High School. This was probably a regional meeting, including Black teachers from area counties. One of the women in the photograph may be Bertha Bowman, near the door, behind the white-haired woman. The Bate School was a leader when it came to Black education in Kentucky.

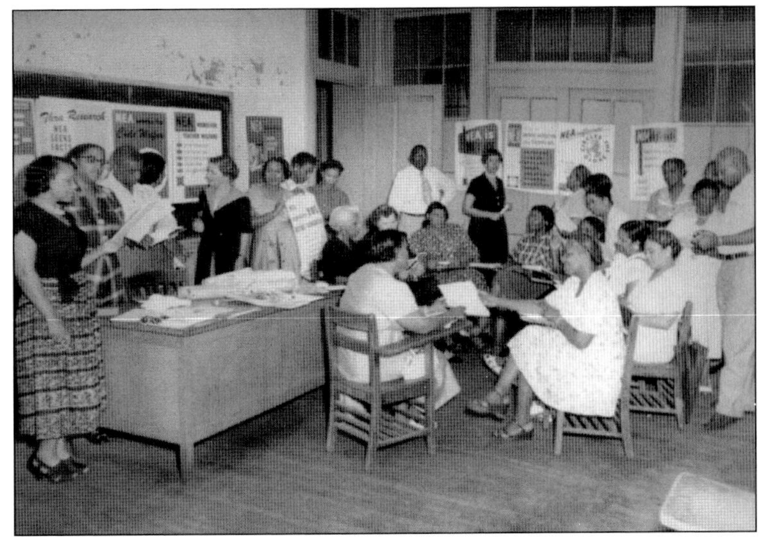

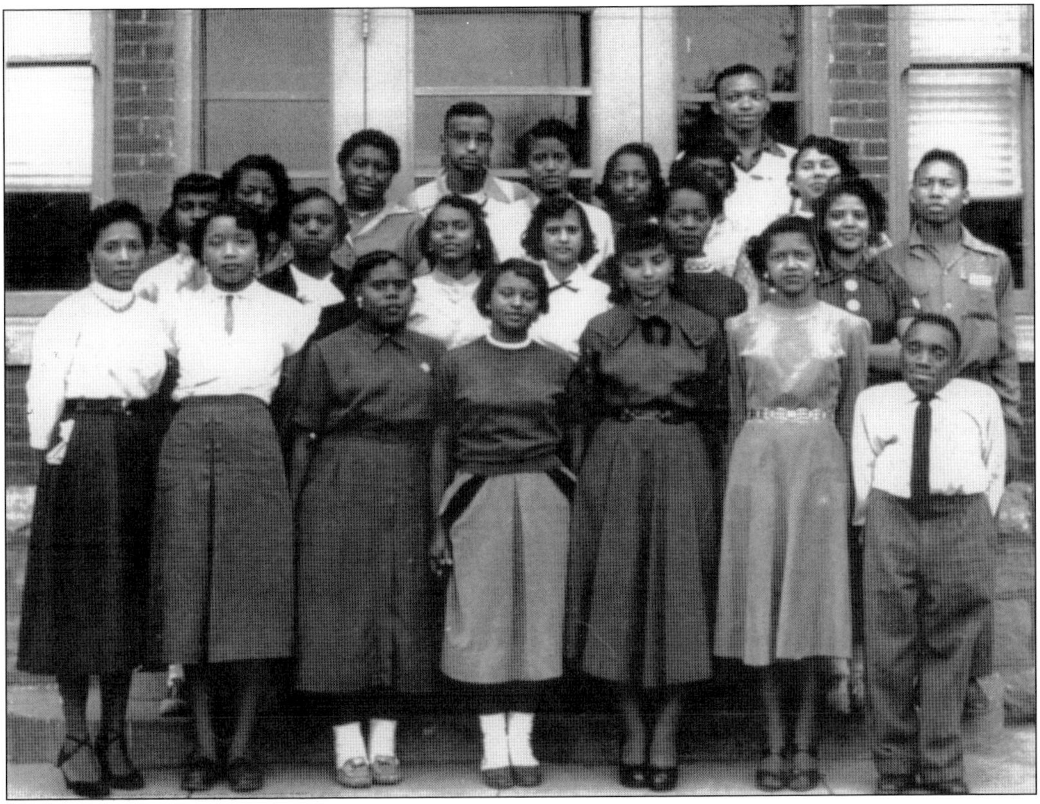

The *Bate Chatterbox* newspaper staff is pictured in 1954. From left to right are (first row) Bertha Bowman, Agnes Neal, Della Bridgewater, Jenetta Smith, Josephine Young, Martha Simpson, and Charles Chitterson; (second row) Lena Napier, Patricia Smith, Emma Rose Routt, Gladys Revely, Monie Ross, Mary Doneghy, and Earl Leverette; (third row) Robina Johnson, Geraldine Tucker, Paul Smith, Doris Routt, Laura Higgins, Corrine Carpenter, George Woods, and Odell Bradshaw. (Charles D. Grey.)

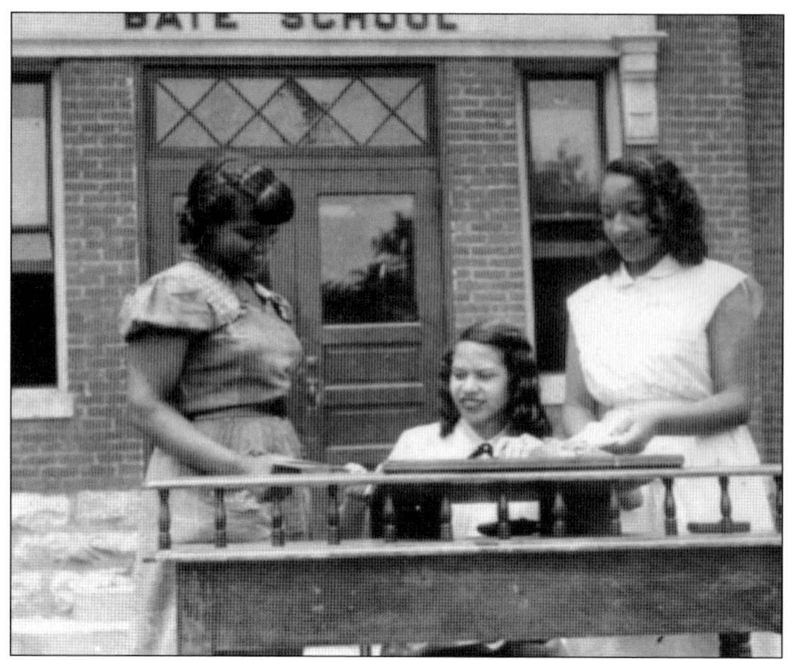

The Bate School banking committee, pictured here in front of the school in 1951, included, from left to right, Eleanor (Segar) Kavanaugh, Melinda (Revely) (Titus) Bufford, and Sarah (Boner) Riffe. The purpose of a school bank was to encourage saving and to teach financial responsibility along the way, and it was a good introduction to the banking business as well.

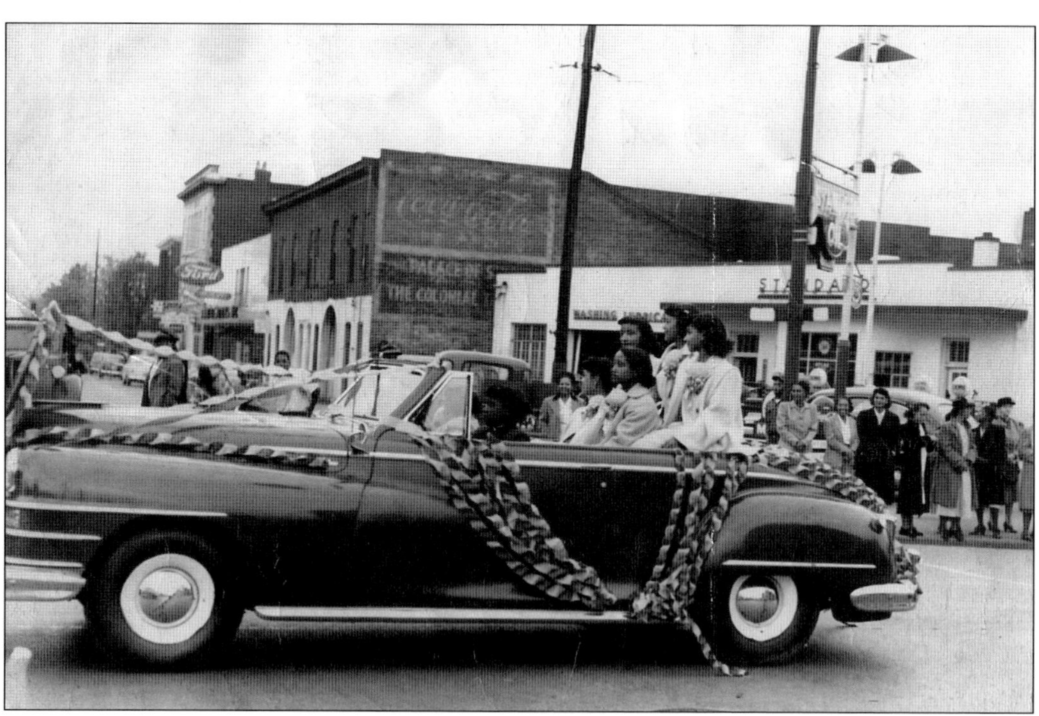

Homecoming 1948 featured queen Eleanor (Segar) Kavanaugh, center; on her right is Ann Carolyn (Jones) Prince. The three young women in the back are, from left to right, Mary J. (Young) Smith, Delores Adams, and Sarah (Bonner) Riffe. The driver of the car is Ella Pryor. The car is going east on West Main Street, just past Fourth Street near the courthouse. None of the buildings in the photograph are still extant.

Ann Carolyn Jones, a junior (Bate School, 1951), was voted 1949 homecoming queen. She was the daughter of Jesse and Sonora Mae (Owsley) Jones. Other candidates were Eunice Ford, Mary Adams, Lena Walker, and Anna Washington. This information from the *Bate Chatterbox* was published on December 2, 1949. (Carolyn [Jones] Prince.)

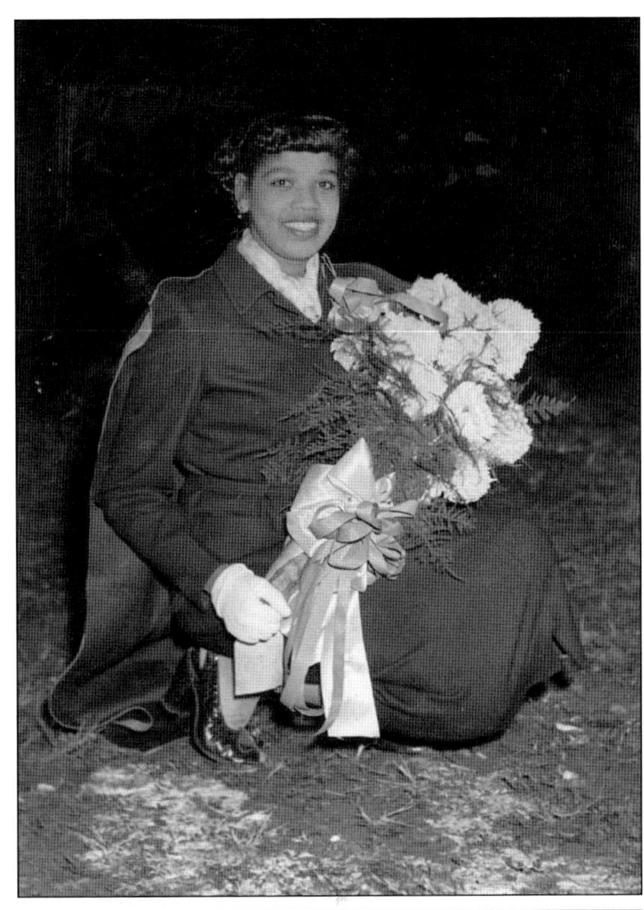

A typing class in the late 1940s is seen here. Pictured from left to right are (first row) Delores Adams and Annie Burdette; (second row) Mary Riffe, Isaac Burke, and Zola Rice; and (standing behind the projector) Carl Rice. In the 1940s, it was unusual for a boy to be in a typing class, as those classes were almost always segregated by gender.

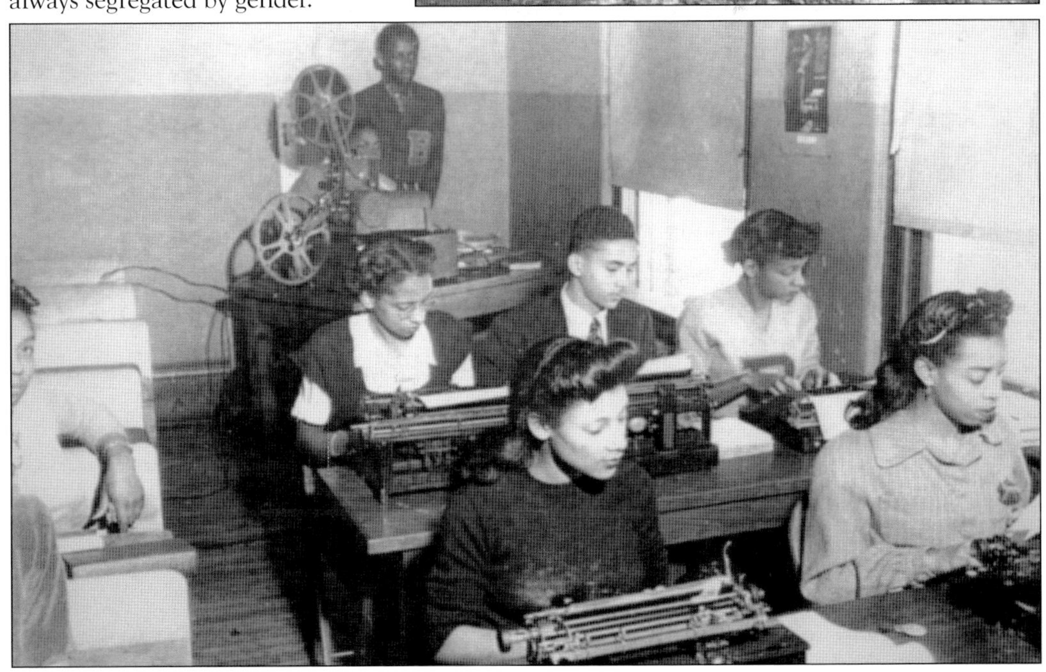

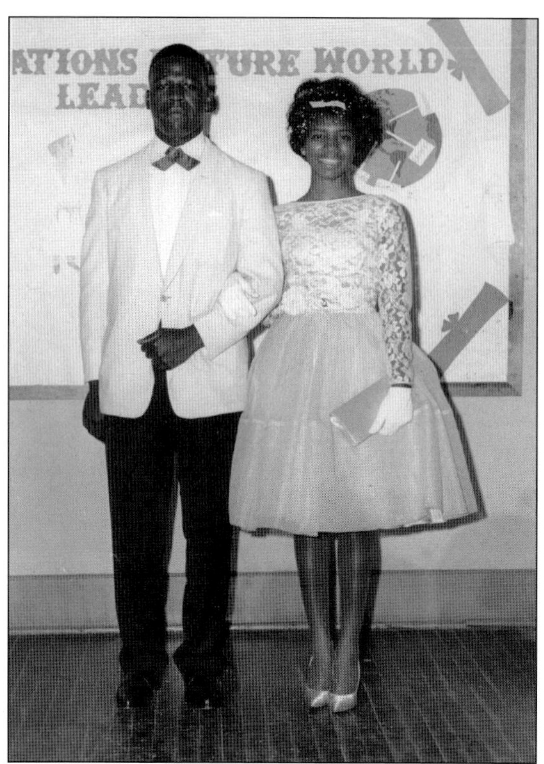

George Hamilton and Gloria Jean Johnson are seen at the Bate Prom in 1963, Hamilton's senior year. Hamilton was born January 9, 1944, the son of James Paul and Fannie Price (Cowan) Hamilton, the seventh of eight sons. He had joined the US Navy by 1965 after graduating from Bate, where he played several sports.

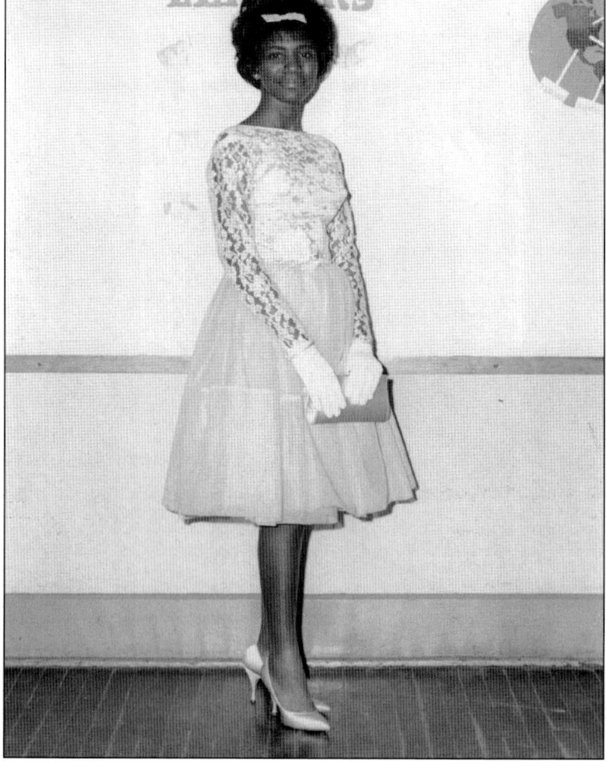

Gloria Johnson Frye is pictured at the prom at Bate High School. Gloria was the daughter of James and Opal (Ford) Johnson; she married Dallas McCowan first, followed by second husband Rev. Isaac Frye. Even though Bate was a segregated school, it provided its students with much of what the "white" schools did.

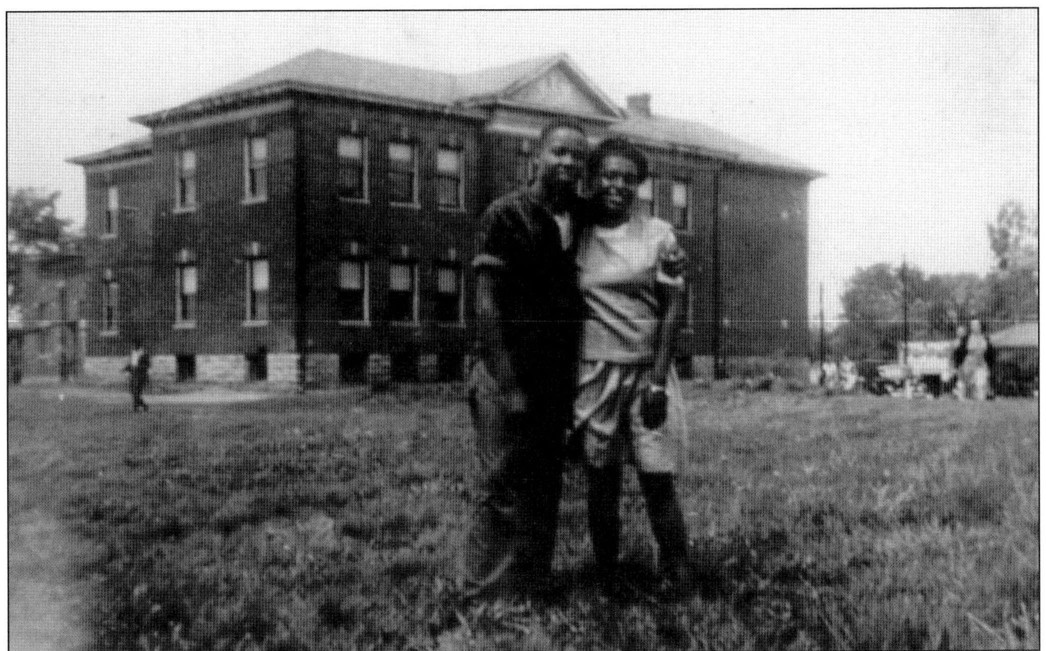

DeRoy Coates and Dorothy Crowdus pose in front of the Bate School in 1945, prior to the building of the last addition to the school. Coates graduated in 1947, though he enlisted in the US Army in 1946, and was discharged after three months. Crowdus was born in 1929 and married Rev. David Chenault in 1947.

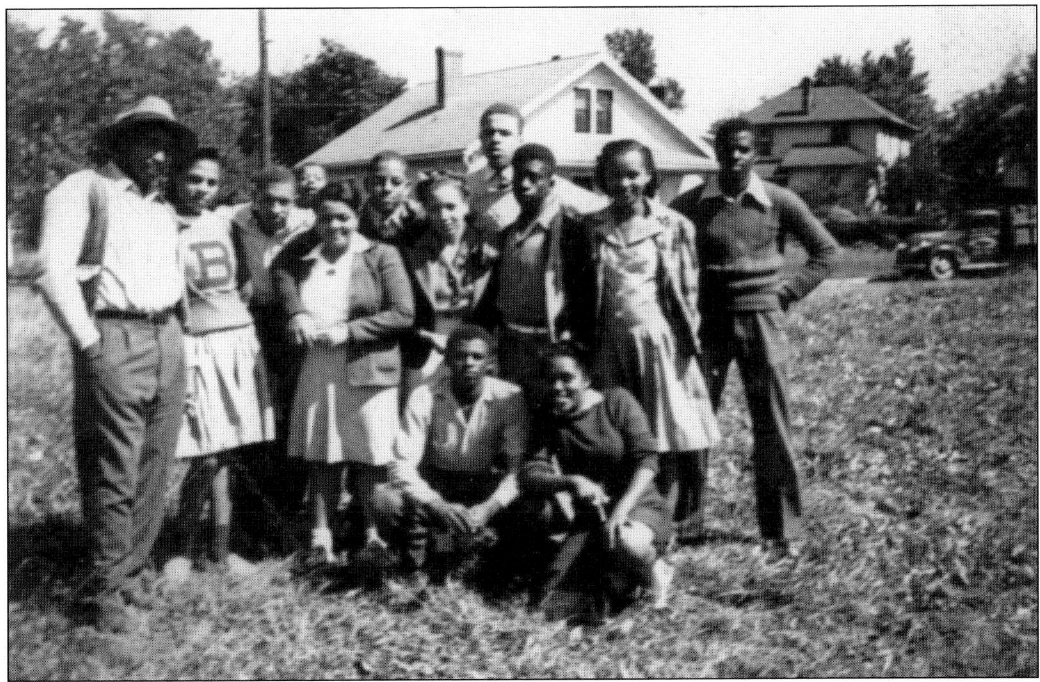

This may be the Bate class of 1945; however, only six people are listed on the graduation records: Susie Ellen Graves, Robert Harding, Marie Johnson, Ozenia Hawkins (on far right), Margaret Young, and Howard Seawright.

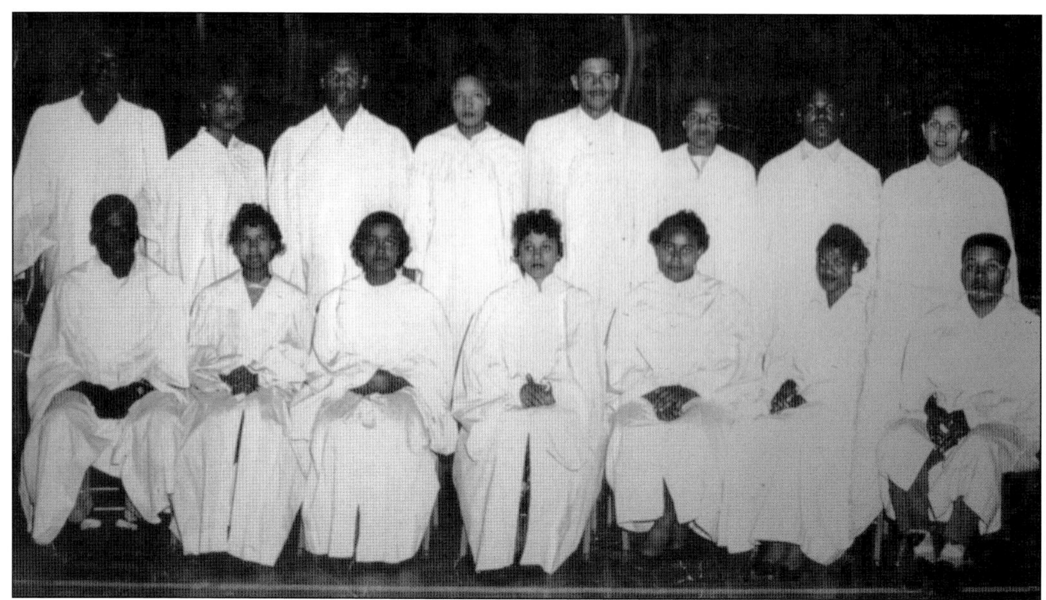

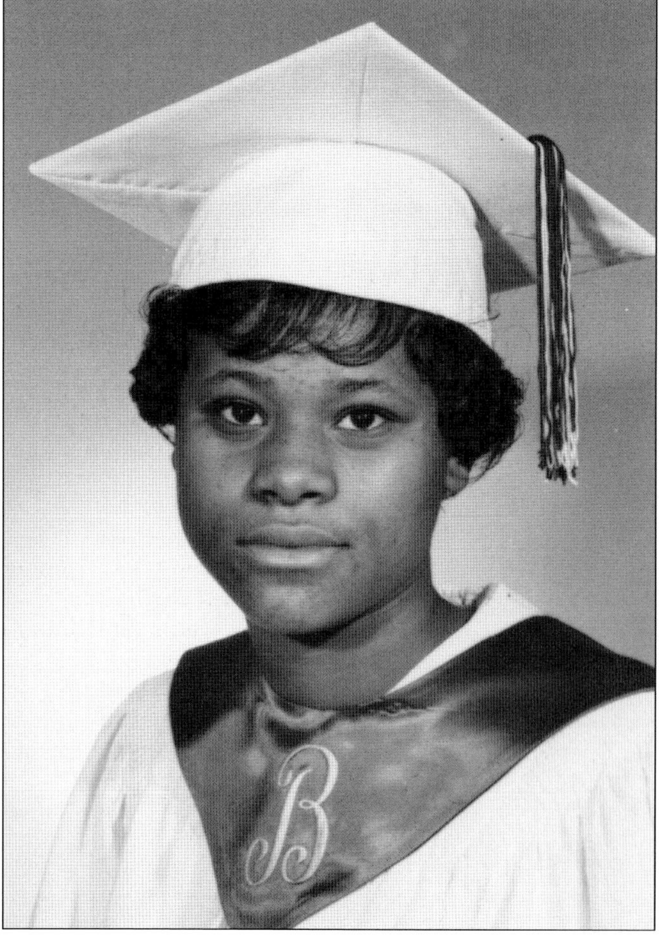

The Bate High School class of 1956 was made up of, from left to right, (first row, seated) John Davis, Sally Gay, Bettye Segar, Audrey Singleton, Dorothy Girten, Dolores Whitley, and Norman Faulkner; (second row) John Adams, Lucinda Fields, Coleman Singleton, Agnes Neal, Raymond Warren, Minnie Caldwell, William Pitman, and Odell Bradshaw. (Charles D. Grey.)

Ann Maxine (Faulkner) Revely, Bate class of 1963, was the daughter of Richard Thrower and Sylvia Bernice (Faulkner) Kennedy and the step-daughter of Rev. Thomas Kennedy. She was born in Cincinnati, Ohio, in 1945 and died there in 1988. She married Thomas Revely III in 1965; he is the little boy in the photograph on page 12, with his father.

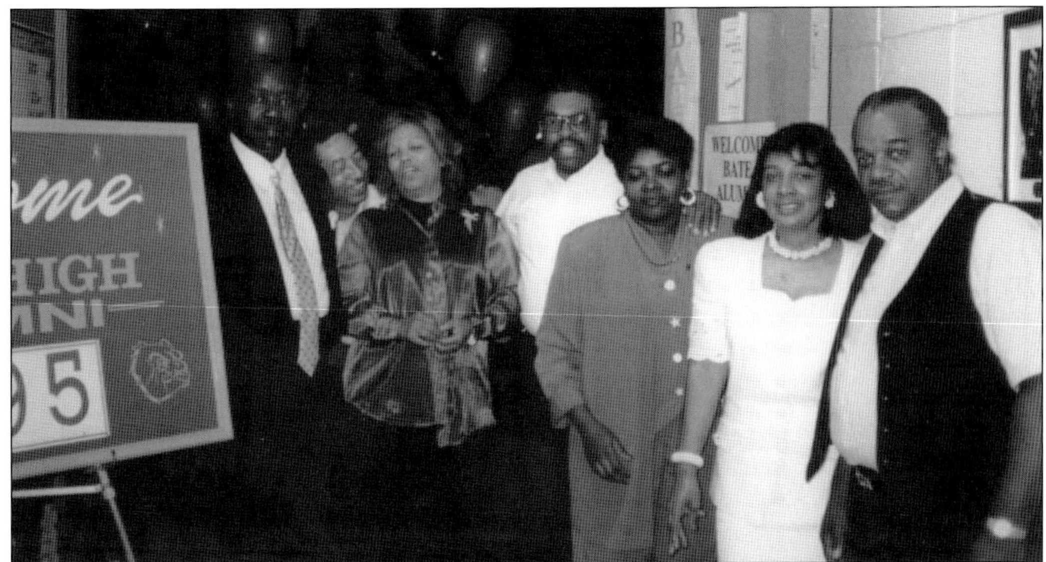

A candid photograph taken at the Bate School reunion in 1995 shows mostly members of the class of 1960, including, from left to right, James Stallworth, James Johnson, Yvonne (Doram) Weathers, Glenn Ball, Florence (Marshall) Maye, Lonnie Sue (Walker) Smith, and James "Jackie" Lewis. The Bate reunion association held reunions that were more like homecomings, every two years. Members of any class were welcomed back to Bate.

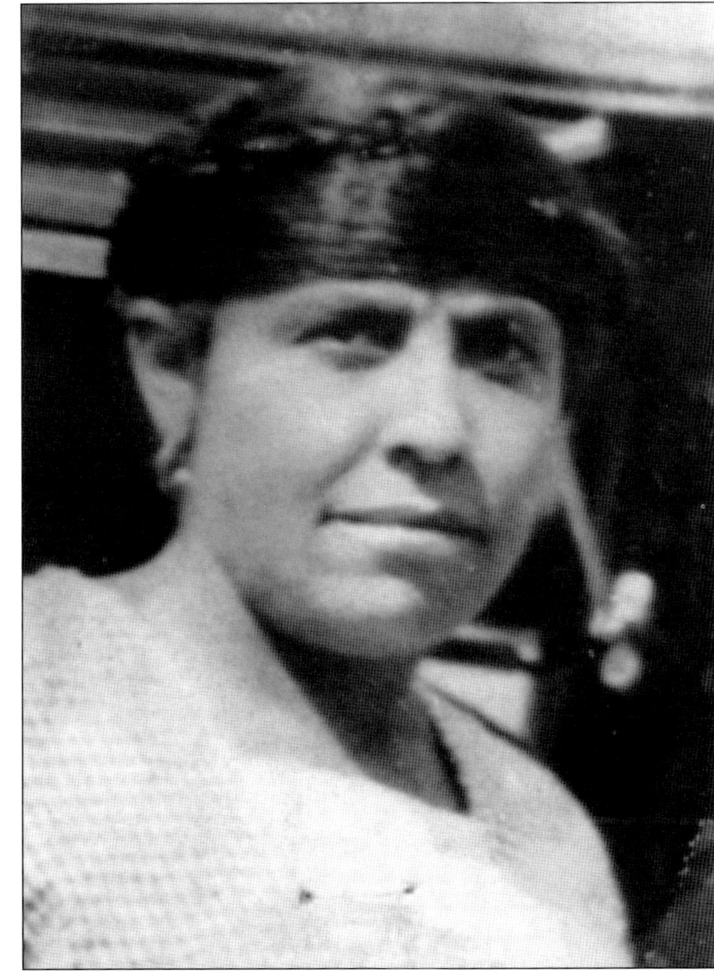

Susie Bell (Rochester) Fish (1882–1961) taught in Danville schools for 54 years. She was the daughter of Archie Rochester, who held several civic offices, and Anna R. Taylor. In 1955, she was honored for her long teaching career at the Kentucky State Fair.

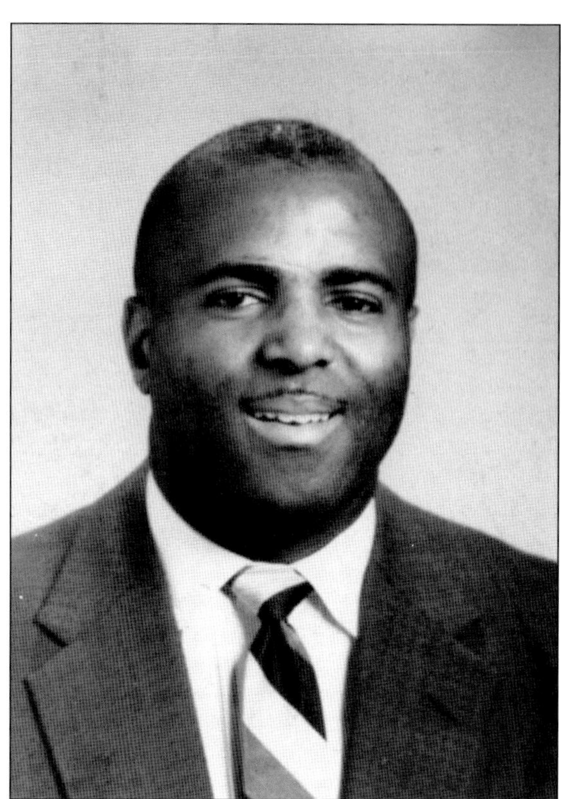

Robert Ozenia Hawkins (1927–2016) graduated from Bate High School in 1945 and, later, from Tennessee State College in Nashville. He later returned to Bate as a teacher and a coach. Coach Hawkins was known to be an effective coach, a teacher who taught thousands of students in Danville as well as the school system at Dillard and Goldsboro High School in Goldsboro, North Carolina.

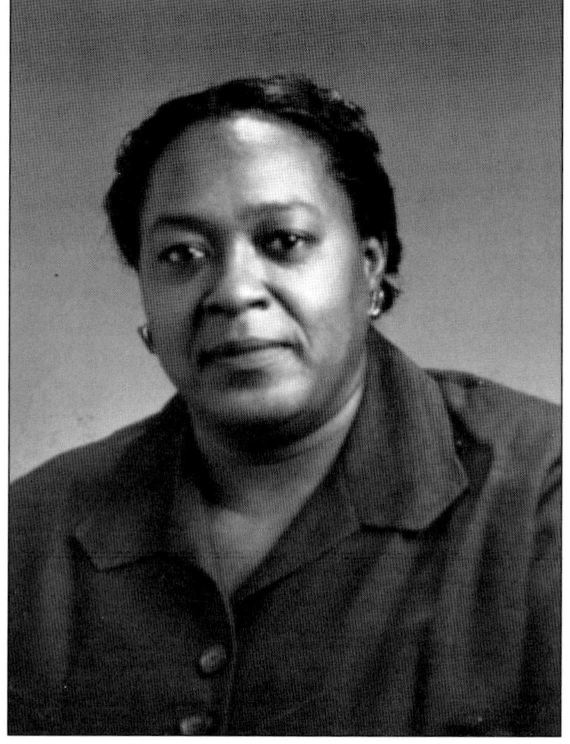

Ella Pauline Pryor, the youngest of eight children, was born in either 1916 or 1917, died in 1983, and is buried in Bowling Green, Kentucky. She taught at Bate High School for almost 40 years. Pryor was educated at Kentucky State University; she was also active in the KSU Alumni Association, a charter member of the local Alpha Upsilon Chapter and Phi Delta Kappa, and a member of several women's clubs in Danville.

From left to right are (first row) Hubert Floyd, Donald Davis, Eugene Johnson, John Davis, and Roscoe Tucker; (second row) Carl Singleton, Earl Leverette, Arthur Napier, William Pitman, James "Poonie" Coulter, and James Ogle; (third row) coach Charles Dabney, Benny Garr, John Whitley, Bobby Johnson, Michael Smith, and Curtis Kinley.

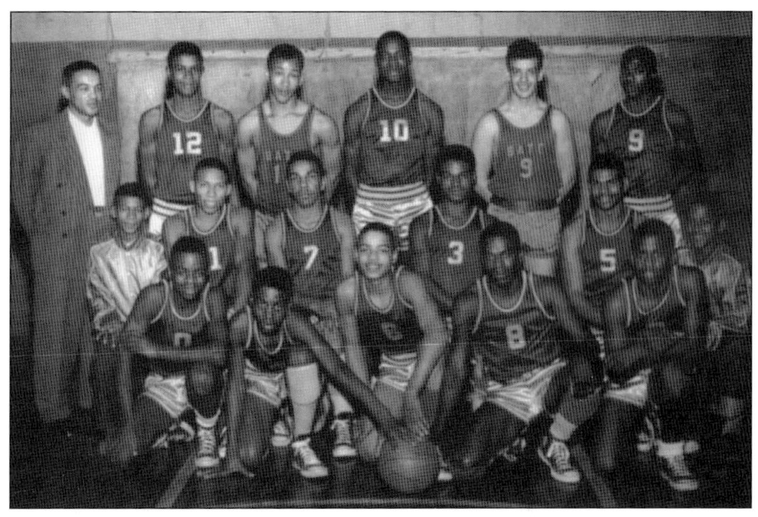

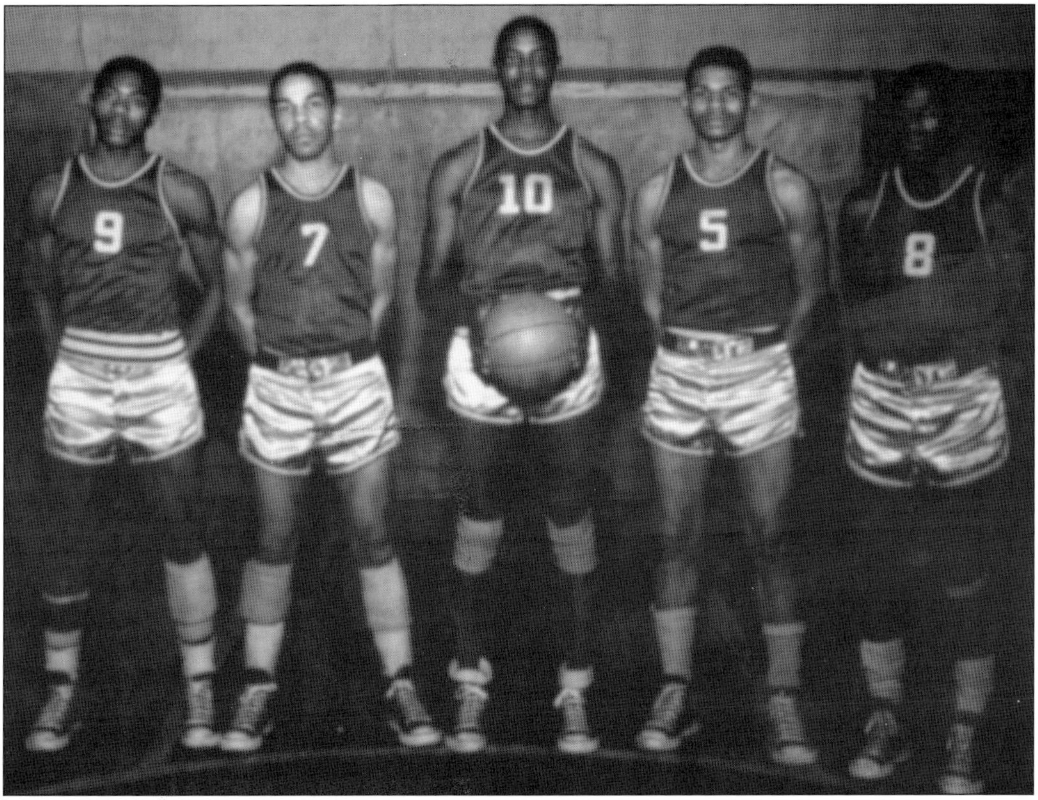

The Bate Bulldogs basketball team of 1955 included, from left to right, Curtis Kinley (class of 1957), Arthur Napier, Robert Johnson (class of 1956), James "Poon Eye" Coulter, and John T. Davis (class of 1956). The *Advocate-Messenger* noted that this was the shortest Bate team in many years. This season, former coach Charles Dabney was replaced by new coach Ozenia Hawkins, of football fame. (Charles D. Grey.)

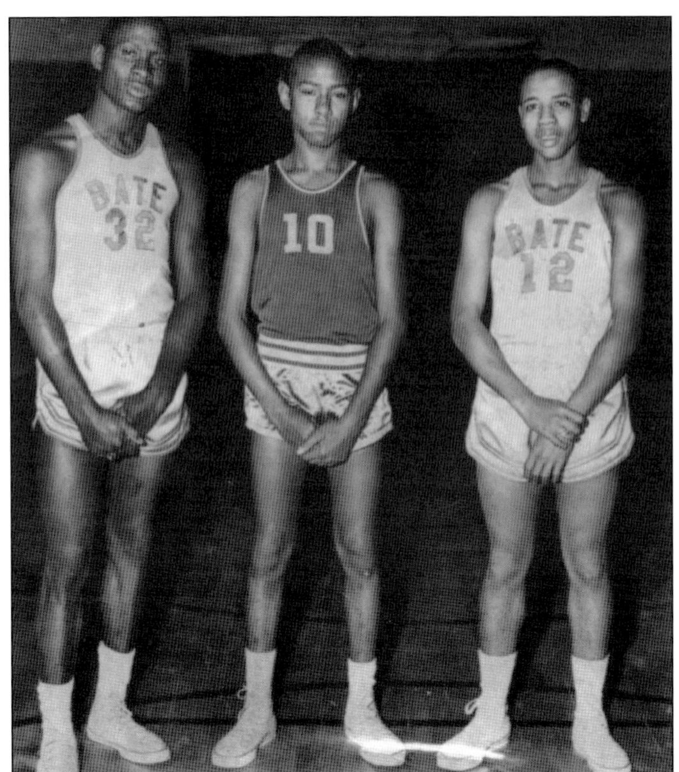

Pictured from left to right, Jessie Adams, Craig Gillam, and Charles Grey are at a benefit basketball game against Hustonville on February 15, 1960, to raise money for a swimming pool in the Bate-Wood Homes project. Many members of the male student body at Bate participated in athletics, including football and basketball. (Charles D. Grey.)

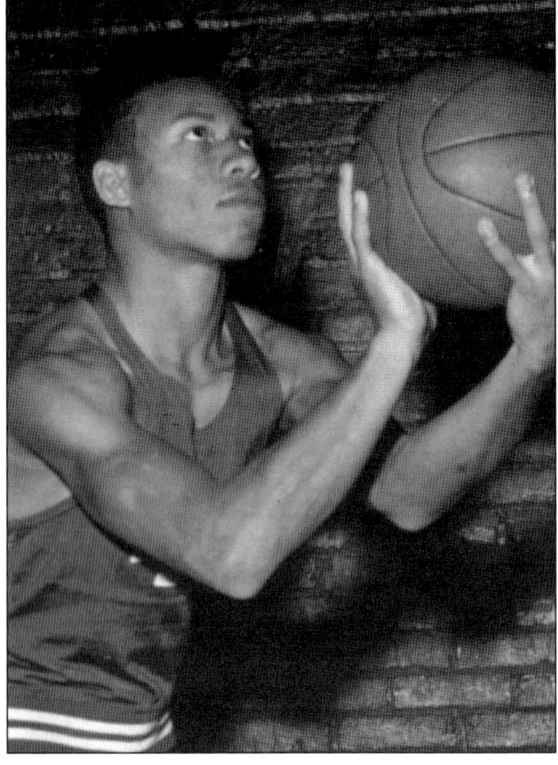

Earl Leverette (1938–1985) was listed as a five-foot-nine senior with the 1956–1957 Danville Admirals; yet the previous year, he played football and basketball at Bate. In 1953, he was listed on the basketball team. He was born in Augusta, Georgia, and died in Danville. He is still listed as a "student" living on West Green Street in the Danville city directory of 1958, however.

Theodore Shurrel Davis Jr., on the basketball team, was on the 1962 football team as well as the last Bate football team in fall 1963. Listed as graduating in 1963, he was the son of Theodore S. and Mayme (Cowan) Davis and nephew of Bunny Davis. His brother Donald, another member of this athletic family, was at one time the recreational director at the Bate Playground.

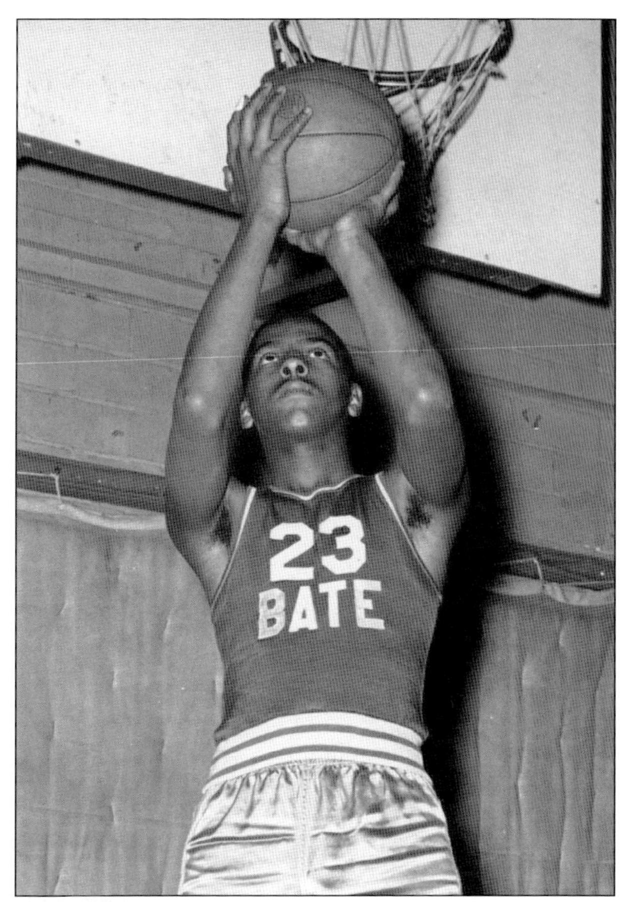

Pictured from left to right, Robert Harding (class of 1945), June "Mutt" Christy (class of 1950), and George Wickliffe (class of 1947) made up three-fifths of the "Fab Five" basketball team. Harding graduated in 1945, enlisted in 1946, was discharged, attended Kentucky State, and was only the second Black student admitted to the University of Kentucky College of Law. He was ultimately admitted to practice before the US Supreme Court. (Christy's unusual story is told on page 95.)

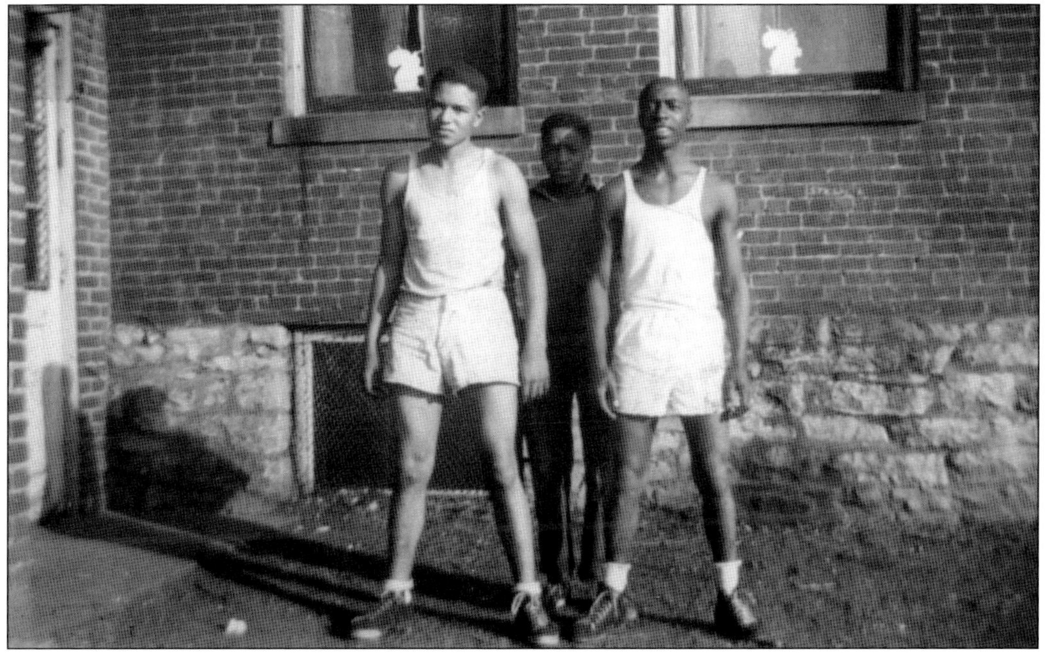

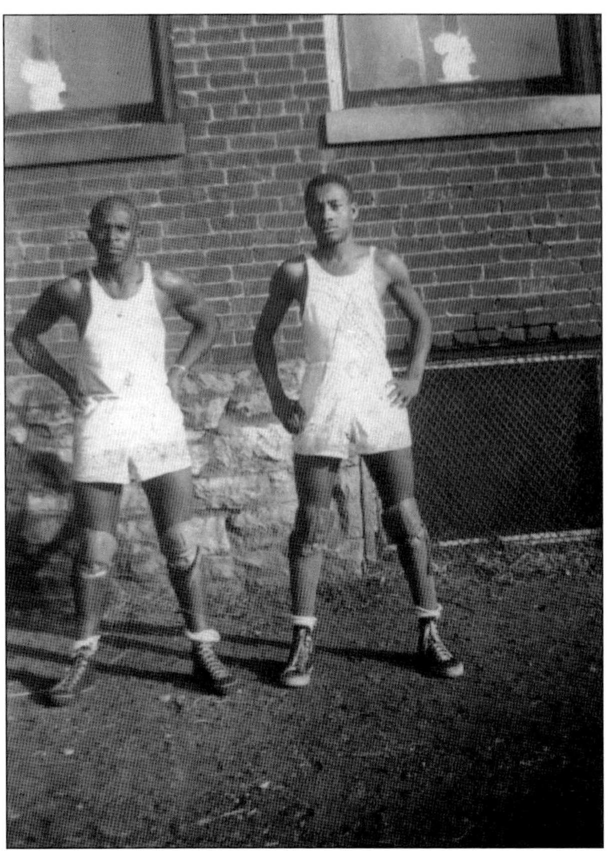

James Edward "Tracy" Tresenwriter and James Simpson are seen here in 1944, the year they both graduated from Bate High School. The basketball coach that year was Sanford T. Roach. Tresenwriter was born in 1925, the son of Willis and Melvinia (Hazelwood) Tresenwriter, and at his marriage in 1945 to Eva McPherson, he was listed as a "soldier." Simpson was born in 1926, the son of Roy and Louise (Chitterson) Simpson.

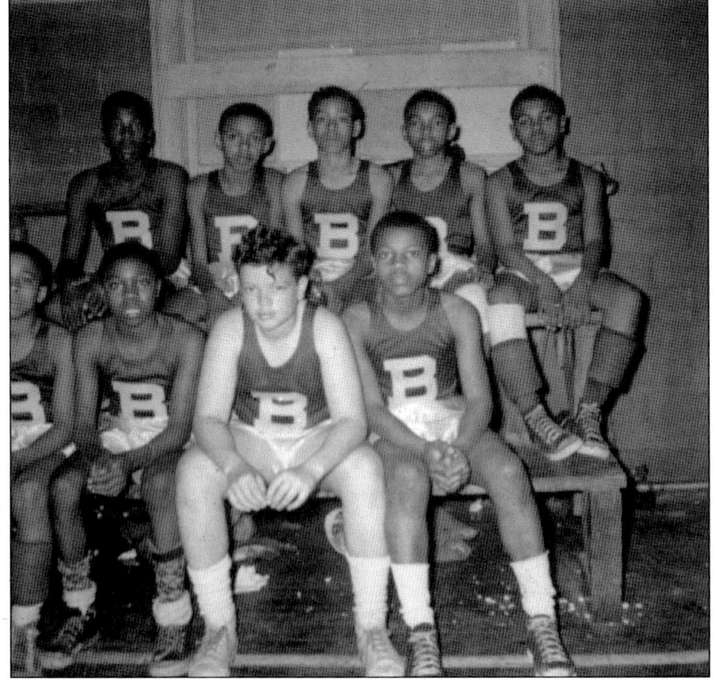

The Bate junior varsity basketball team is pictured here in the late 1950s; from left to right are (first row) William "Billy" Harlan (graduated 1961), Billy Joe Carpenter, Norman Smith (graduated 1962), Jay Henry Walker (graduated 1962); (second row) Roscoe Scott, Joe Paul Routt (graduated 1961), Tyrone Doram (graduated 1960), Glenn Ball (graduated 1960), and Glenn Grey.

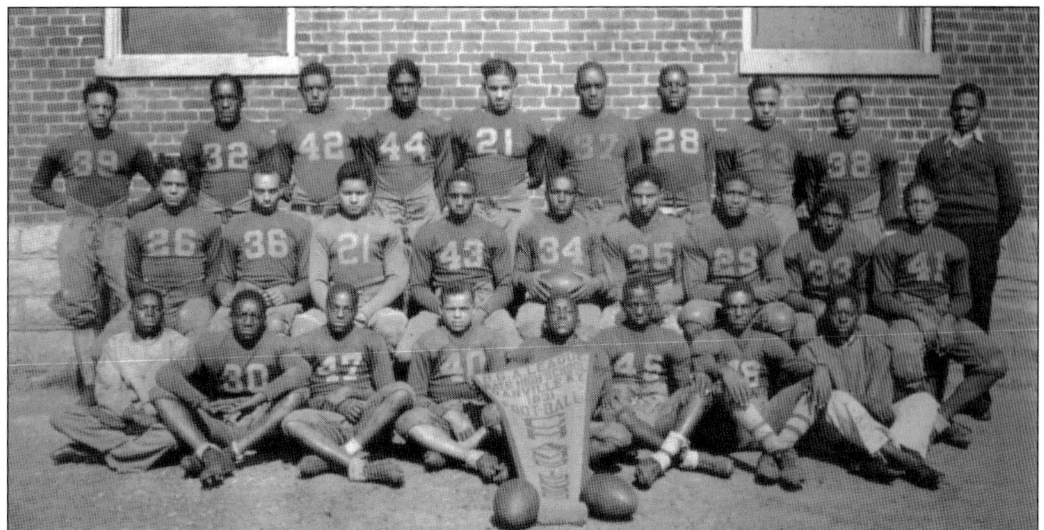

The GGA League Champion Football Team is pictured here in 1931. From left to right are (first row) John Turner, Elwood Saunders, William Davis, Roscoe Doram, Francis Saunders, James Coates, Theodore Davis, and Herman Warren; (second row) James Doram, Porter Smith, Robert Trumbo, Robert Jackson, Worthington Beasley, George Coffey, John Taylor, Paul Routt, and Sanford Roach; (third row) Allen Caldwell, Eugene Stewart, Robert Rowe, David Routt, Ralph Smith, David Hale, Frank Fisher, James Baughman, Joe Gaines Reed, and coach William Goodwin.

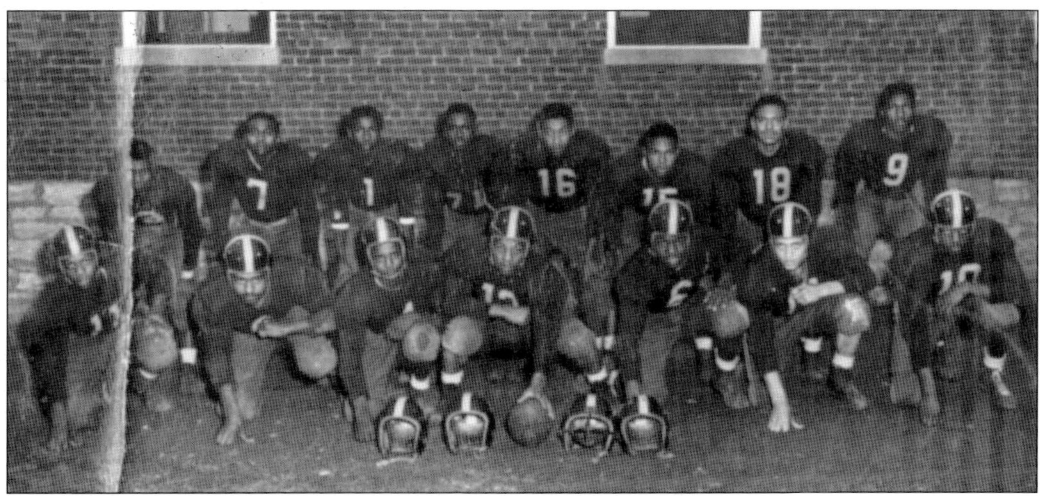

The 1949 Bate football team is seen here; from left to right are (first row) Harry Whitley, Larue Patton, Donald Segar, George Cowan, Kenneth Prince, Marvin Swann, and David Wade; (second row) Derwood Garr, John Henry Marshall, Josh Shannon, Eugene McGill, Donald Redd, John Segar, Matthew McCowan, and William Falkner.

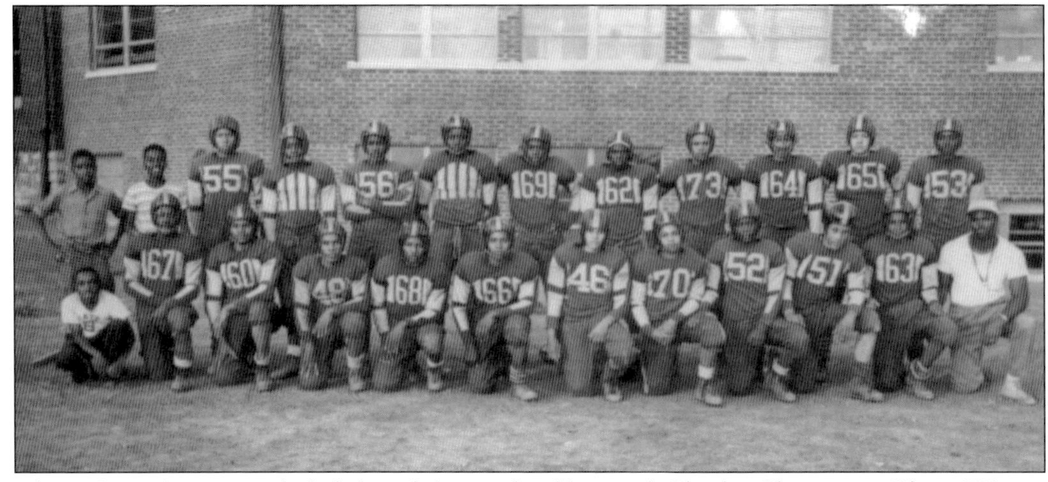

The 1953–1954 team included, from left to right, (first row) Charles Chitterson, Oliver Wheat, James Coulter, Arthur Napier, William Shannon, Gene Bright, ? Brown, Eugene Johnson, Johnny Whitley, Benny Garr, and coach Ozenia Hawkins; (second row) trainers Joe Lewis and Donald Davis, Earl Leverette, Hubert Floyd, Eugene Pope, Samuel Johnson, Curtis Kinley, John Davis, Coleman Singleton, Raymond Warren, Charles Langford, and Robert Johnson.

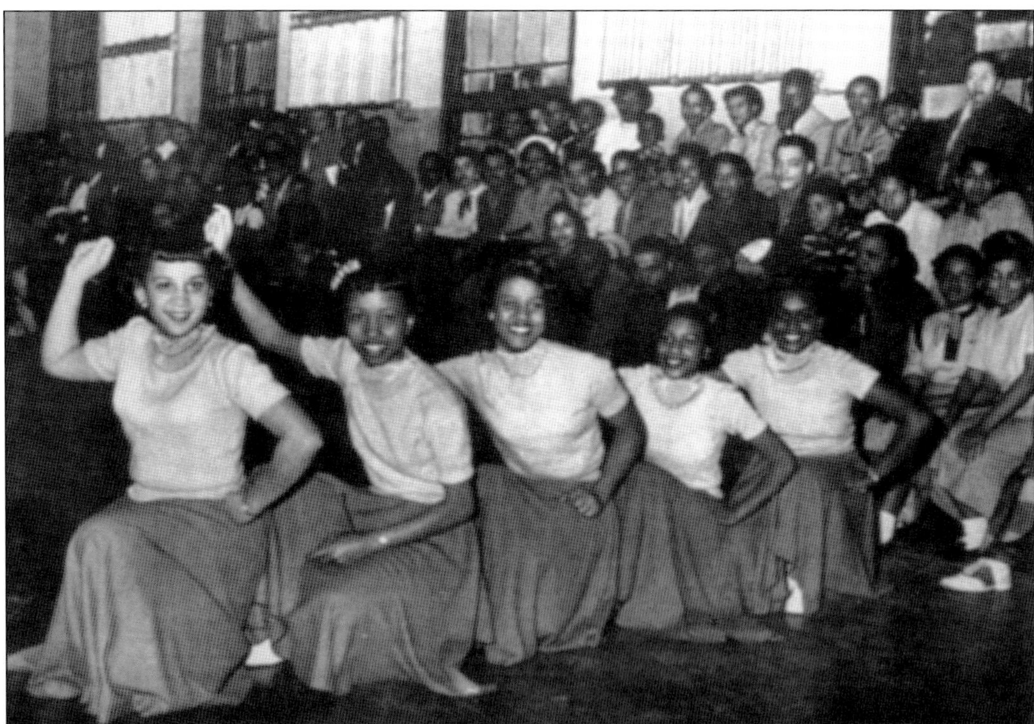

These cheerleaders, pictured in 1952, included, from left to right, Martha Bradshaw, Louise Wheat, Eunice Ford, Charlotte Turner, and Shirley Tucker. Absent from the picture was Doris Routt. While the local newspaper frequently carried stories about the Bate sports teams and the scores of their games, all the teams were male. Cheerleading was about the only activity for girls, and only a few of them at that. (Charles D. Grey.)

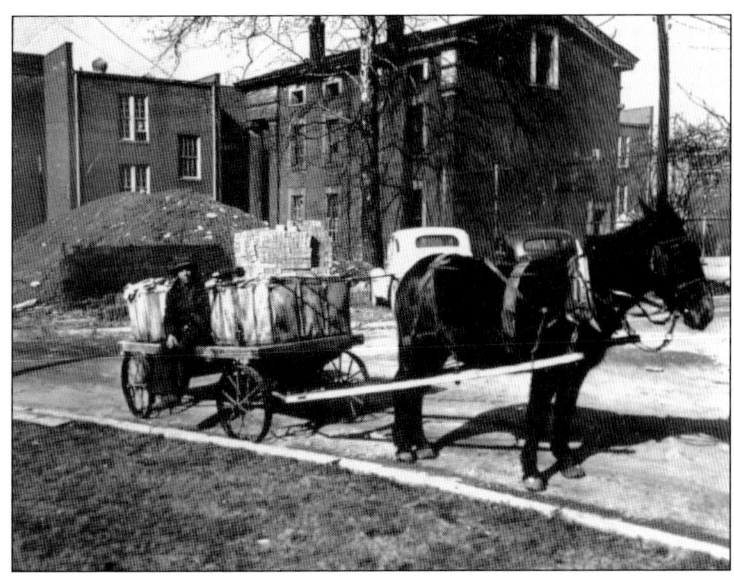

Ulysses Grant Burdette and his horse carry laundry to the "new" power plant at the Kentucky School for the Deaf, 1948. Burdette was born in Lancaster in neighboring Garrard County about 1890 and died in Danville in 1953. He was a deaf-mute and was long associated with the Kentucky School for the Deaf. His son Theodore ("Theo") and wife Annie are shown in Chapter Seven. (Jacobs Hall Museum, Kentucky School for the Deaf.)

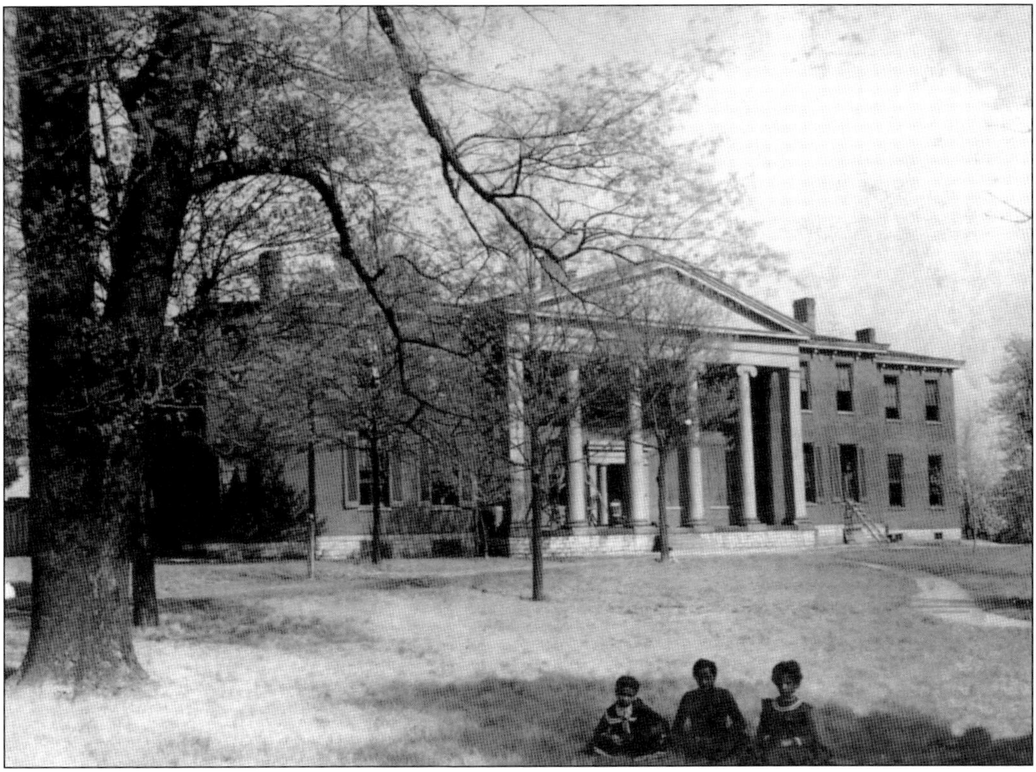

Though the Kentucky Asylum for the Tuition of the Deaf and Dumb was established in 1833, one of the first state-supported schools for the deaf in the United States, the "colored" department of Kentucky School for the Deaf was established by 1885 on the former property of Col. J.W. Grigsby's Warwick Hall. This building was replaced in 1952 with present-day Washington Hall. (Jacobs Hall Museum, Kentucky School for the Deaf.)

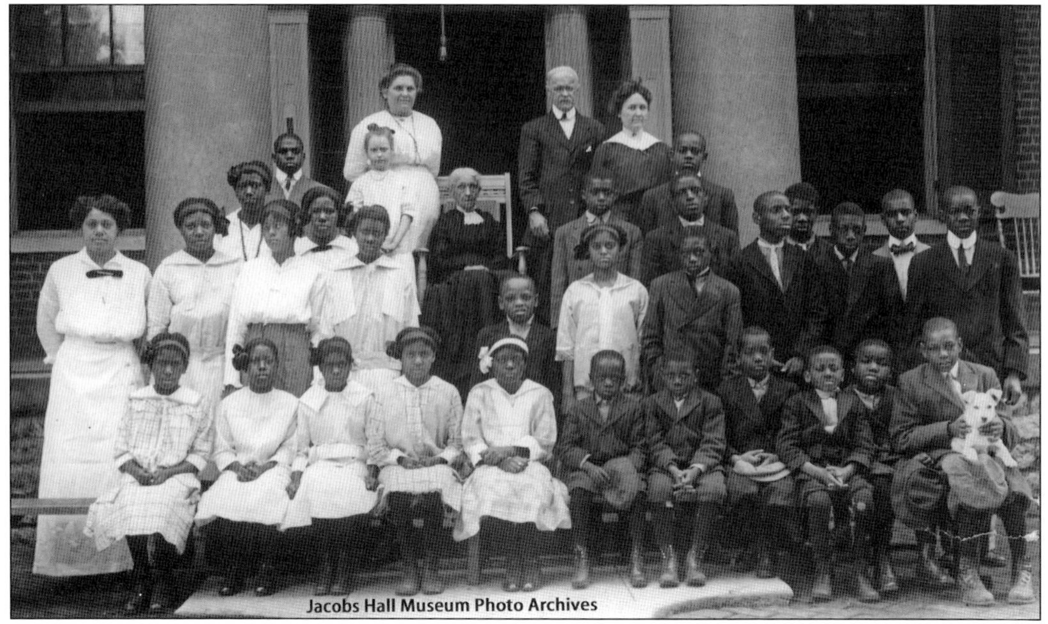

Students in the Kentucky School for the Deaf colored department are seen here in a photograph taken about 1910. Students from Boyle County attending included Ellen Rice, admitted on February 1, 1885; Robert Hays, September 15, 1885; John Taylor, September 15, 1886; John Caul, January 10, 1887; Rachel Davis, February 25, 1887; Robert Hays, September 19, 1906; and Frank Hays, October 10, 1917. (Jacobs Hall Museum, Kentucky School for the Deaf.)

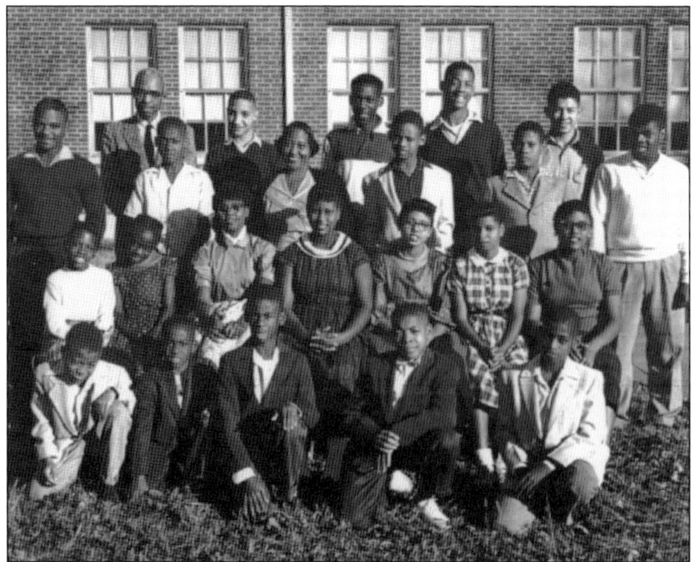

At the 1952 opening of Washington Hall, which replaced the colored division's Warwick Hall, supervisor Warren Livingston and the African American students pose for this group photograph. According to KSD, the school integrated gradually, with vocational classes first in 1954, then all classes in 1959, and finally by 1963, dormitories and dining halls. Interestingly, Danville schools did not fully integrate until 1964. (Jacobs Hall Museum, Kentucky School for the Deaf.)

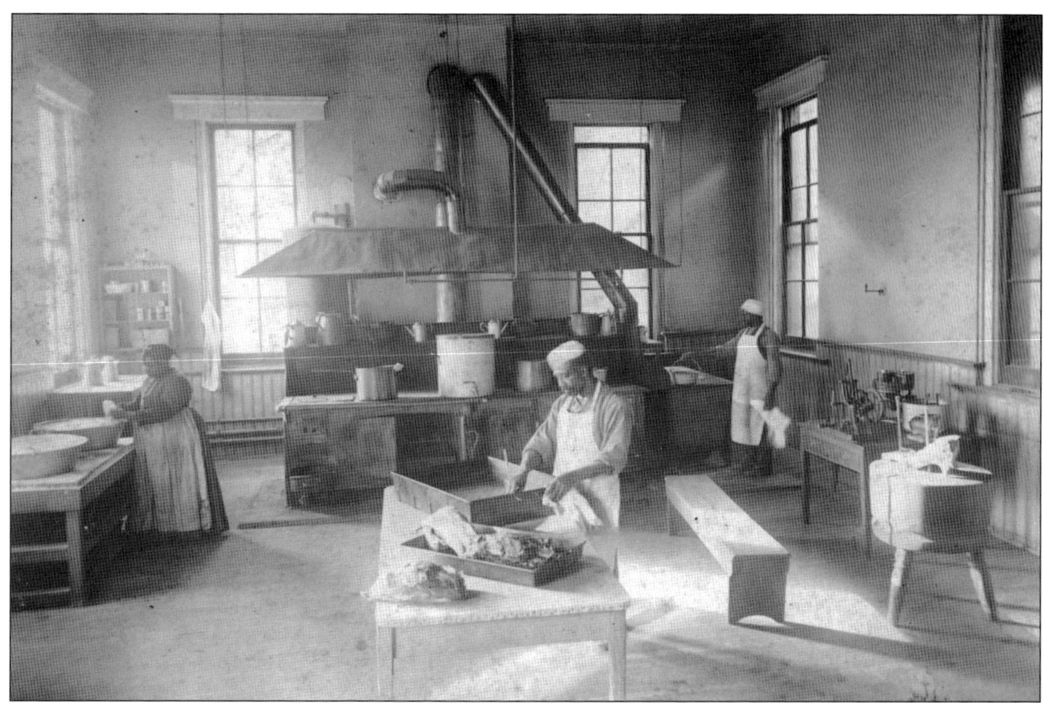

Mr. Harren is the head cook in the colored division kitchen in Warwick Hall at the Kentucky Asylum for the Tuition of the Deaf and Dumb, now known as the Kentucky School for the Deaf. The school began admitting African American students in 1885, with eight students in the beginning. By 1923, a total of 216 African American students had attended. (Jacobs Hall Museum, Kentucky School for the Deaf.)

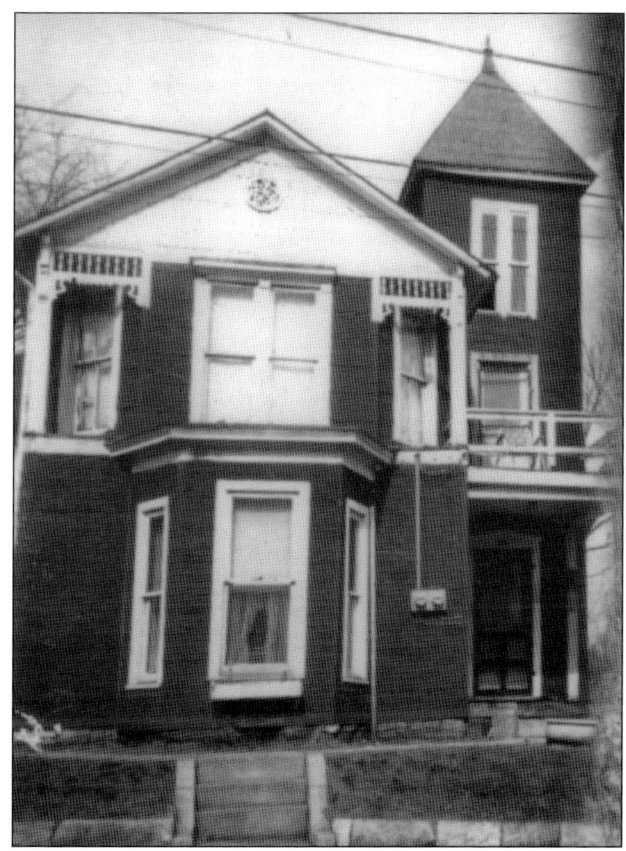

Benjamin Tibbs's home was on the site of Willis Russell's school. Russell, a freed black, operated a school in his home in the 1840s and 1850s. Tibbs, a wealthy Black barber, built his home on the site directly opposite St. James African Methodist Episcopal Church. Now, a multi-apartment building is on the site

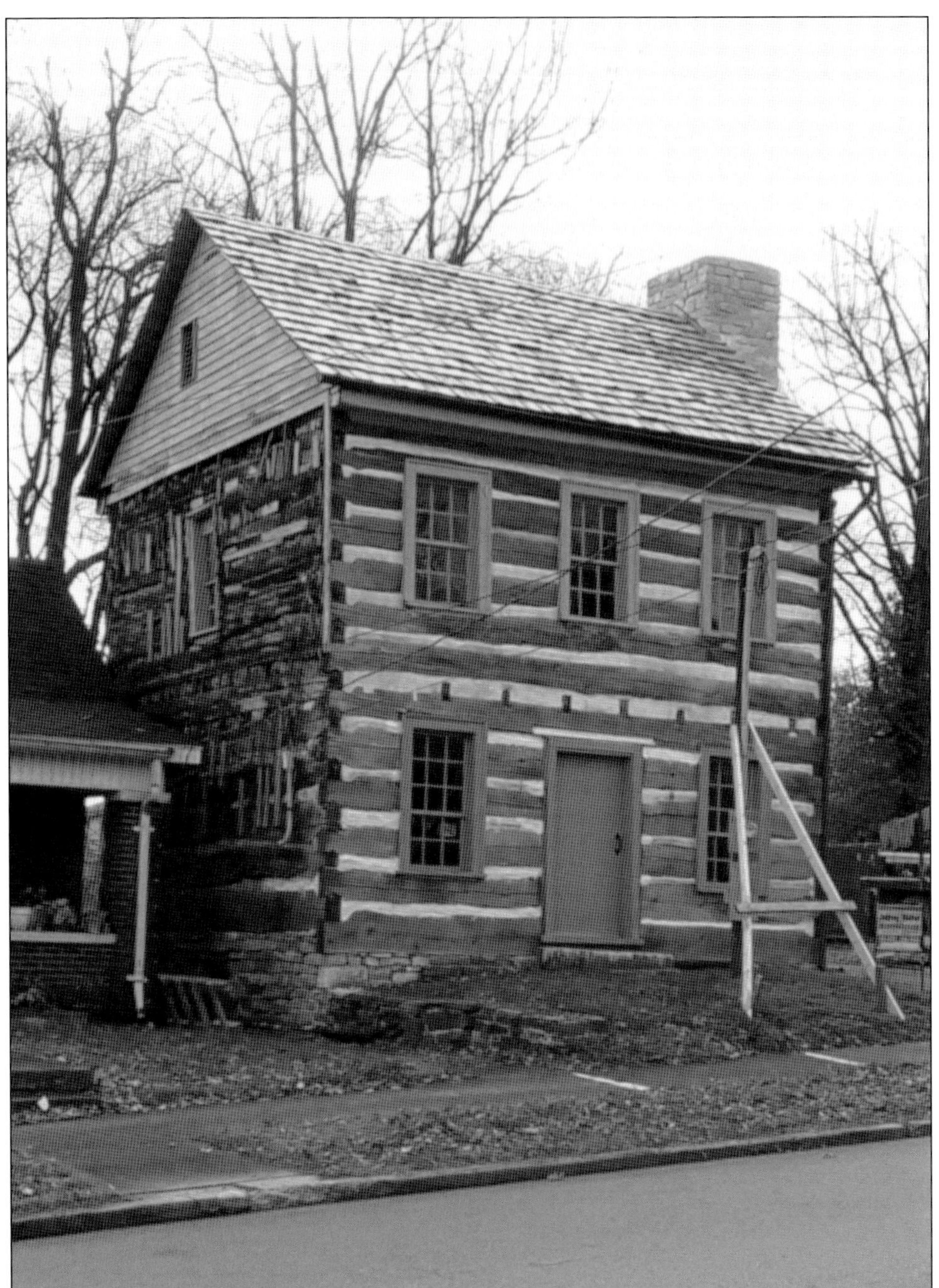

This building was long thought to be Willis Russell's home and school. Recent research shows that it was not, but it is important enough historically to preserve, and it was renamed the Willis Russell Memorial Cabin. The original Willis Russell home was directly across East Walnut Street from the St. James AME Church, and on the site once occupied by Benjamin Tibbs's home. This building is undergoing renovation and stabilization to preserve it for many years to come. Although it is not what it was believed to be, it is nonetheless an important example of early-19th-century log construction. Danville has many "log cabins" that have been rebuilt and covered over with more modern materials to look like modern homes. (Michael Denis.)

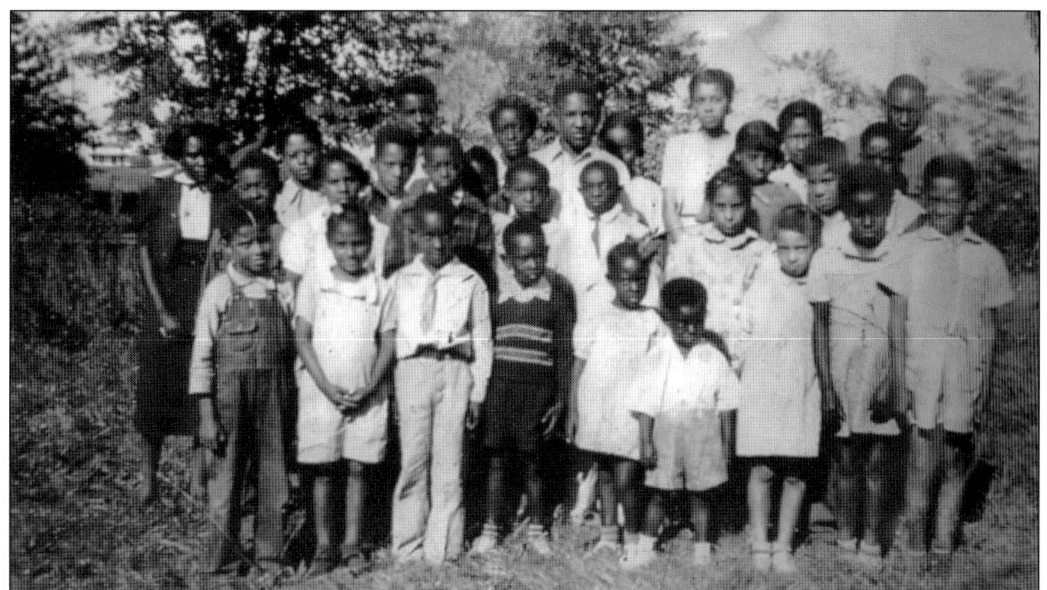

Students at the Wilsonville School in the late 1930s are pictured with their teacher Ella Marshall. Though most students are unidentified, Samuel Letcher is somewhere in the back row. Alma (Bruce) Overton (Bate School class of 1941), Matthew "Pistol Pete" McCowan (born 1931, Bate School class of 1950), John Franklin "Frank" Bruce (born 1923), and Sam Bruce (born 1925) are also in the photograph.

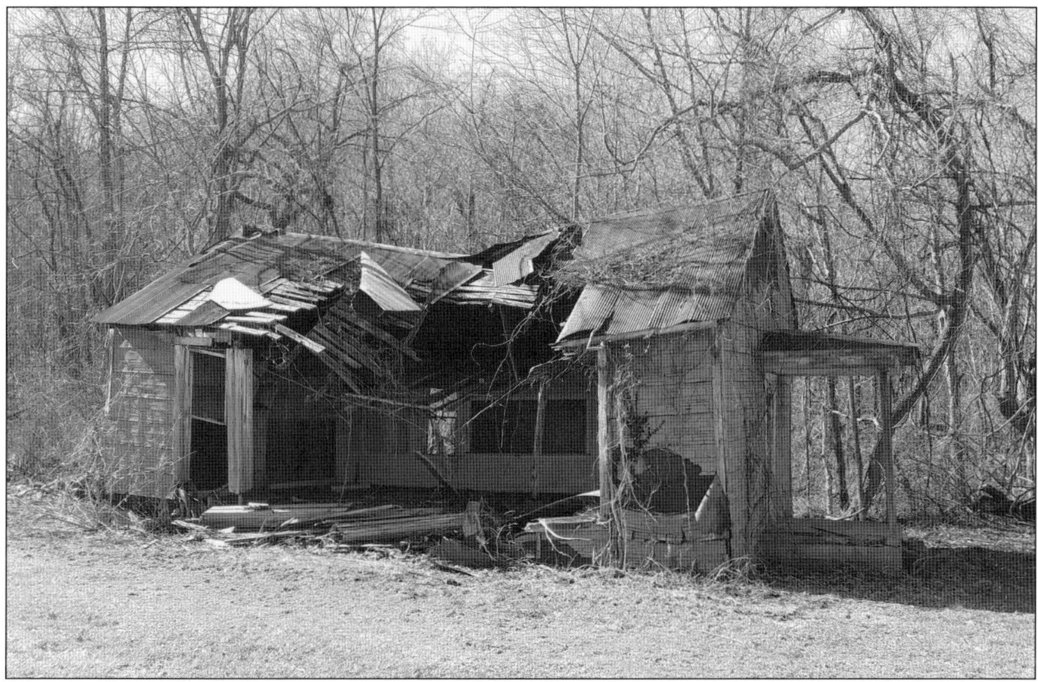

What is left of the Wilsonville School is shown here. Built before 1876, this school at one time housed up to 50 students from all over the southwest part of the county. It is now almost totally gone, but the Danville Boyle County African American Historical Society has saved the coat hooks and a bookcase, which are now in the DBCAAHS History Center. (Michael Denis.)

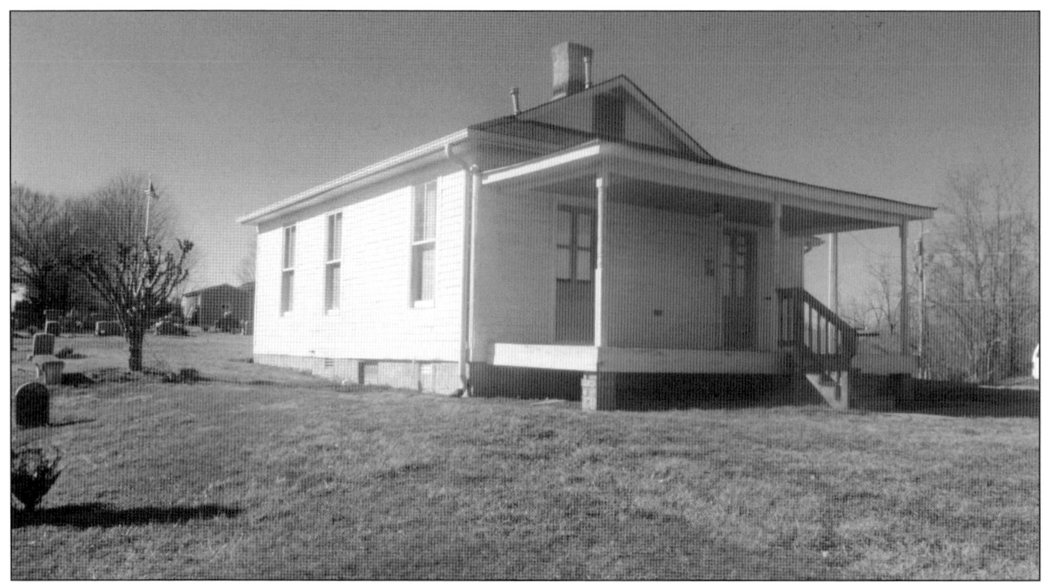

The Perryville "colored" school is seen here as it looks after restoration, being dedicated on August 24, 2014. This was, along with Wilsonville, one of the last two colored schools in the county. It is now restored and named the Amelia Sleet Burton Colored Schoolhouse for its longtime teacher. (Michael Denis.)

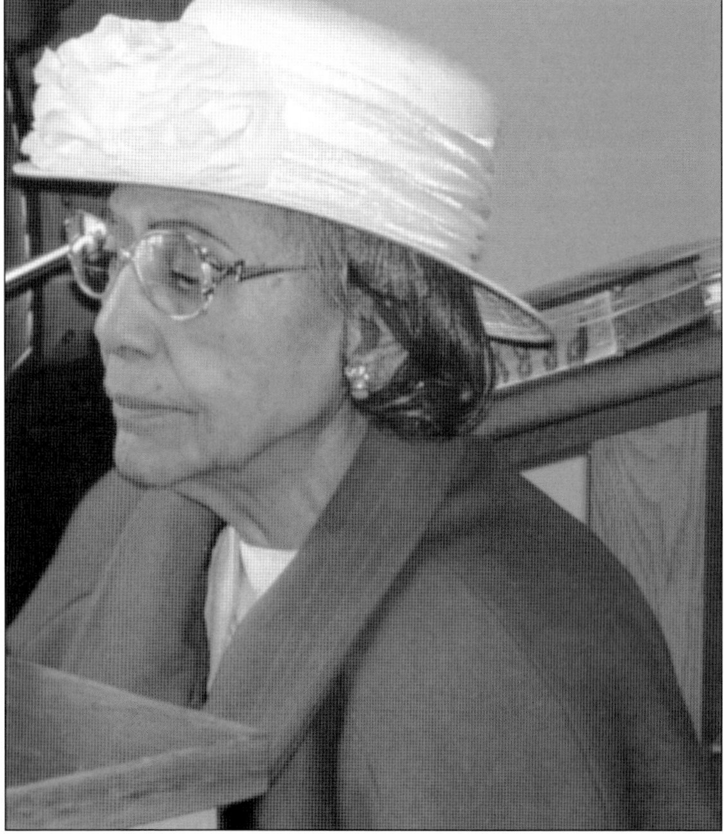

Amelia Sleet Burton began teaching at age 16 in September 1935 in Perryville and continued there until the school closed. She spent 14 years at Bate School in Danville and was the first Black teacher at Jennie Rogers School in Danville in 1967 and taught for another 15 years. In 1983, she received Kentucky's first Distinguished Teacher Award. She retired in June 1982 after a teaching career that spanned 47 years.

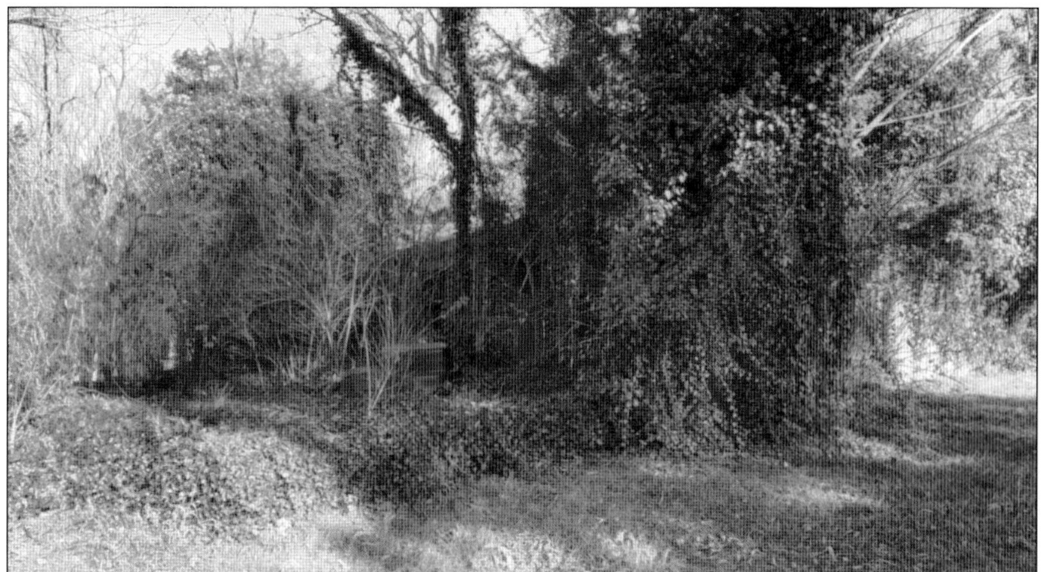

The Clifton School, seen here in 2021, shows it is almost completely gone, having been closed in the 1940s, then turned into a private home, and abandoned by the 1970s. Nearly all the African American school buildings in the county, except Stony Point and Perryville, are now gone or almost so. (Michael Denis.)

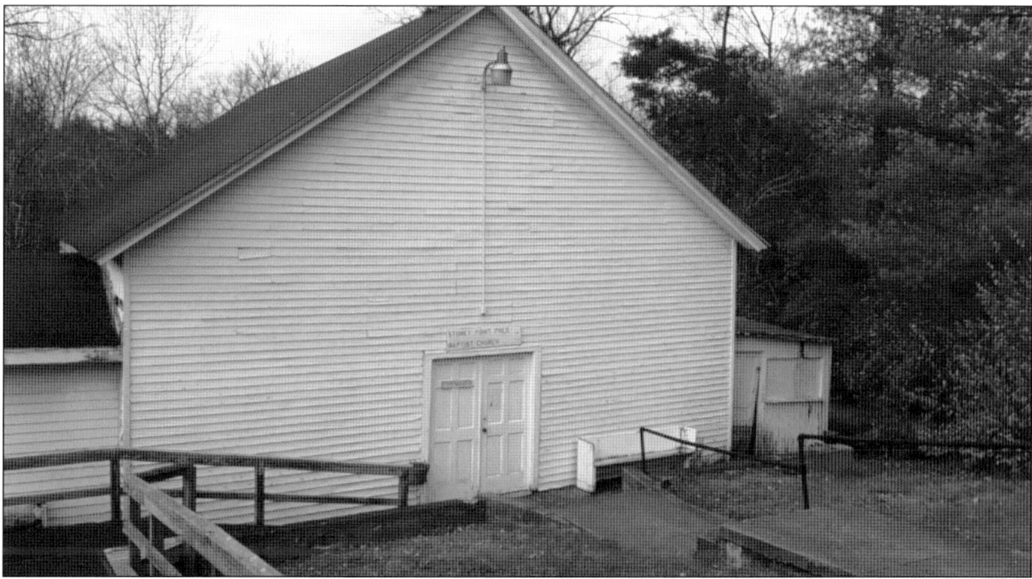

The Stony Point School, in existence since at least 1898, was moved from its original location about a mile north of its present location about 1945, and now serves as the Stony Point Predestinarian Baptist Church. The DBCAAHS has on loan the original school bell from this school. Rev. Wallace Fisher staged a meeting here in 1898, with 34 converts. (Michael Denis.)

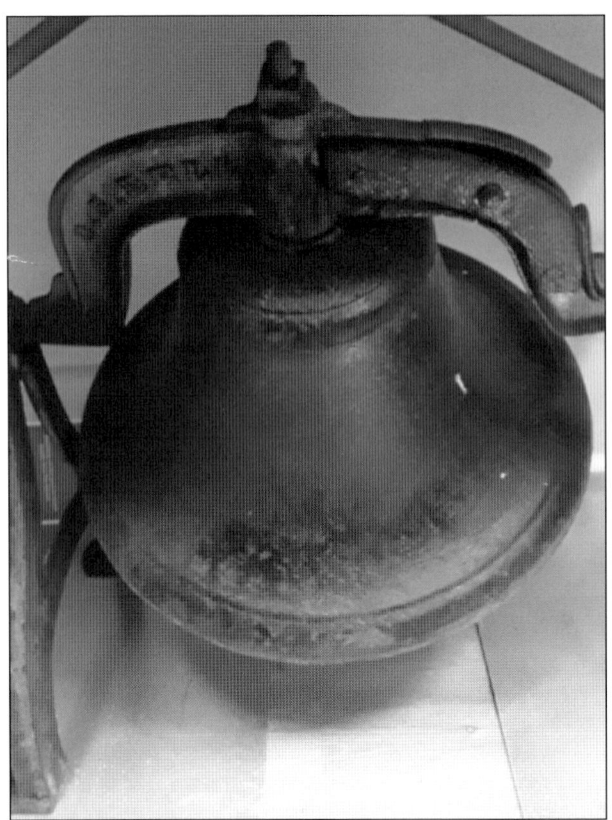

The original school bell from the Stony Point School is now at the Danville Boyle County African American Historical Society's History Center. The bell is on loan from Dr. John Hankla. Stony Point itself is confusing in that some records call it "Stony" while others call it "Stoney." The school dates from at least 1915 until it was closed in 1945 and sold to the Stony Point church. (Michael Denis.)

The names and the location of this photograph are unknown. It could be of any colored school in Boyle County. All of the names are uncertain, though the girl on the far right may be Theora (Tarrance) Coates, who was born in Chicago, Illinois, in 1918 but lived in Danville, according to the 1920 and 1930 Census records. The photograph was donated to the DBCAAHS by Coates.

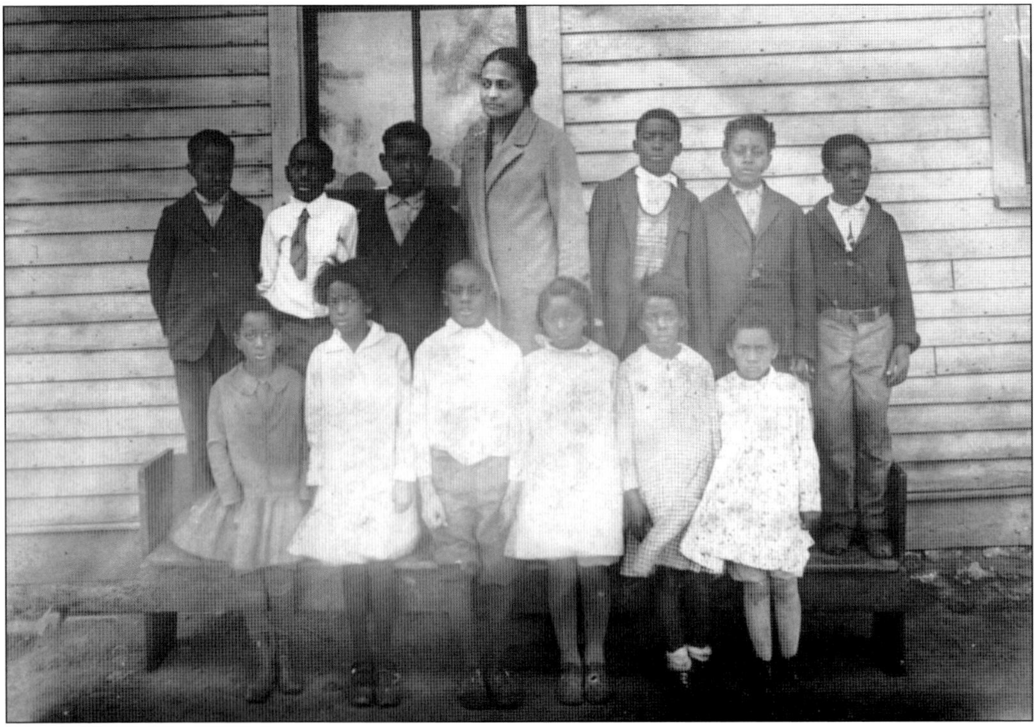

Five

Neighborhoods and Outlying Communities

Aside from Danville, there were numerous settlements where African Americans lived. In some cases, these settlements were established well before the Civil War, but for the most part, they were settled afterward and, more often than not, by former enslaved individuals and families. These settlements included (generally from west to east) Aliceton, Mitchellsburg, Sleettown, Wilsonville, Worldstown, Shelby City, Atoka, Faulconer, Zion Hill, Needmore, Clifton, Stony Point, and Wells Landing.

Of these communities today, the only one with more than a handful of African Americans is Perryville. Most of these settlements have no African American residents now and have not had any for years, or even decades.

Within Danville itself, areas of Black settlement included South Second Street, East and West Walnut Streets, Seventh Street, Rowe Street, East and West Green Streets, Russell Street (now renamed Martin Luther King Jr. Boulevard), Bate Street, Oak Street, and a few others. Duncan Hill, formerly outside city limits, was almost exclusively black, and understandably, Hilldale Cemetery, the colored cemetery, was established there by 1869. Much of West Danville by the 1960s was African American. However, the Black population of Boyle County has dropped from about 25 percent in 1900 to about 9 percent today.

But South Second Street was the African American business district from the early 1900s until urban renewal ripped it out of the heart of the city. South Second Street had barbershops, restaurants, grocery stores, civic organizations, service stations, and any kind of business the Black community needed at various times.

Instead, the very fabric of the African American community in downtown Danville was destroyed, pushing residents out of the area, shutting down what few businesses were left, and shredding any sense of belonging that Black residents of the area had. Social institutions were devastated, and the area was "renewed" as a state historic site and park—Constitution Square—where with the exception of two historical markers almost every mention of African Americans was erased.

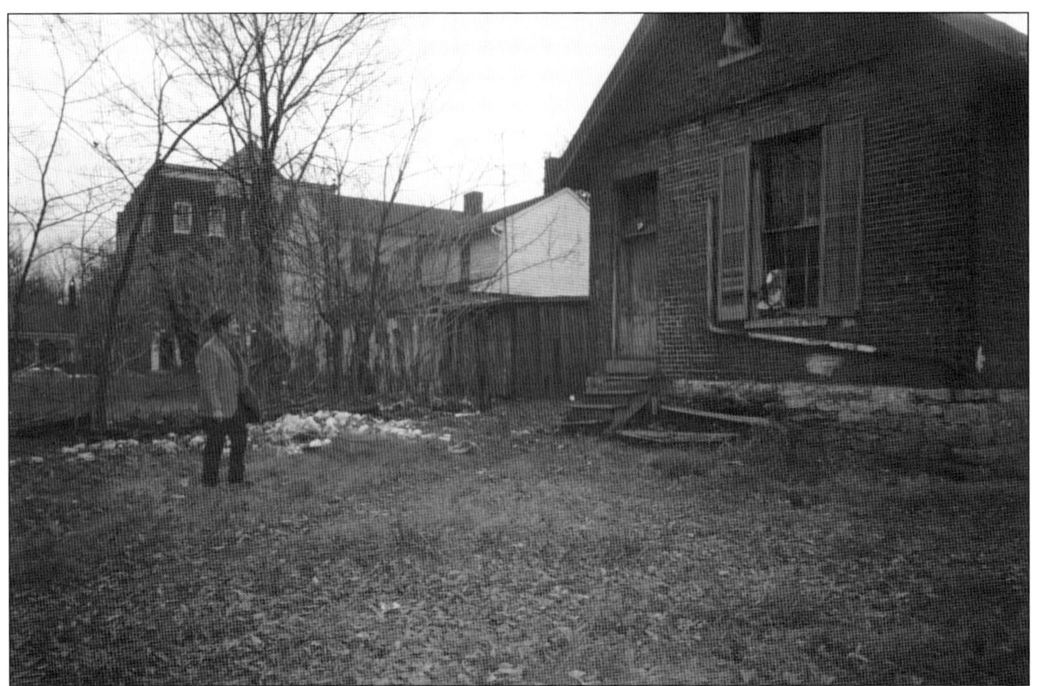

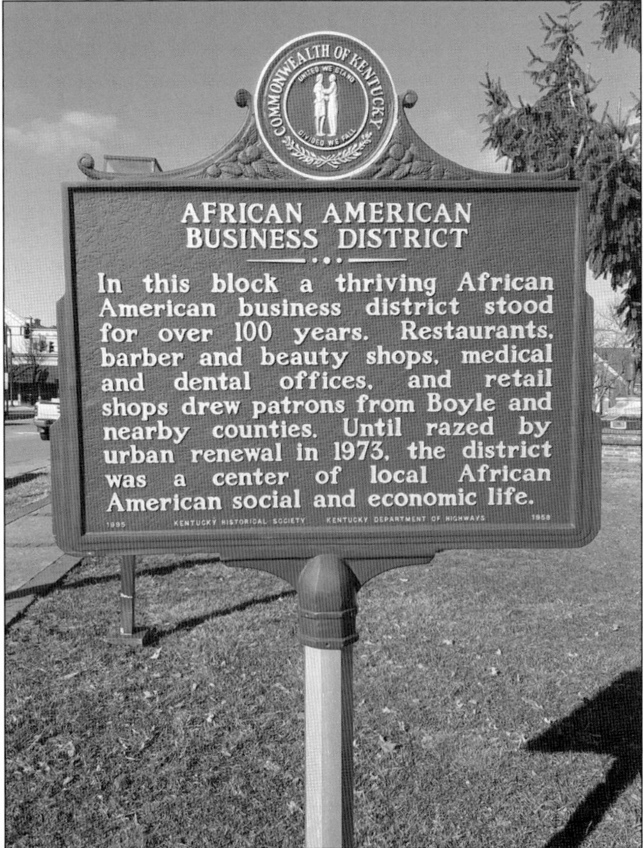

Head of urban renewal in Danville, Guy Best, is inspecting the dilapidated brick schoolhouse on South First Street. The three buildings seen here are, from left to right, the brick UBF Hall, the white Grayson Tavern, and the old brick schoolhouse, dating from about 1820. The latter two were restored, and the schoolhouse is now the McKinney Conference Center. (Charles A. Thomas Collection, BCPL.)

This historical marker was placed on September 16, 1995: "In this block a thriving African American business district stood for over 100 years. Restaurants, barber and beauty shops, medical and dental offices, and retail shops drew patrons from Boyle and nearby counties. Until razed by urban renewal in 1973, the district was a center of local African American social and economic life." (Michael Denis.)

The front side of a historical marker in Danville notes that beginning in May 1864, many Black men, formerly enslaved, marched to Camp Nelson in Jessamine County, about 20 miles away. When passing through Danville, they were stoned and shot at by residents. At first, they were not accepted as army recruits. This marked the formation of the US Colored Troops in the Civil War. (Michael Denis.)

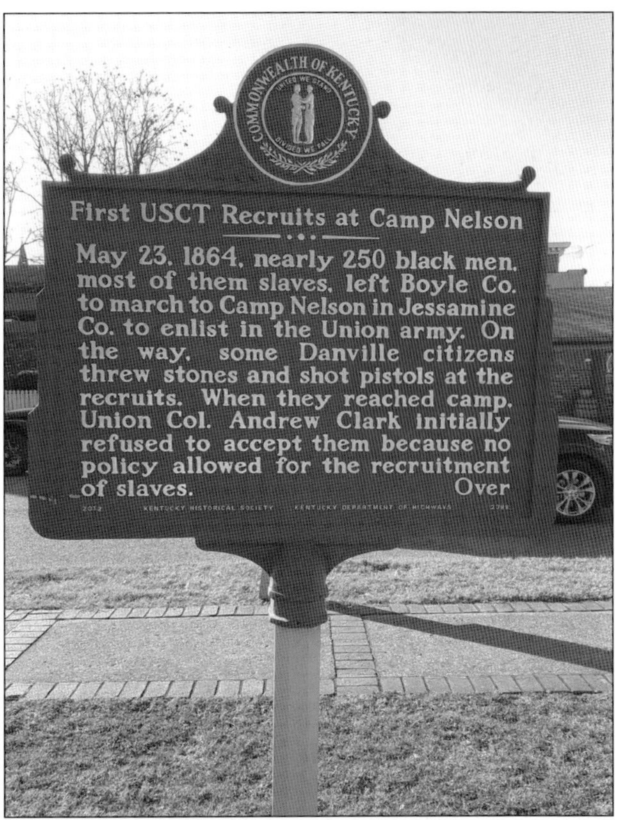

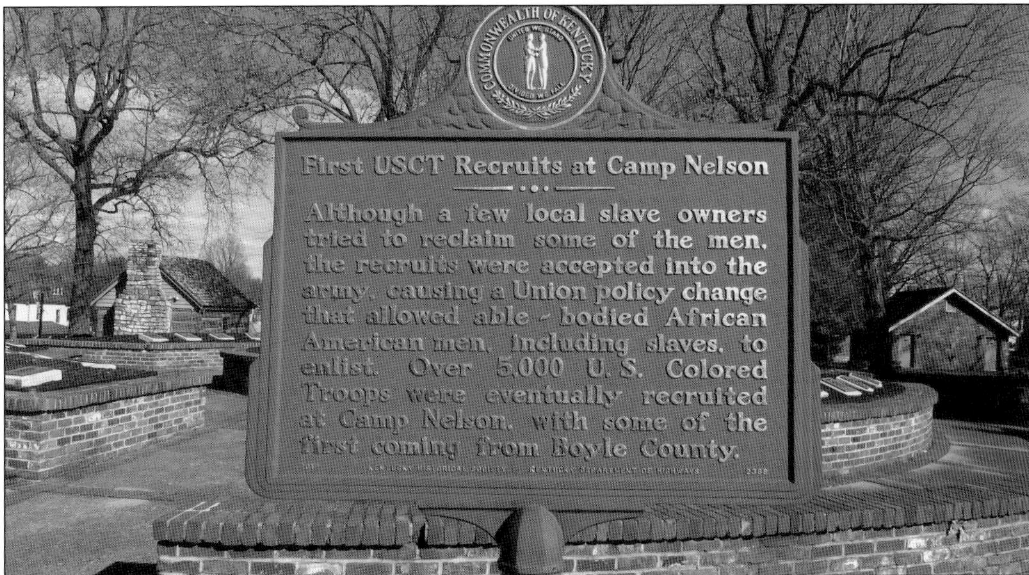

The backside of this marker reads, "Although a few local slave owners tried to reclaim some of the men, the recruits were accepted into the army, causing a Union policy change that allowed able-bodied African American men, including slaves, to enlist. Over 5,000 U.S. Colored Troops were eventually recruited at Camp Nelson, with some of the first coming from Boyle County." (Michael Denis.)

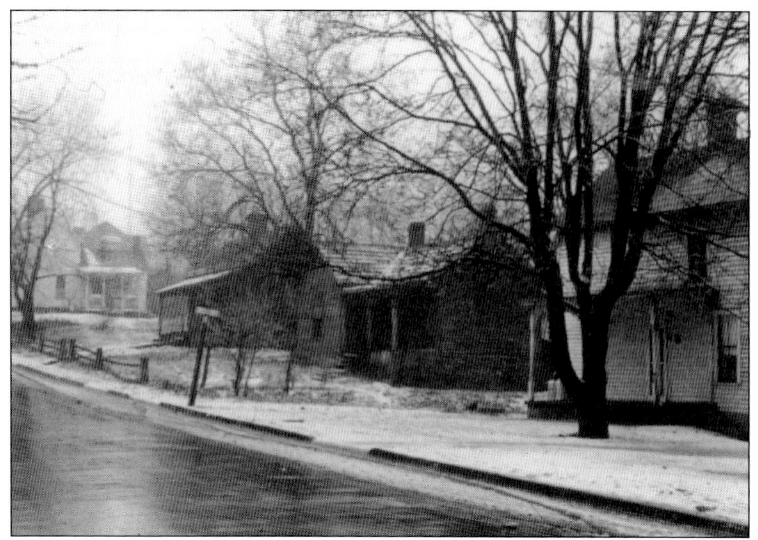

Seventh Street, between the houses, off Lexington Avenue, was the first Black neighborhood of Danville to come under the wrecking ball of "urban renewal" by 1963. Many promises were made to the residents, but few were kept. Homes on this street were torn down, and then much of the area was sold to Centre College. Residents were left to find housing wherever they could

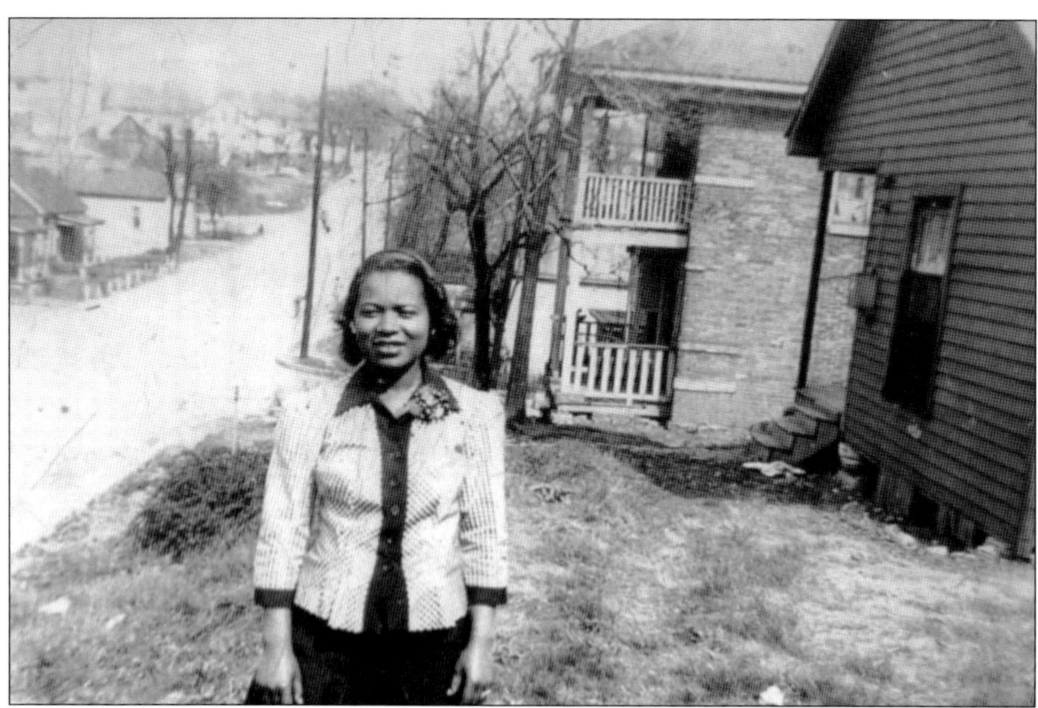

The background of this photograph shows what Seventh and Rowe Streets looked like before urban renewal. Both streets were almost exclusively black, and by the early 1960s, had become quite run down. As other areas of the city prospered, Black residents did not. Centre College purchased much of the land after urban renewal removed Black families from the area. The woman in the photograph is unidentified.

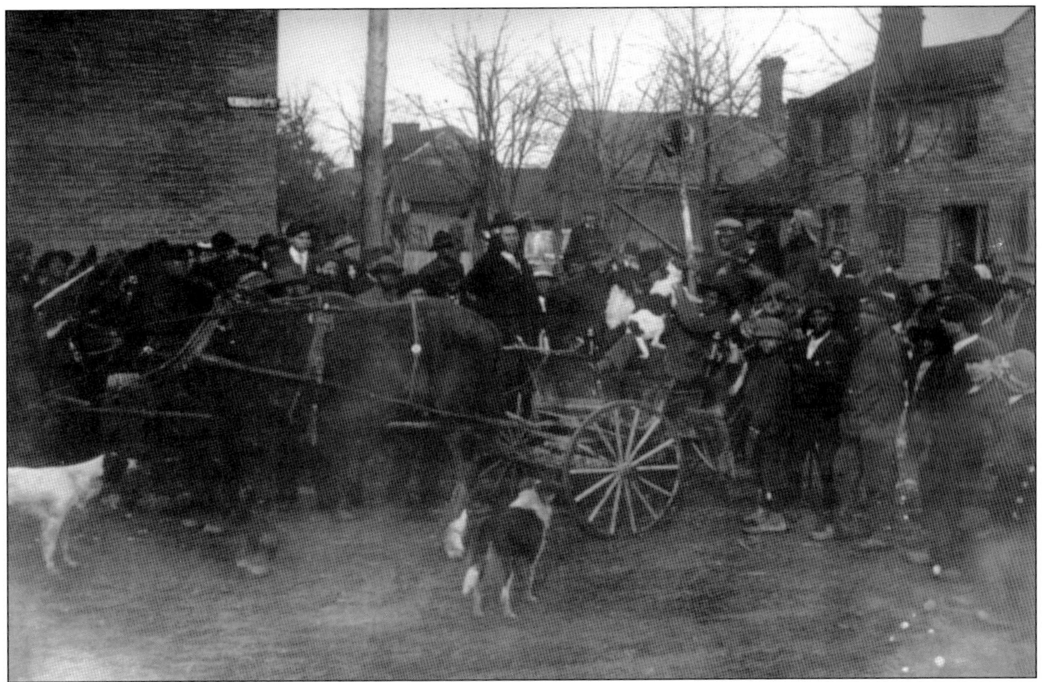

Taken on West Walnut Street at South First, it is unknown what was going on, but it appears to be a sale of hunting dogs in about 1900. The building on the right is present-day Grayson Tavern. The brick building on the left is shown on the 1914 Sanborn Fire Insurance Maps as a "hose house," probably for the segregated Black fire department.

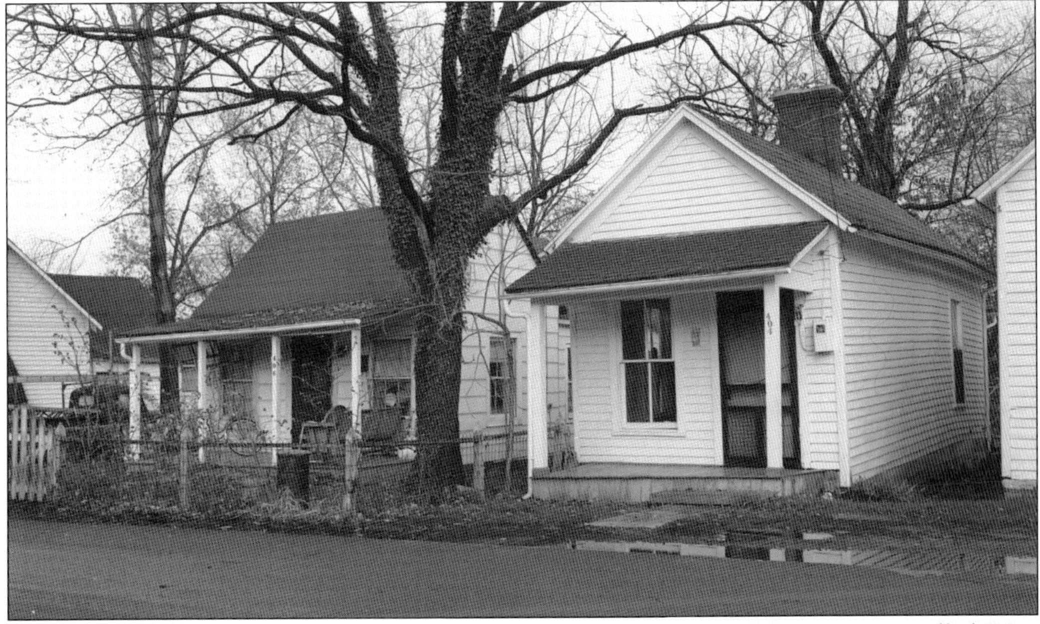

These buildings at 404 and 406 Cecil Street in the northeast part of the city, were called "Van Houses" in the Charles A. Thomas Collection. Cecil Street, in the early part of the 20th century, was a mostly Black neighborhood, consisting of many of these small homes. (Charles A. Thomas Collection, BCPL.)

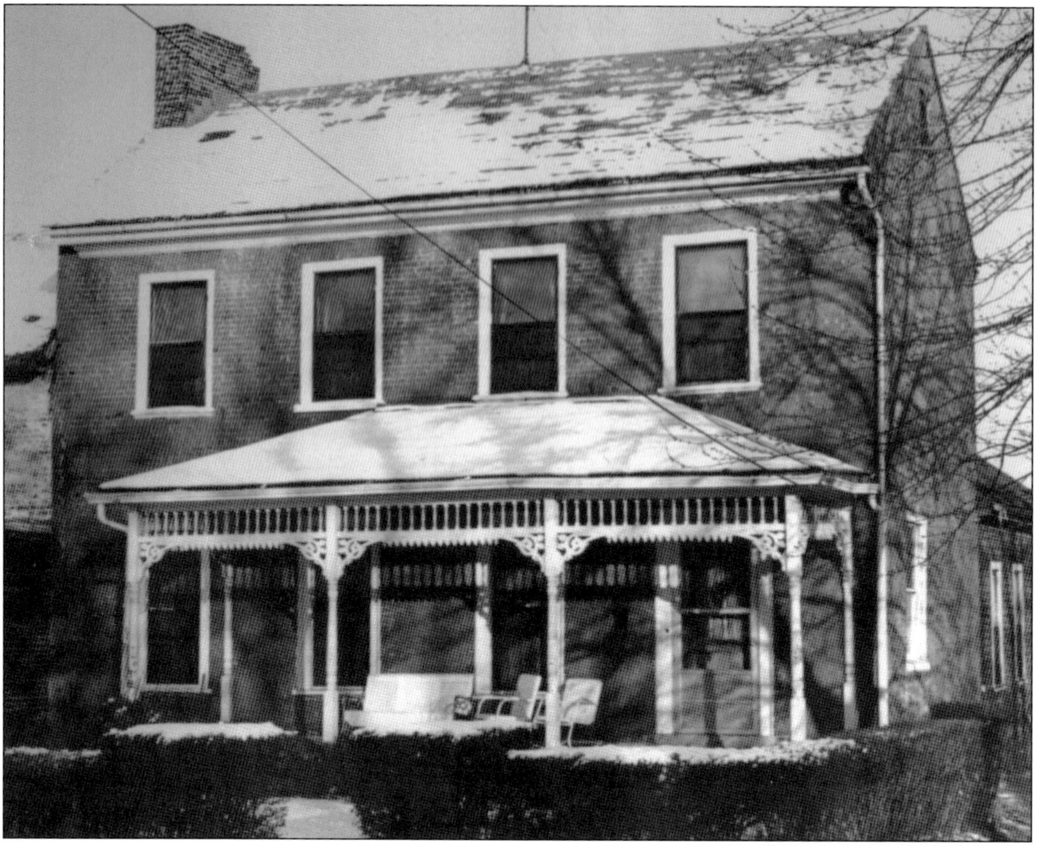

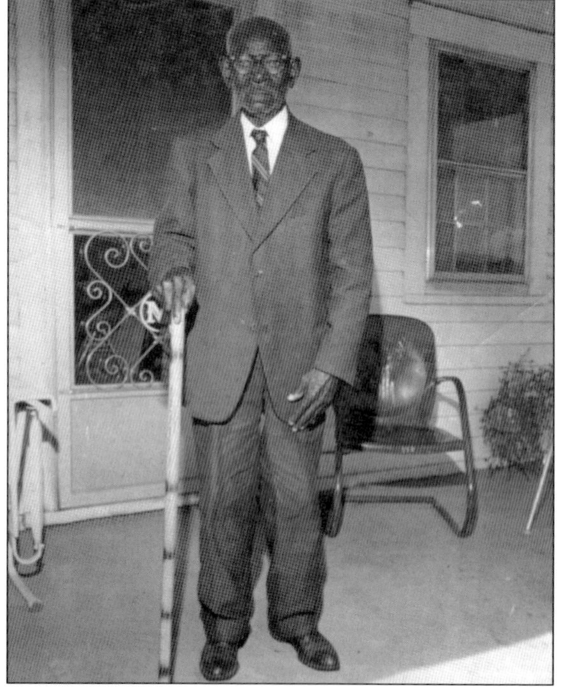

The Richardson House was located at 108 South First Street. Barber Either One Richardson owned this house until it was purchased by urban renewal. When he was born, there was a question of what he should be named. Apparently, there were two names suggested, and his mother or father said, "Call him either one." He was the son of George "Pap" Richardson, who bought the City Barber Shop on West Main Street.

John Henry Marshall of Wilsonville was born between 1868 and 1871 and died in 1976. The father of 17 children, he was the subject of an article in the *Advocate-Messenger* on June 13, 1971. Marshall retired from the railroad in 1937 and was the oldest pensioner on the railroad rolls. The *Messenger* reported on October 20, 1927, that he had suffered a badly mashed foot as a section hand on the Louisville & Nashville Railroad (L&N).

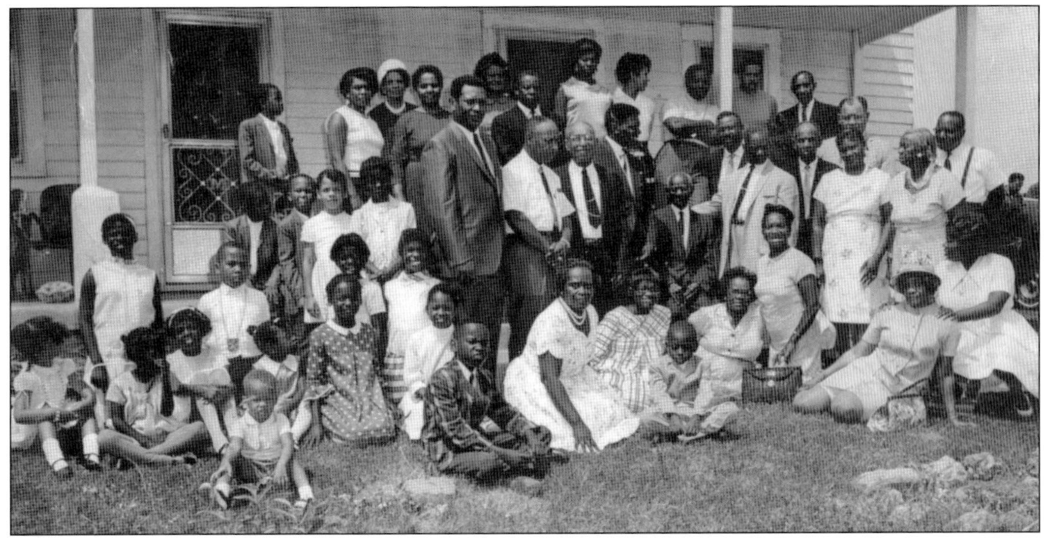

This was a reunion of the Marshall family of Wilsonville in front of Ella Marshall's house, which is now long gone. Ella is the lady wearing pearls and a light dress in the first row. Her father, John Marshall, is the seated gentleman behind her and to her left. In profile on the right side of the photograph is Sally Bruce, and her husband London Bruce, two people to her right.

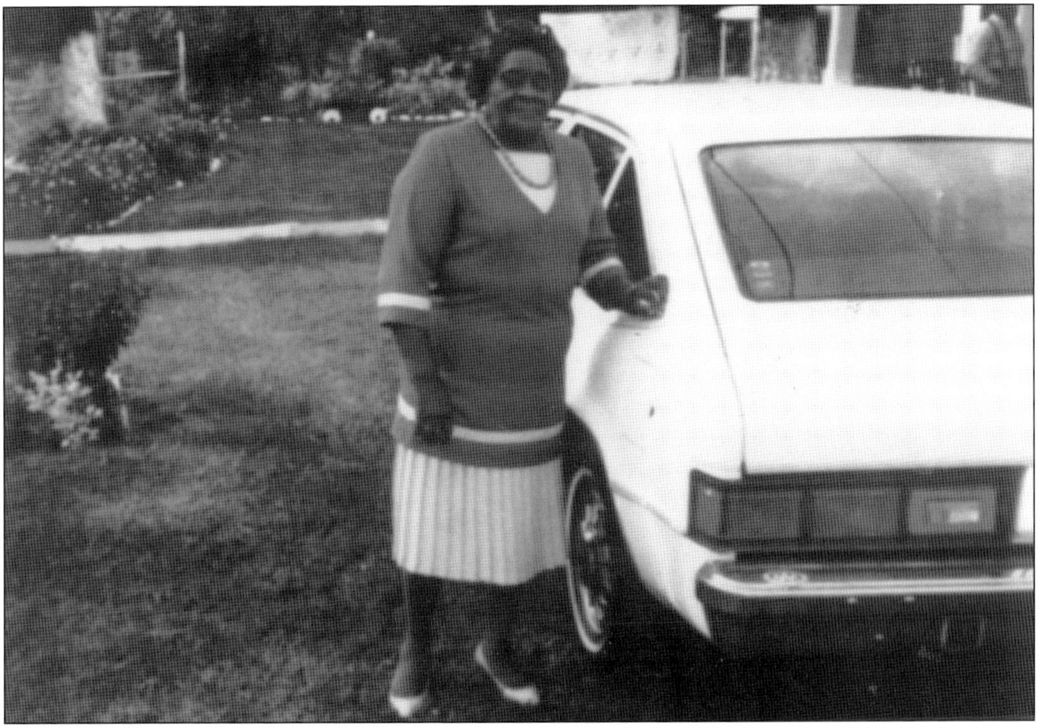

Continuing with the Marshall family, a later photograph shows Ella Mae Marshall. She was born September 24, 1913, and died April 9, 2003. She attended the Wilsonville School, then Bate High School, later earning both a bachelor's and master's degree. She taught for over 50 years, at Wilsonville, in Casey County, and finally in Junction City. She was named Kentucky Teacher of the Year in 1981.

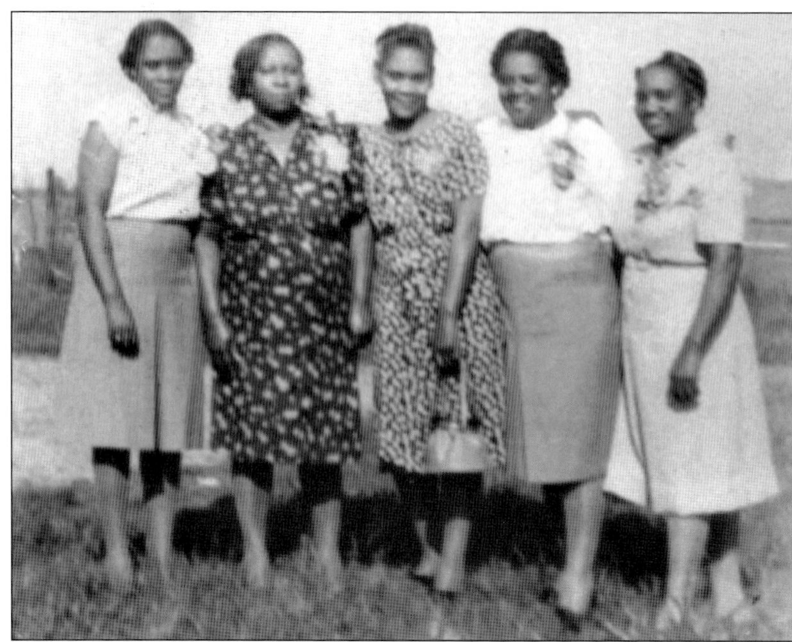

Ella Marshall is with four of her sisters in the photograph taken about 1935. From left to right are Ella, Sally (Marshall) Bruce, born 1900; Odessa (Marshall) Ensley, born 1900; Elizabeth (Marshall) Davis, born 1902; and Helena "Lena" (Marshall) (Mays) Wilhite, born 1908. There was a fifth sister, Thelma, born in 1918, who died in 1919.

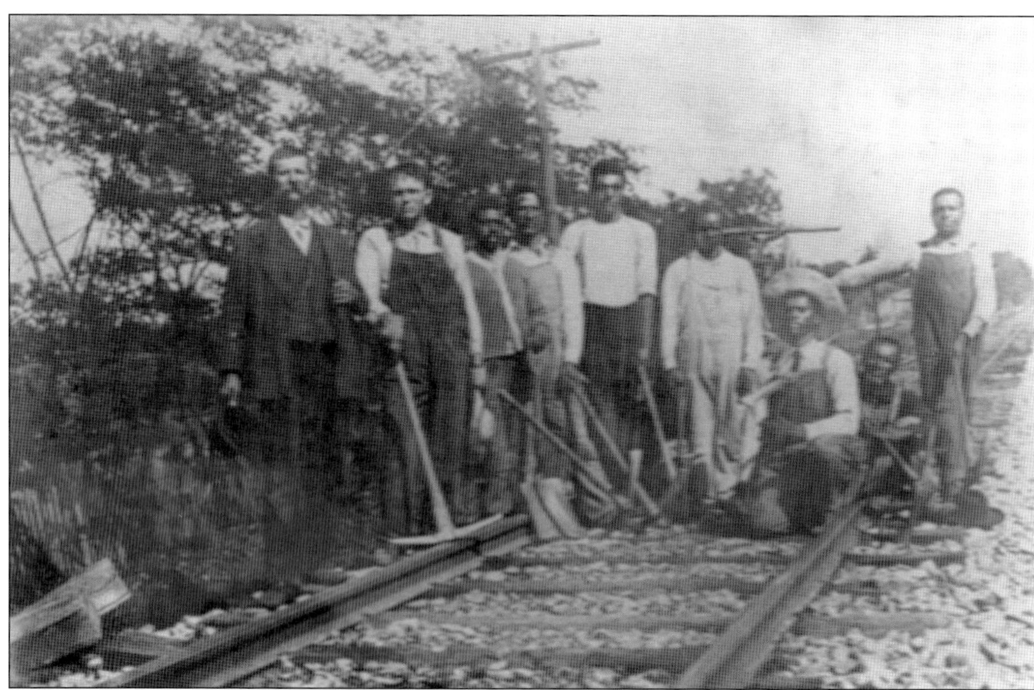

Many residents of the Wilsonville community worked on the Louisville & Nashville Railroad, which passed within feet of the Wilsonville church and school. In this 1898 photograph, John Henry Marshall, about age 22 at the time, was one of thirteen children and is fourth from the right. His father, Stewart Marshall (?1845–1922), is second the from the right.

Longtime Clifton resident Smith Yeager Tarrance (1846–1919) is pictured here with his grandchild. A one-time slave, he was one of several African Americans attending a party, so the story goes, and rather than being reintroduced into slavery, they left and walked about 20 miles to Camp Nelson and joined the Union army. The uniform picture has been looked at by an expert and is determined to be authentic.

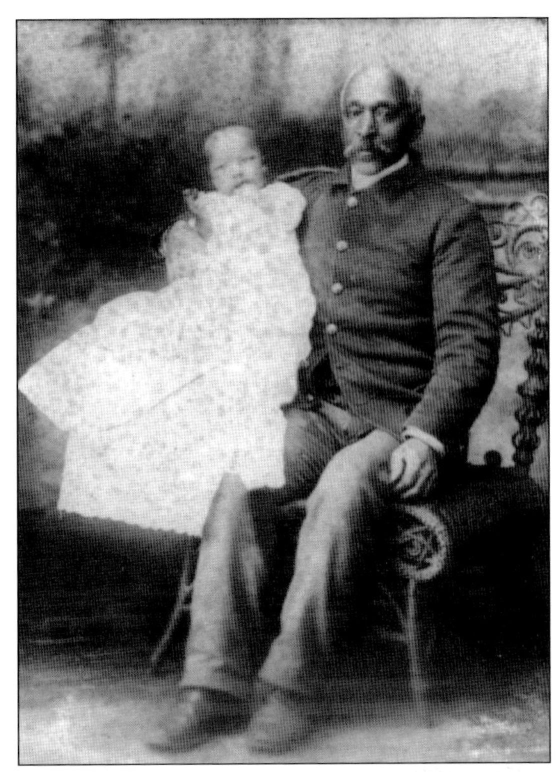

Clifton residents seen here are, from left to right, (first row) Mary Eliza (Tarrance) Baughman (1903–1995), daughter of James Thomas and Mary (Alford) Tarrance; Bessie Carmaleet (Walker) Tarrance (born 1904, wife of John Thomas Tarrance); Leona E. (Doram) Burdette (1905–2000, daughter of Eleazar and Nancy (Walker) Doram, wife of Andrew Burdette; (second row) unidentified and Madison Tarrance (1908–2002), brother of Mary Eliza.

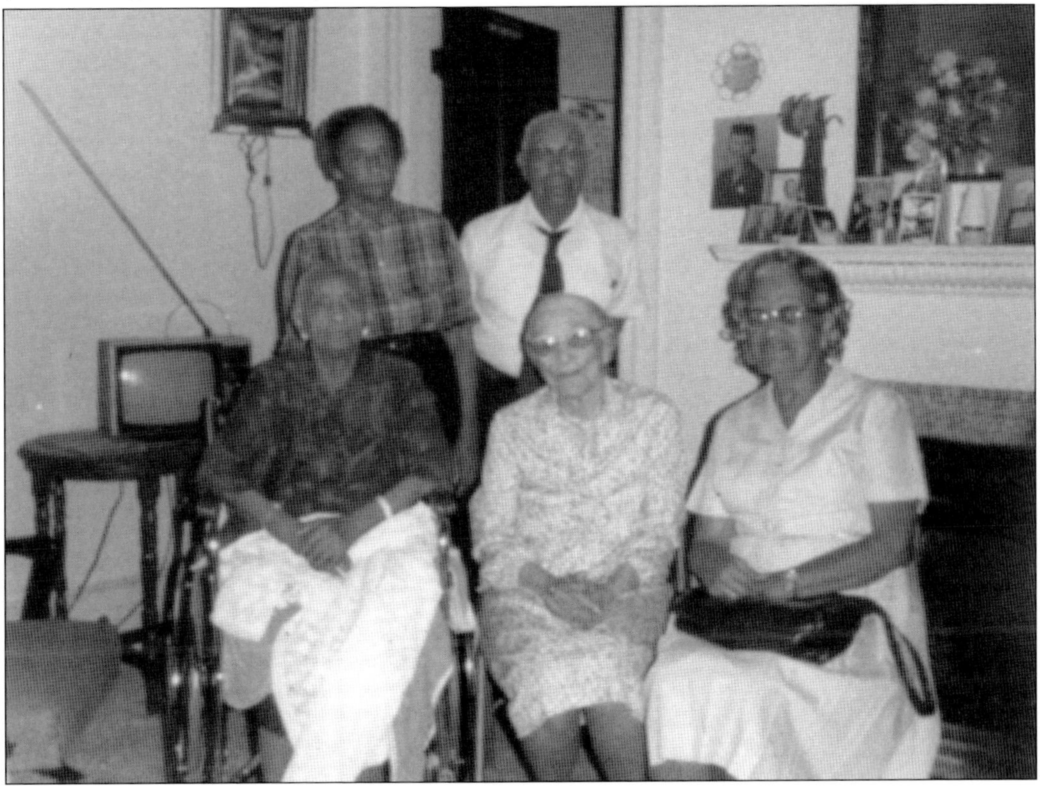

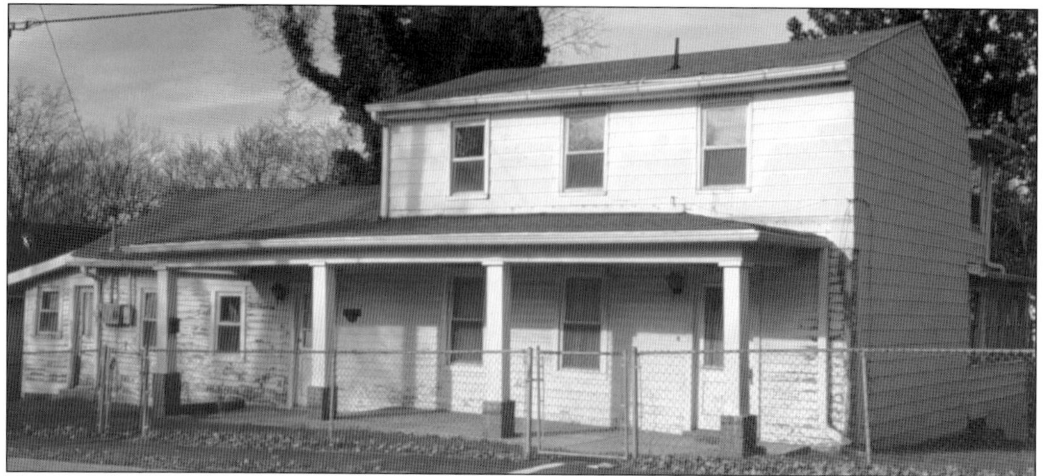

The Doram-Sledd House, East Martin Luther King Boulevard, was built by Dennis Doram (1797–1869), who owned more than a thousand acres of land and several town lots in Danville, Junction City, and Clifton. Prior to the Civil War, he also purchased a number of slaves for the purpose of freeing them. This house was later owned by Gertrude (Spillman) Sledd, a longtime teacher at Bate School. (Michael Denis.)

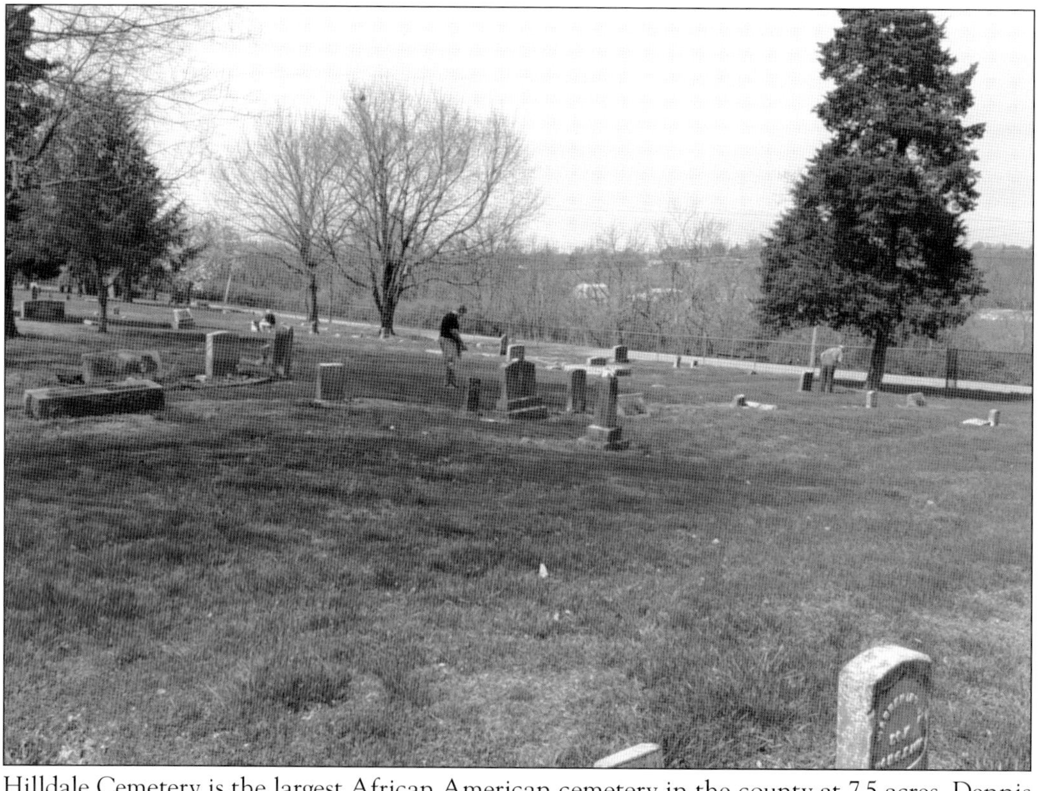

Hilldale Cemetery is the largest African American cemetery in the county at 7.5 acres. Dennis and Diadamia (Taylor) Doram were the first buried here, with Dennis in 1869. Over the years, the main story of this cemetery has been neglect, but that may have changed now with more attention being paid by the city. (Michael Denis.)

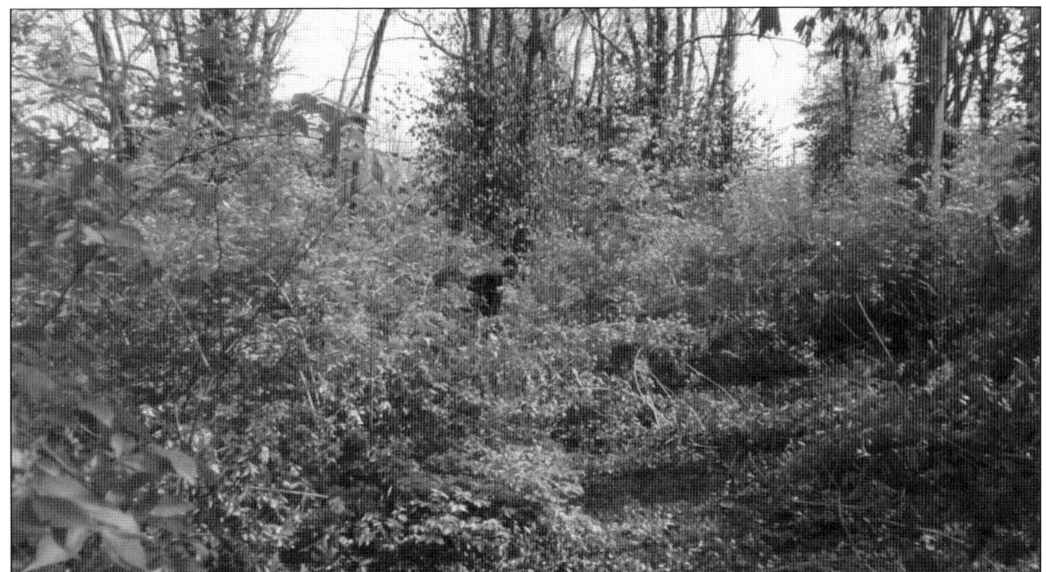

Meadow Lane African American Cemetery, as it appeared in April 2018, was originally located on the plantation of Lawson Moore, and is the oldest Black cemetery of which absolute records exist. Many of Moore's enslaved persons were buried here beginning probably in the 1830s, including "Simon," born about 1793 but recorded in the county records as dying August 10, 1853, while still enslaved. (Michael Denis.)

Patricia Ann (Harlan) Jones was photographed before South First Street was closed, about 1965. She married James Richard Jones in 1967. The two-story wooden building on the left is Grayson's Tavern, one of the few buildings that were spared the urban renewal wrecking ball. The three-story building across Walnut Street was the UBF hall, which did not survive urban renewal.

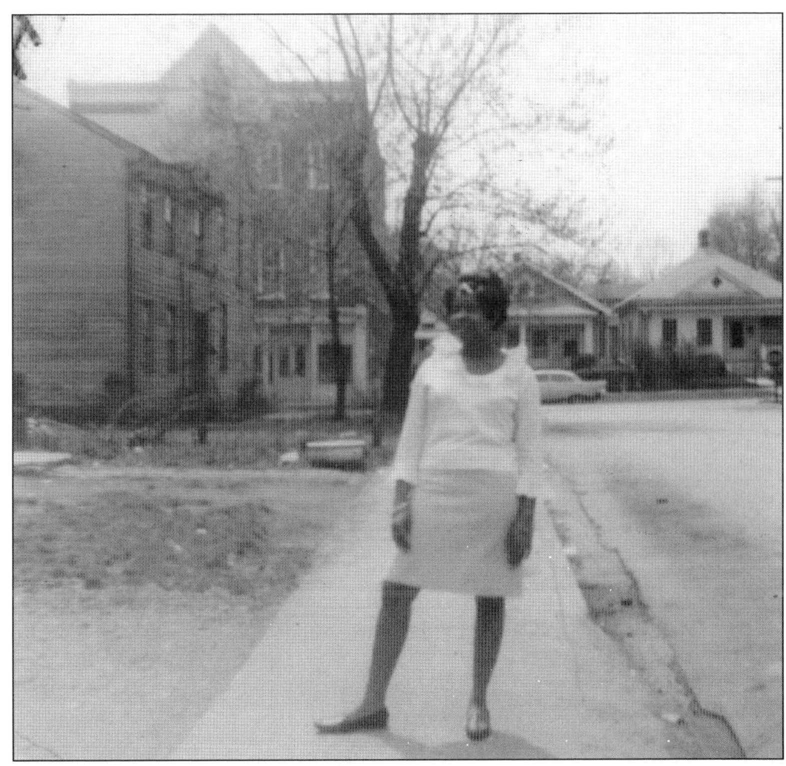

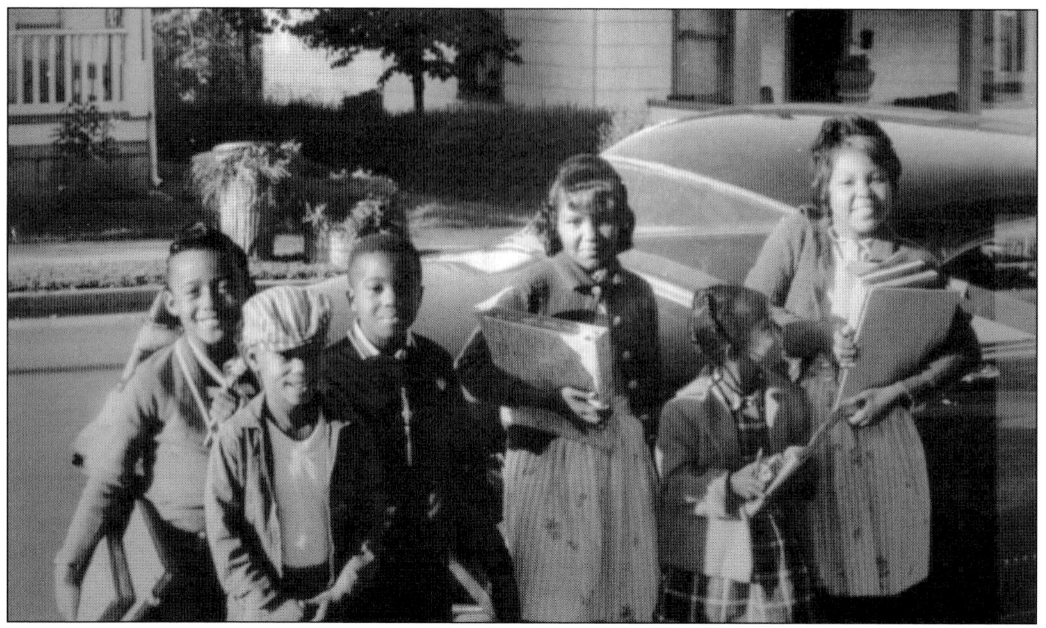

Russell Street children, pictured from left to right, James Jones, Jerry Jones, James Simpson, Alberta (Taylor) Lewis, Justine Singleton, and Francine (Taylor) Thompson are on their way to school in the mid-1950s. These children would have attended the Bate School prior to 1964, the distance being between one and one-and-a-half miles. They all would have graduated from Danville High School.

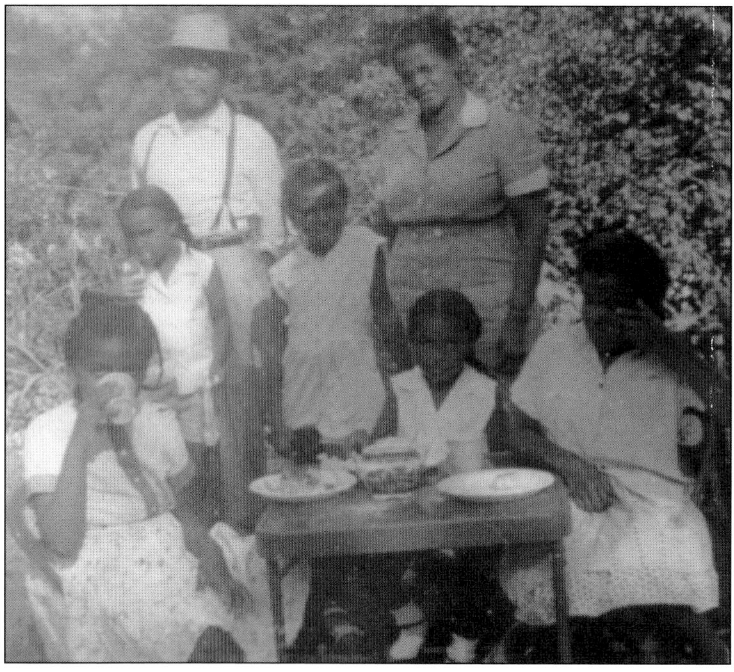

Russell Street neighbors in the mid-1950s here include (standing) Montague and Agnes Adams, and (around the table, from left to right) Benetta Penman, Francine (Taylor) Thompson, Delores Penman Townsend, Alberta (Taylor) Lewis, and Delores Briscoe. Many Russell Street residents worked at Centre College as cooks and maids and in other menial jobs, as Russell Street was an easy walk to the Centre campus. The street was named for Robert Russel, but its spelling has changed to "Russell" over time.

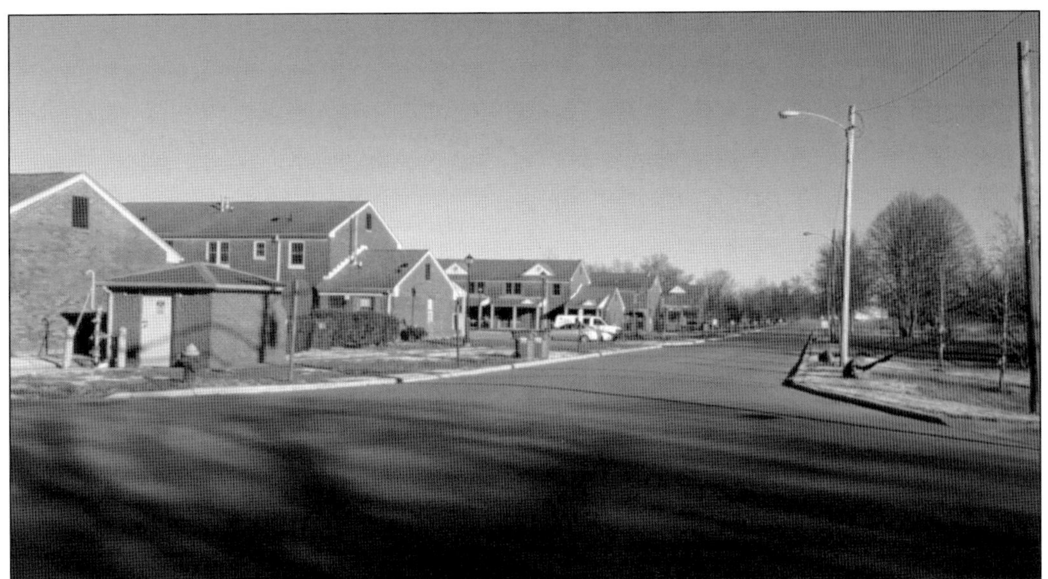

When public housing came to Danville in the 1950s, it was segregated, with the result being the colored Bate-Wood Homes on South Second Street, named after educator John Bate and minister J.W. Wood. But after the Civil Rights Act of 1964, segregated housing became illegal. Both the colored and white projects were dedicated at the white project site. (Michael Denis.)

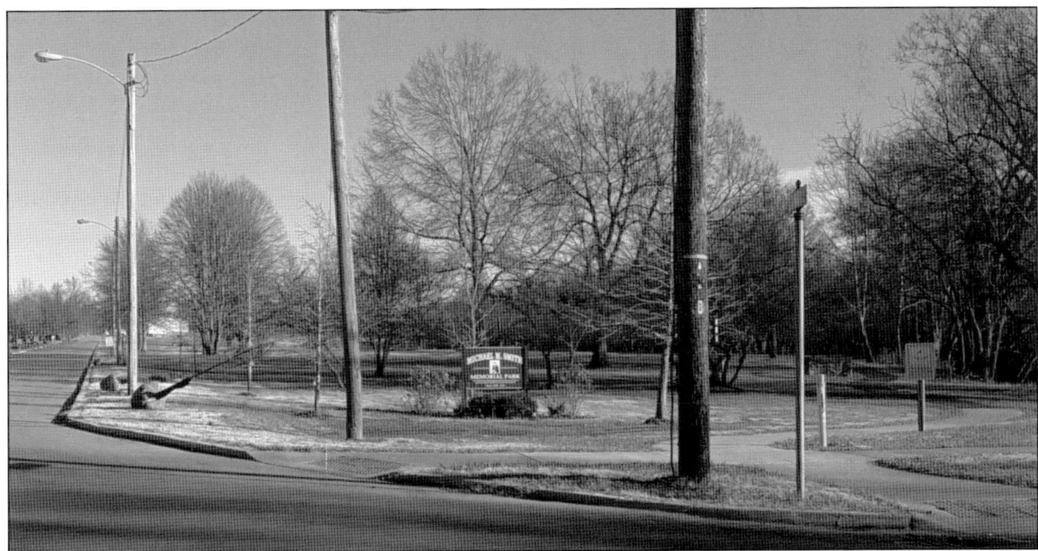

Michael Smith Memorial Park is located at Bate-Wood Homes. Smith was the owner, with others, of the Smith-Jackson Funeral Home, which had the honor of burying most Blacks in Danville. When he died, the city considered renaming a street in his honor, but it was decided instead to name the park and walking trails at Bate-Wood for him. (Michael Denis.)

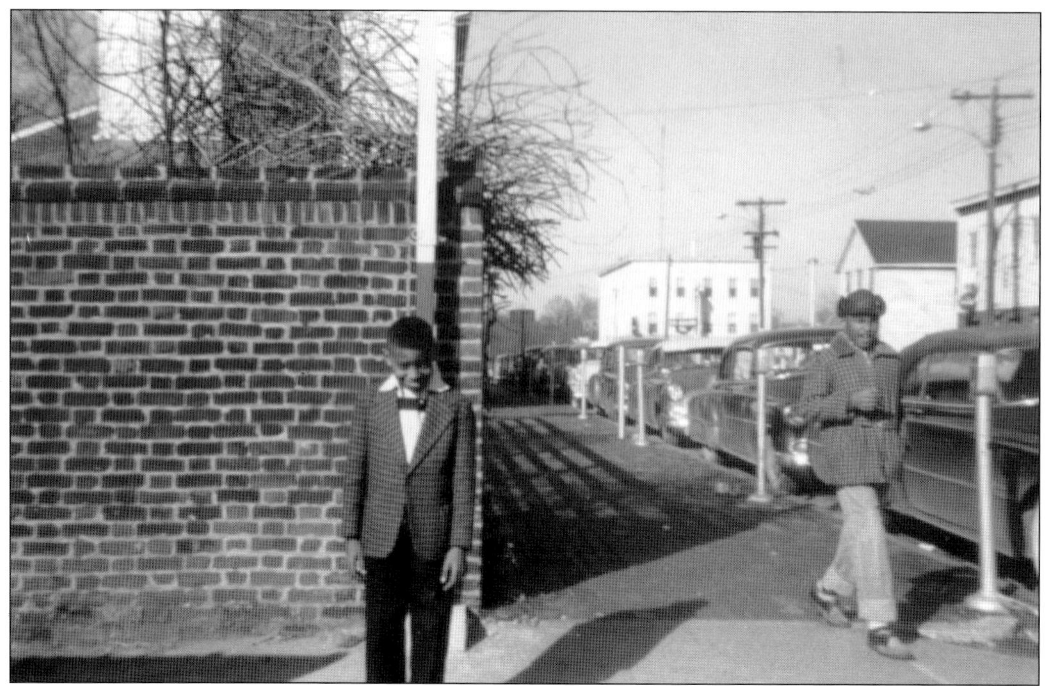

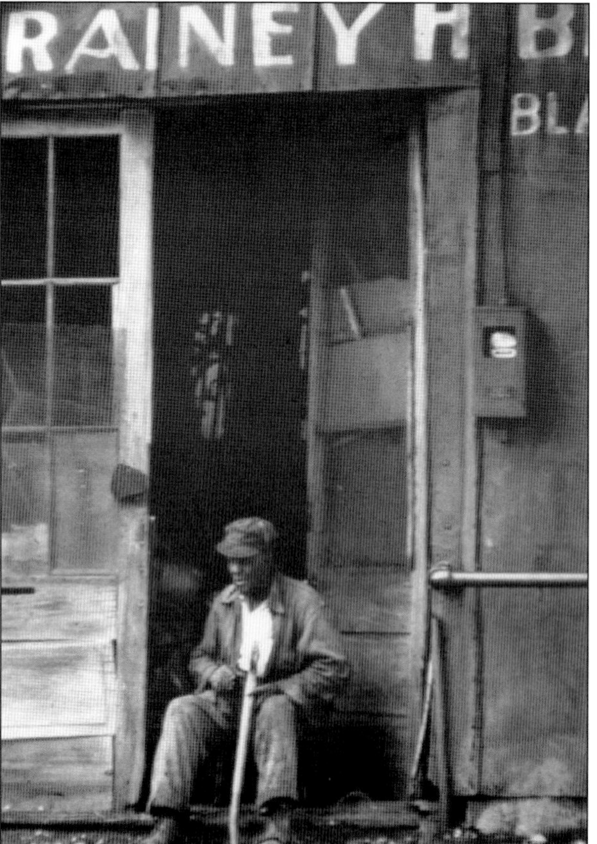

Donald Lee Faulkner, born in 1947, was the son of George and Cornelia (Simpson) Faulkner. Steve "Butch" Mays was also born in 1947, the son of Bentley L. and Jewel (Gregory) Mays. They are here on South Second Street, with the McDowell House behind the brick wall. They are almost opposite the Elite Pool Room and the Elite Cab Company buildings.

Rainey Bridgewater owned one of the few Black businesses on West Walnut Street. He was the last blacksmith in Danville, selling his shop (pictured in 1952) in 1964. This is now the Farmer's National Bank parking lot. Born about 1877, he never married and died in neighboring Marion County in 1971. Described as the "best blacksmith Danville ever had," he was frequently seen around town with his horse and wagon.

Six

Recreation

Baseball is a sport that almost anyone can play, with a minimum of equipment and expense— one reason why it was so popular with African Americans. Beginning in the late 1800s, Danville was lucky to have two "fields" where the game was played and several teams over the years. Nearby Junction City also had a team in the 1920s, coached by World War I veteran and "Harlem Hellfighter" Wallace Gaines.

People went out to Duncan Hill's ballpark, variously named Davis Park, Sportsman's Park, Foag's Park, Old Fort, or Yankee's Park. This park also served as the home field for Bate High School. Some of the best athletes at Bate School played, and many members of the Danville Yankees and the Danville Cubs actually played semi-professional baseball in Lexington. The Danville teams played other teams from all over central Kentucky and, at first, traveled to away games in a converted cattle trailer. Later, the Victory Bus Lines bus replaced the cattle trailer.

As seen in the chapter on schools, football and basketball were also major recreation events. Community events often revolved around a baseball game, particularly on holidays. Though both the Cubs and the Yankees attracted large crowds on game days, it was as much a social event as it was an athletic competition.

A sign next to Arcy's "Bunny" Davis (page 98) reads in part:

> William "Bunny" Davis, the grandson of former North Carolina slaves, was born in 1917, in Perryville, KY. Throughout his life, Davis broke racial barriers and achieved great success as a leader in sports, business and government.
>
> Davis played baseball, basketball, football, and track and was inducted into the Kentucky High School Sports Hall of Fame. He truly excelled at baseball, playing in the 1940s for the Lexington Hustlers, the first integrated team in the south. He played against baseball greats Jackie Robinson, Willy Mays, Satchel Paige, and Roy Campanella. He was also the first black umpire in the Southeastern Conference.
>
> After sports, Bunny's Moving and Storage was his business and he was affiliated with numerous service organizations in Danville. He was active politically, elected to the Danville City Commission six times, and was Mayor Pro-tem for ten years. He is also fondly remembered statewide for his 28 years of service as the doorkeeper for the Kentucky House of Representatives.

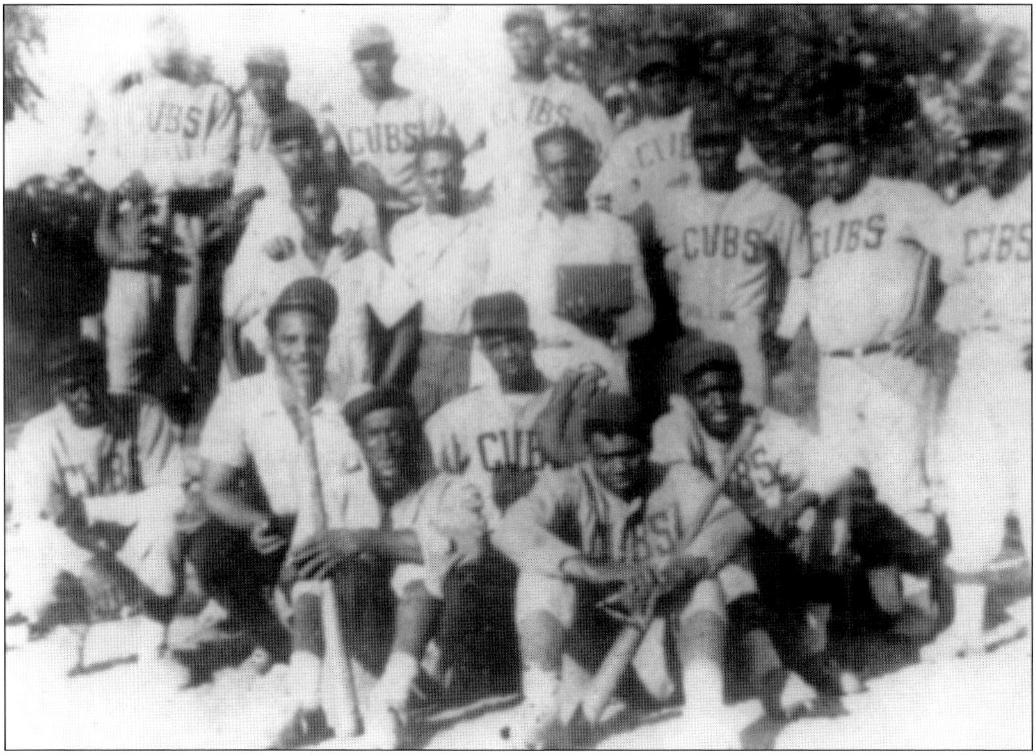

Danville Cubs, playing from the early 1920s to about 1950, had their "home field" at "Foag's Park" on Duncan Hill, and later moved to West Danville's Fairview Park after about 1941. Players over time included Bunny Davis, James Caldwell, Rich Frye, Ben Jenkins, Tom Kennedy, Pete McCowan, Paul Routt, Elwood Spaulding, Eugene "Gene" Spaulding (possibly), James "T.J." Spaulding, and June Sperley, among others.

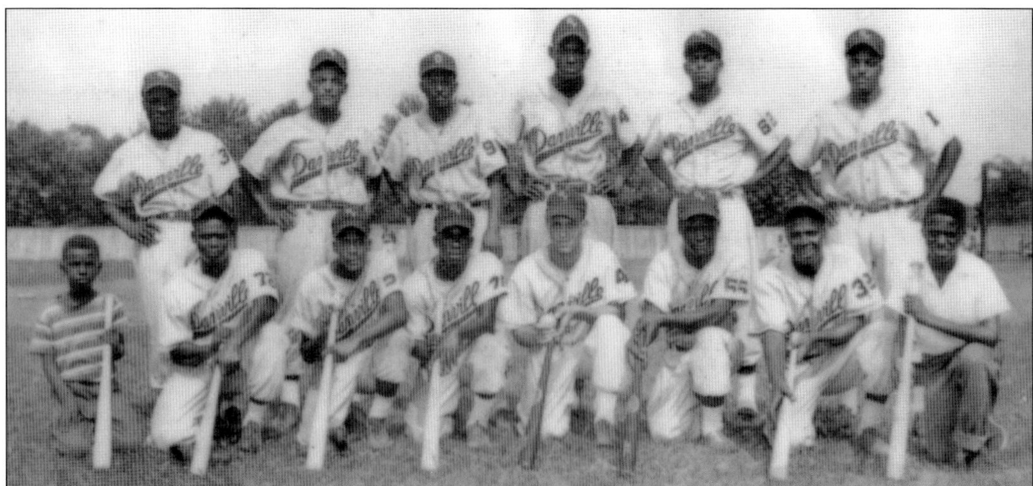

The Danville Yankees baseball team is seen on July 24, 1953, the undefeated team includes from left to right (first row) trainer Theodore Davis, Sidney Stevenson, June Christy, Oliver Wheat, Marvin Swann, William Pittman, J.W. Raines, and Donald Davis; (second row) Tom Kennedy, Archie McCowan, Dowell McCowan, Roy Yocum, Matthew "Pistol Pete" McCowan, and manager Bunny Davis.

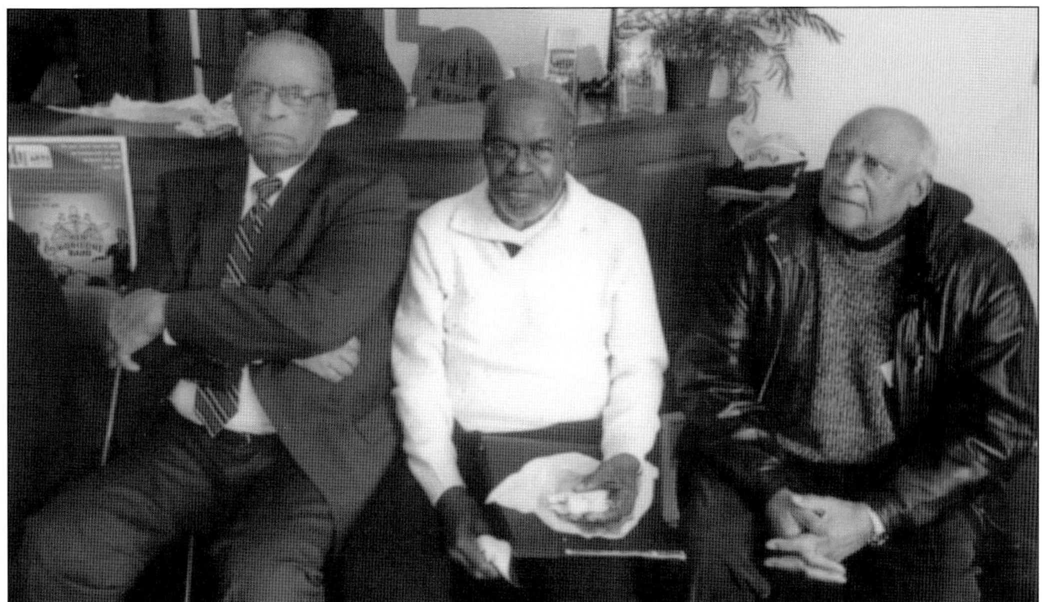

Pictured from left to right, baseball players Matthew "Pistol Pete" McCowan (1931–2020), John Thomas Davis (1935–2018), and Thomas Mutt Christy (1927–2018) all played baseball for various Danville teams. McCowan earned his nickname for the speed of his pitch. Davis, who tried out for the St. Louis Cardinals in the 1950s, was the son of Bunny Davis. Christy also played for the Danville Yankees as a shortstop.

The African Americans on the Kentucky State Hospital team in the photograph are, from left to right, Bunny Davis, Calvin Bedinger Jr., and June Christy. Christy was inducted into the Army Air Corps at the age of 18, in 1945. After his discharge in 1947, he returned to Bate and finished his high school career, graduating in 1950. He was again drafted in 1950 and served almost a year in Korea.

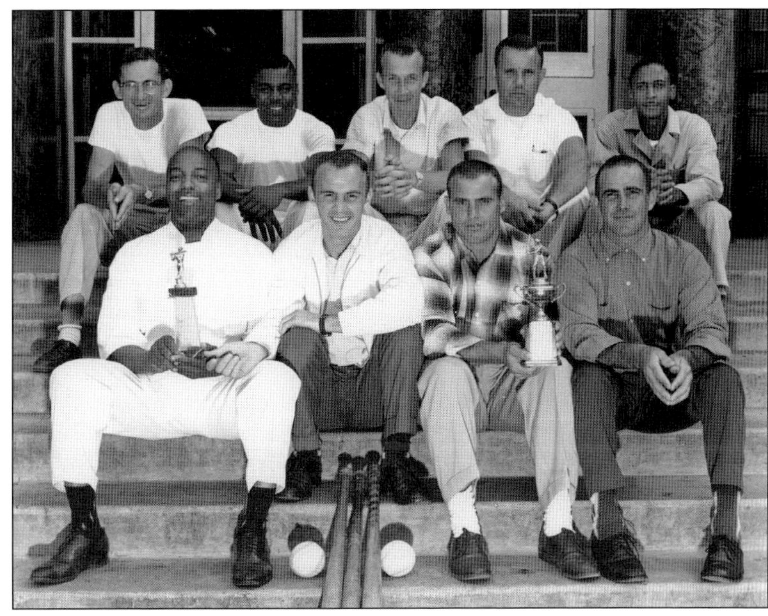

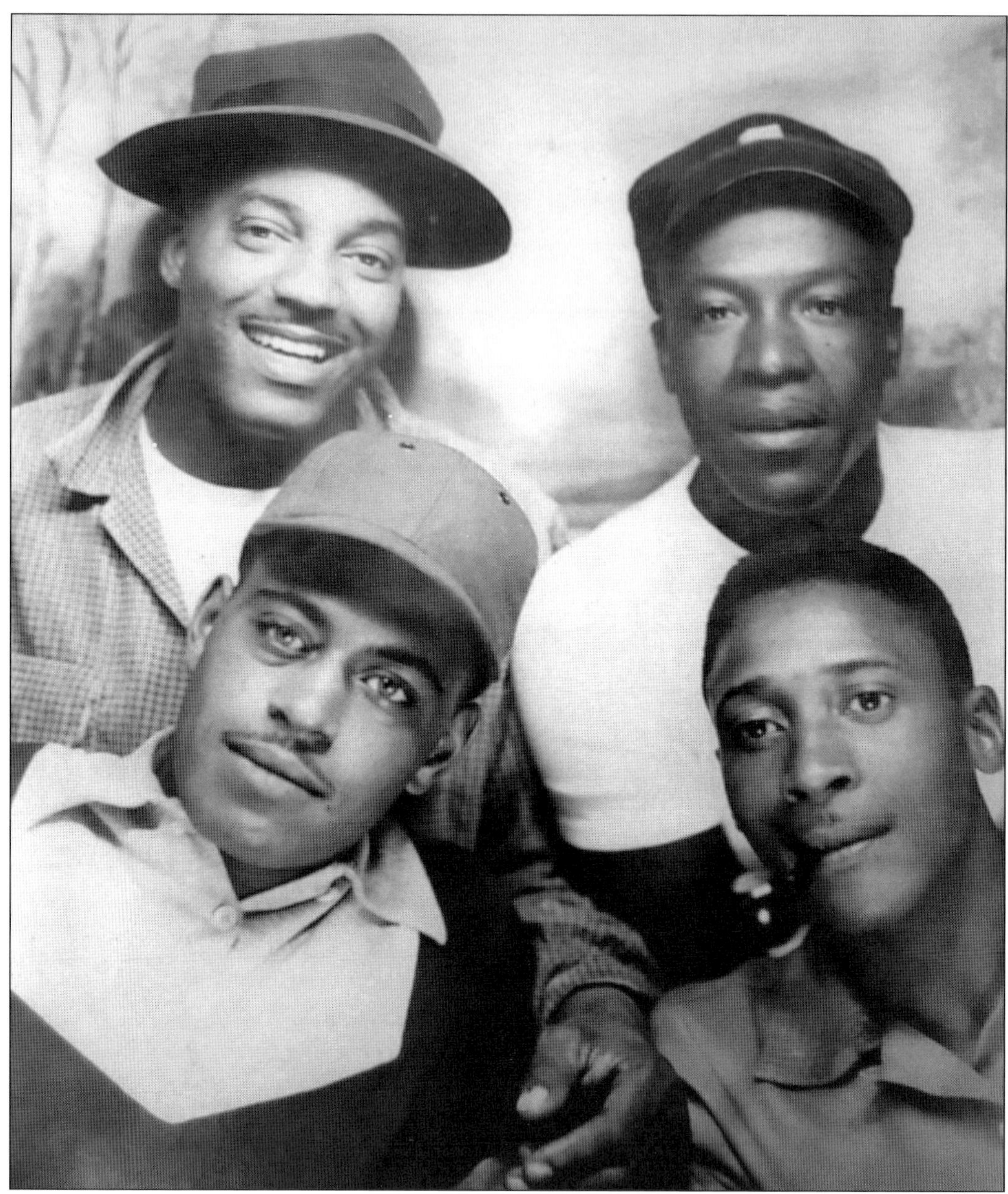

Members of Danville Yankees are shown here. Clockwise from the top right are Rev. Thomas Kennedy, Mutt Christy, Pistol Pete McCowan, and Bunny Davis. McCowan earned his nickname for his fast pitching at Bate, and Davis for his running ability in school, and as a baseball player. All but Kennedy played with other teams, some integrated, and Davis played against some of baseball's greatest stars of the 1950s and 1960s. These men playing our "national pastime" played despite conditions that worked against Black players at the time, and yet they brought a great deal of pleasure, enjoyment, and pride to the African American community in Danville.

Mary J. Smith and her grandson are shown in front of a Victory bus. In the early years, the teams traveled by cattle car for away games. By this time, however, the Victory Bus Line provided transportation. As seen in other photographs, baseball was an integral and inexpensive part of African American lives, and it was a social event as well as a sporting event.

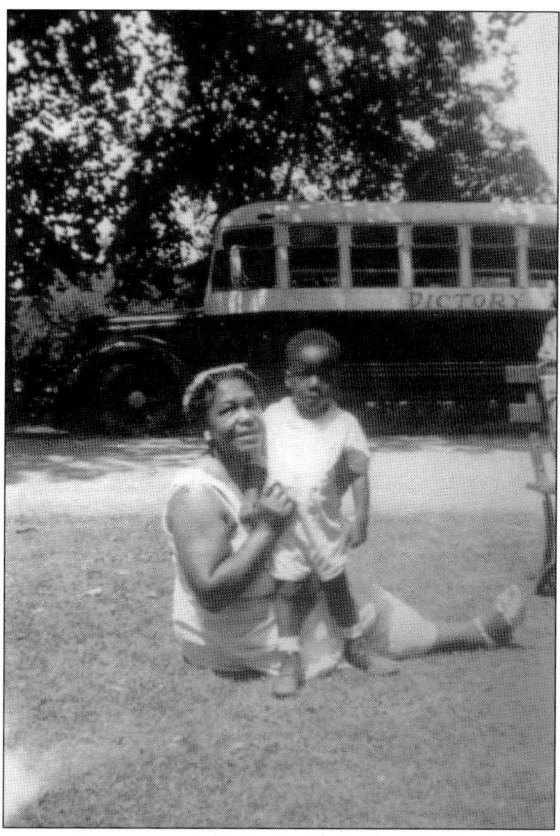

Danville's Bunny Davis played for the Lexington Hustlers baseball team. Also pictured, from left to right, are Robert Mosley, Walter "Beaver Dam" Mason, and John Will "Scoop" Brown. This team was the first integrated baseball team in the South, with white players making up a third of the team by 1949. The field where the Hustlers played was purchased in 1945 and is now the home of the Lexington Legends.

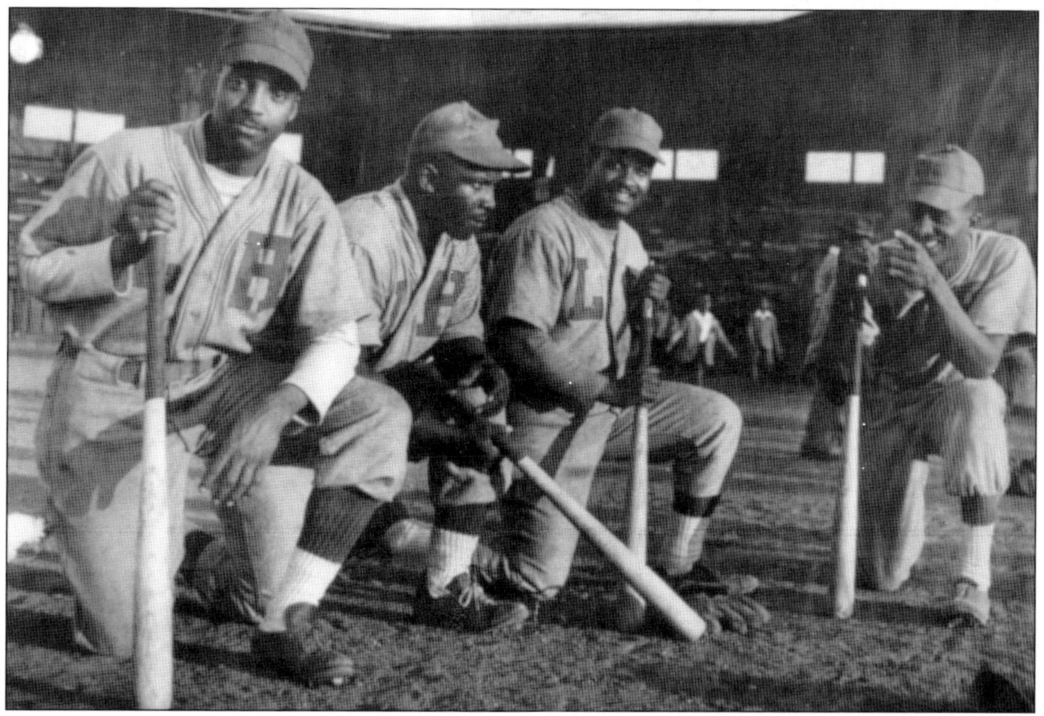

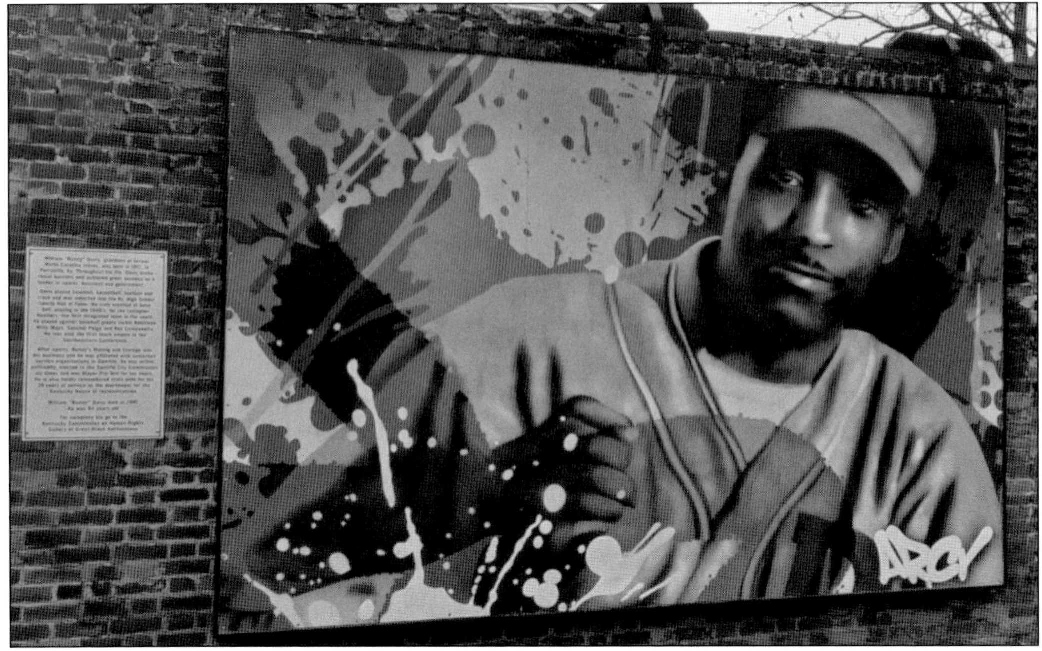

Bunny Davis as a wall mural was created by street artist ARCY for the Soul of Second Street Festival on August 4, 2018. Done entirely with spray-can paint, it captures Davis's essence, in color and in action. It is currently mounted outside on a wall on the west side of South Second Street. The plaque is quoted on the introduction page for this chapter. (Michael Denis.)

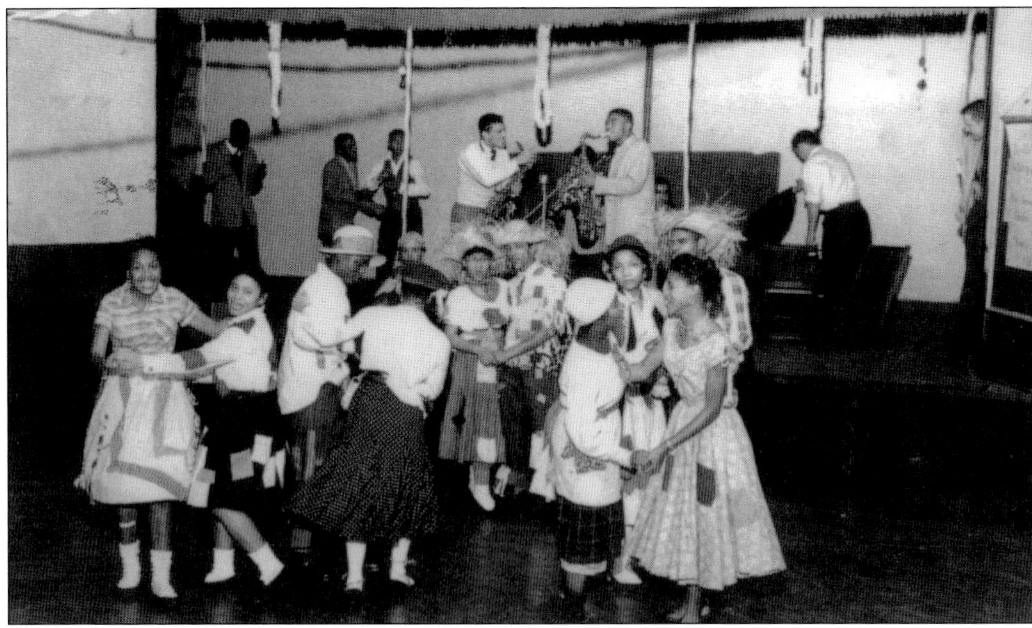

A Sadie Hawkins dance was held in 1954 at the UBF hall. From left to right are Minnie Lou Caldwell, Audrey Singleton, L.J. "Nick" Bates, Lucinda Fields, Bessie Cowan, Doris Routt, Normal Barleston, Joan Neal, George Coulter, Elois Thompson, and Yvonne Doram. Band members, also listed from left to right, are Ira Brand, Craig Penman, Earl Leverett, Michael Smith, James Ogle, James Morris Daugherty, Paul Smith, and two unidentified people.

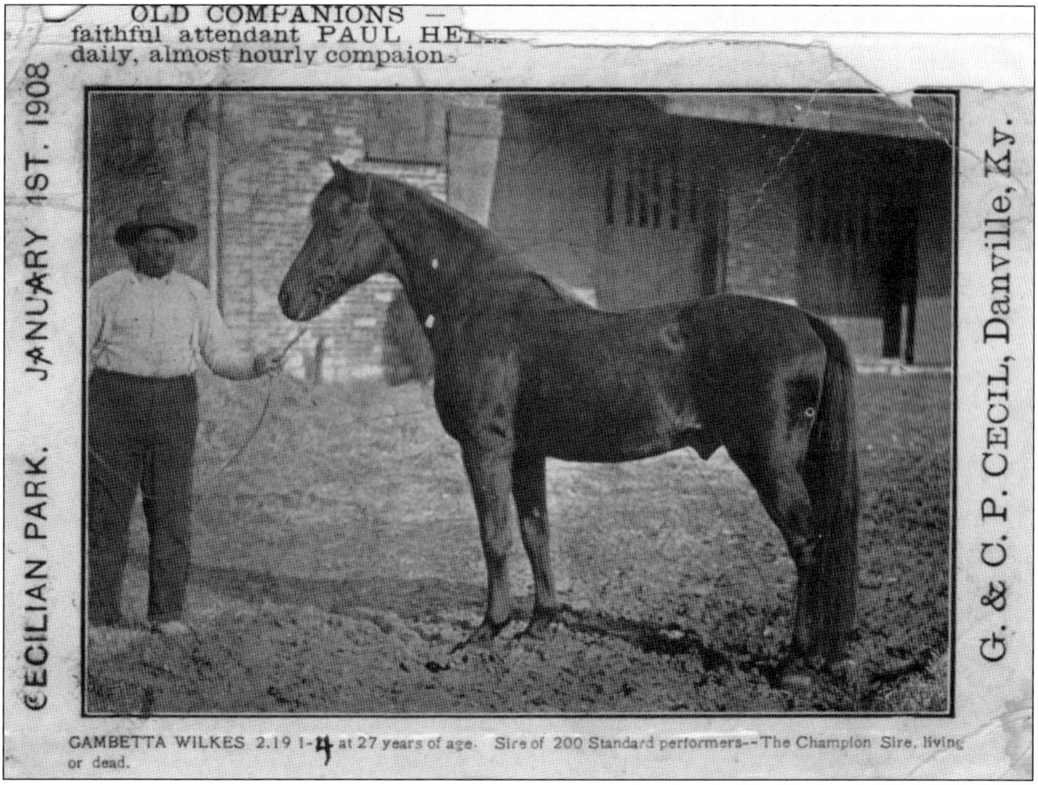

OLD COMPANIONS —
faithful attendant PAUL HE
daily, almost hourly compaion

CECILIAN PARK. JANUARY 1ST. 1908

G. & C. P. CECIL, Danville, Ky.

GAMBETTA WILKES 2.19 1-4 at 27 years of age. Sire of 200 Standard performers--The Champion Sire, living or dead.

The great racehorse Gambetta Wilkes died at age 29 in August 1910. A direct descendant of the famous Justin Morgan, he was not only a great racehorse, but his offspring were as well. His longtime trainer was Paul Helm. As Gambetta's chief trainer for 25 years, Helm "is desolate for he loved this horse and was his companion in his youth, in his prime and in his equine dotage" (Danville *Messenger*, August 23, 1910).

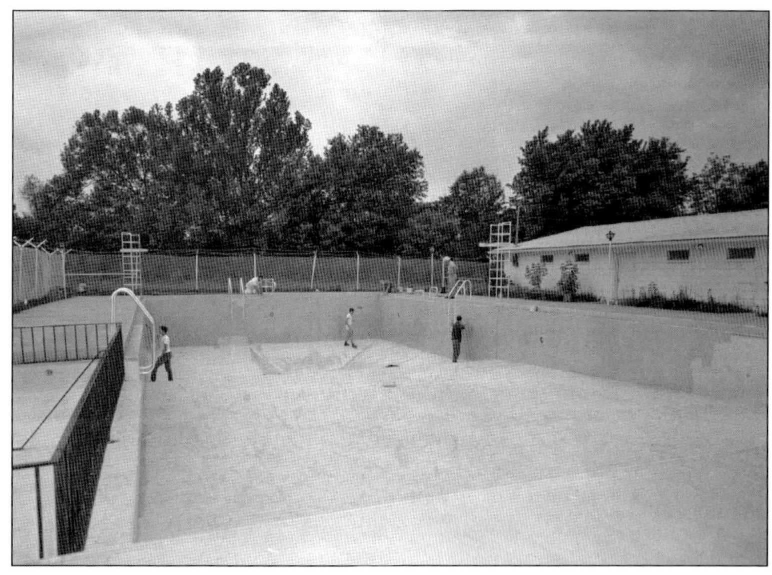

The Terrell Drive swimming pool was built in the early 1960s at the Bate-Wood apartment project. Both the public housing project and the pool were segregated at the time. The pool suffered from mismanagement, however, and was eventually drained and filled in after only being used from 1961 to 1974. (Charles A. Thomas Collection, BCPL.)

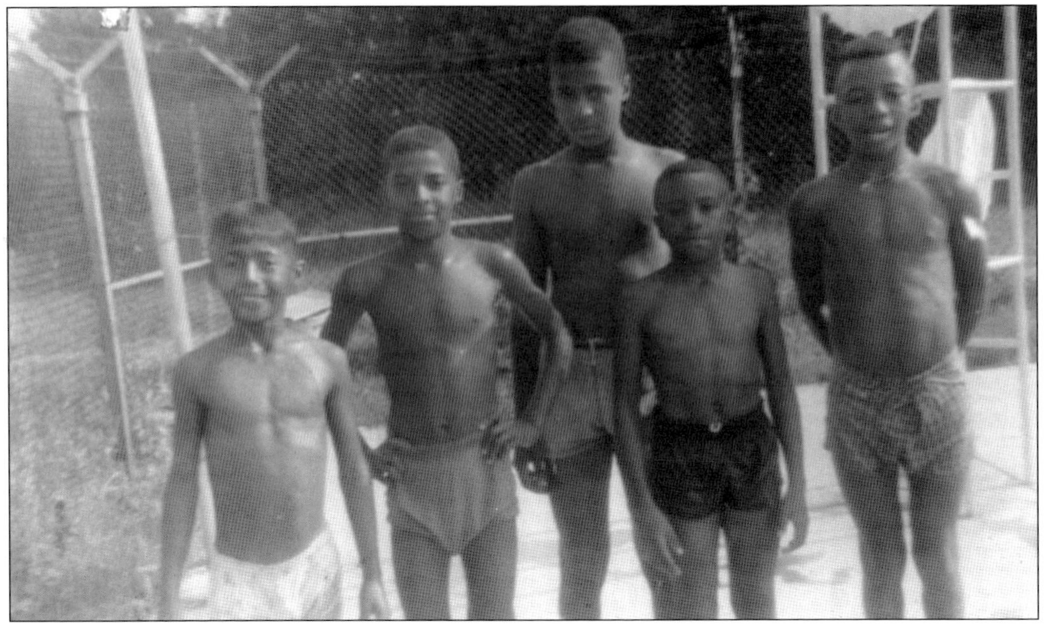

At the pool in 1962 are, from left to right, James Richard "Jimmy" Jones (1947–), son of James and Ophelia (Faulkner) Jones; John W. "Johnny" Raines, (1952–2019), son of John William and Betty (Current) Raines; his brother Ronald Cornell Raines, (1950–2002); James C. "Jimmy" Simpson (1952–2018), son of James and Joy (Caldwell) Simpson; and Robert L. "Bobby" Faulkner (born 1948), son of Robert Eugene and Dorothy (Pope) Faulkner. Simpson earned a doctorate from Texas Southern University.

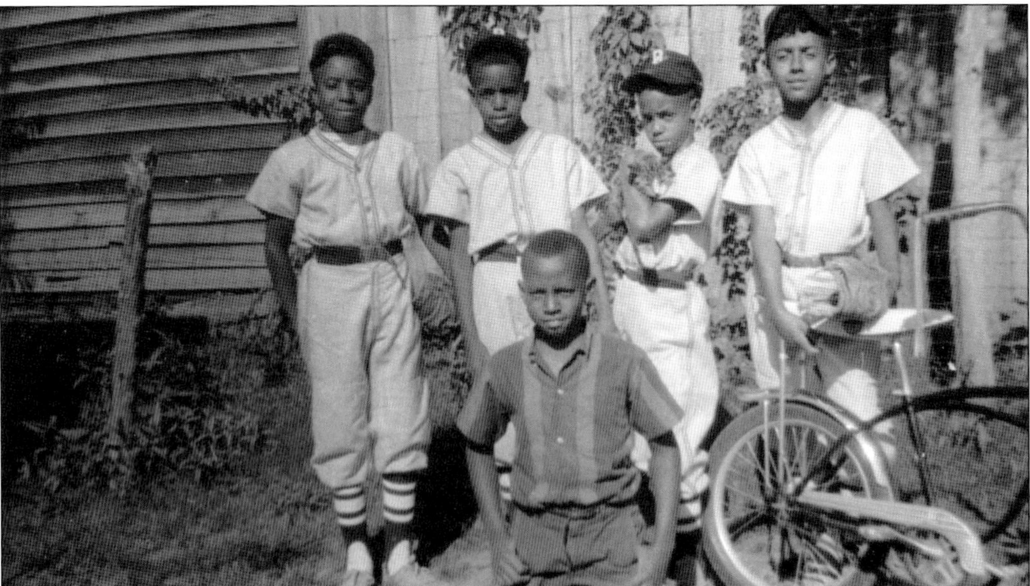

Pictured about 1964 on Russell Street, from left to right, Jimmy Simpson, Jimmy Mayfield, Jerry Jones, Jimmy Jones (sons of James Walter and Hettie (Singleton) Jones), and Marvin Jones (front), were playing for the Porter Smith Braves, Little League team. One Jerry Jones is mentioned frequently in the 1966–1968 newspapers as being an outstanding little league pitcher, but it is not known if the Jerry Jones holding the cat is the same person.

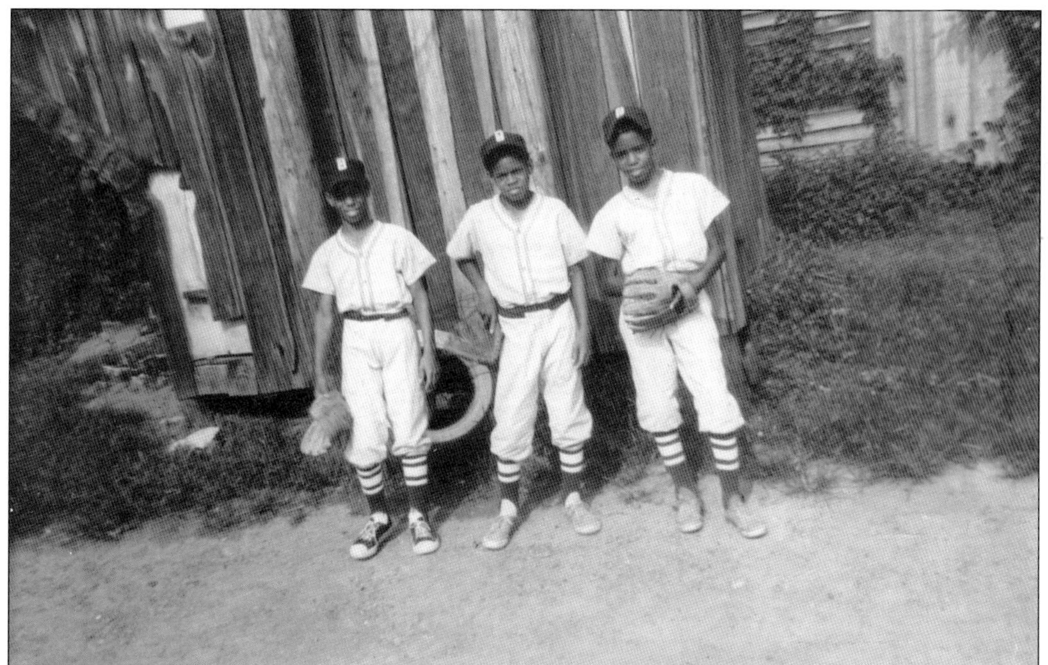

Pictured here on Russell Street in 1966, from left to right, are Jerry Jones, B.B. Gray, and James "Jimmy" Mayfield, who was probably born in 1954 to Fred and Evelyn (Gray) Mayfield, married Pat ?, and resided in Clarkston, Georgia, in 2013. The boys were still with the Porter Smith Braves Little League team.

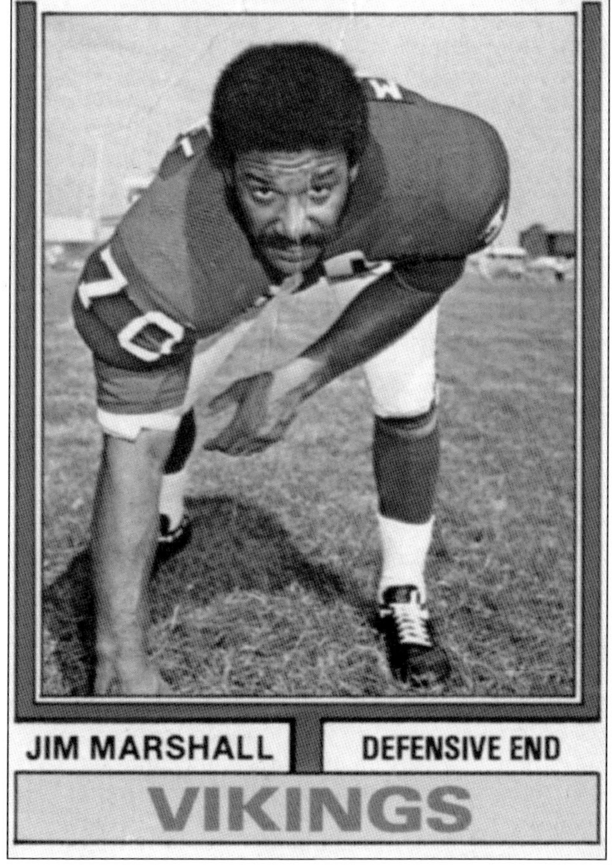

James "Jim" Marshall was born in Wilsonville, on December 30, 1937, but grew up in Columbus, Ohio. He attended Ohio State University but left to play in Canada. In 1960, he was drafted by the Cleveland Browns but was traded to the Minnesota Vikings in 1961, playing every game until 1979, including all four of the Vikings' Super Bowl appearances in the 1970s.

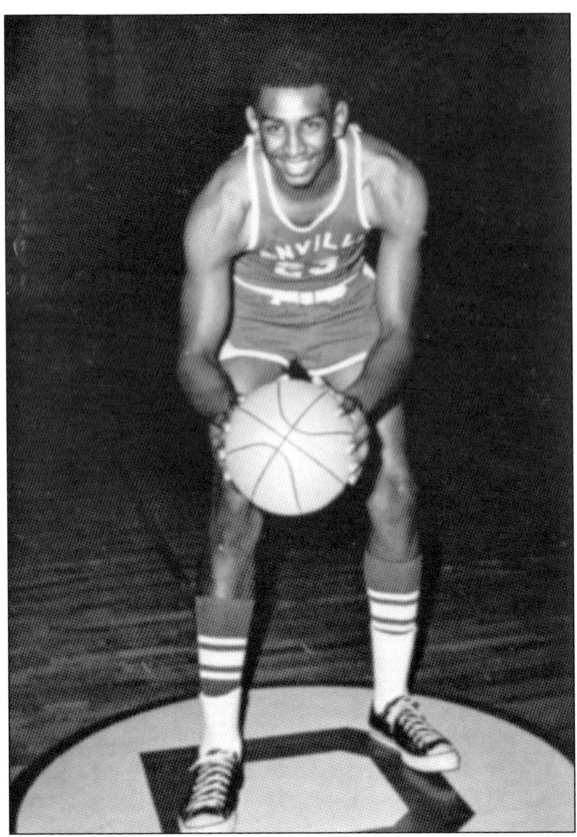

Leonard Coulter (1951–2009) was a star athlete at Danville High School and was, at the time of his death, still the school's all-time leading scorer. At Morehead State University, he was a three-time conference selection in the Ohio Valley Conference and was also Morehead's first Black All-American. He was drafted by the Seattle SuperSonics basketball team in 1974. (Morehead State University Hall of Fame.)

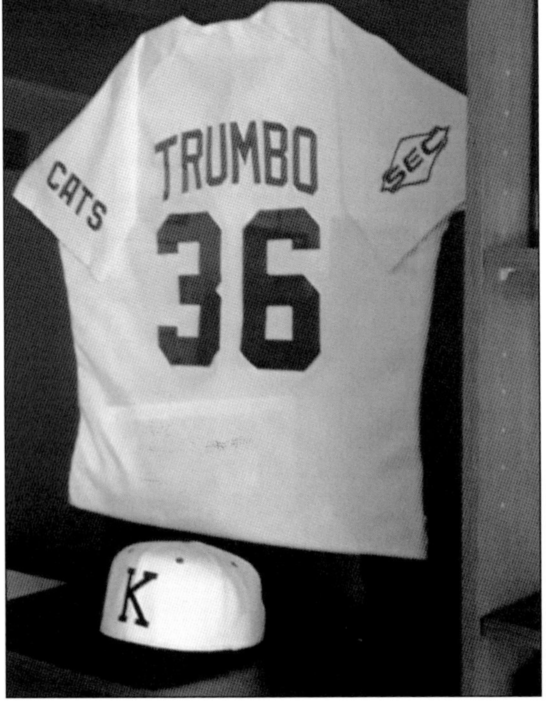

Troy Trumbo was the son of Bobby and Doris (Kinley) Trumbo and was one of Danville's star athletes. In 1992, he attended the University of Kentucky, pitching for the Wildcats. On June 1, 1994, Trumbo's trip to Alaska was to be all business. He tragically died on June 25, 1994, from complications due to an unidentified infection. His baseball jersey is in the DBCAAHS History Center, on loan from his parents.

Seven

People

Many of the photographs in the collection of the Danville Boyle County African American Historical Society's History Center are simply of African Americans pursuing life on a daily basis. There is often no real historical significance outside of Danville or Boyle County to many of these photographs but they do show aspects of African American culture and daily life in Boyle County. There are some that picture nationally famous people such as Willie Mays or Otis Redding. But for the most part, people portrayed in this section are only famous in and around Boyle County. These are the names that pop up everywhere when researching the history and genealogies of African Americans in the county.

This chapter gives the reader a glimpse of everyday life in and around Danville, with some of the more "famous" people and many of the "everyday" people.

Often, the background becomes as important as the subject. For example, one photograph of people sitting on door stoops shows the word "Green" in a window behind them. That one photograph led researchers to the Green Pastures restaurant, which no one knew about or remembered, from the 1930s.

Many photographs that show background buildings from different angles or over time are included here and in other chapters, notably Chapter 3, with pictures showing the evolution of the McDowell House from a tenement building to a restored early-19th-century home and important historic site.

Many of the photographs here seem to have been taken about the same time, namely Easter Sunday, sometime in the 1940s. Certain people appear in more than one picture, as well, but in different situations and from different viewpoints.

Also, because of the dwindling size of the Black population, it seems that many of the subjects in this chapter are related to each other, and certain surnames appear very commonly. Luckily, many of the family genealogies have now been traced, though there is much more work left to do.

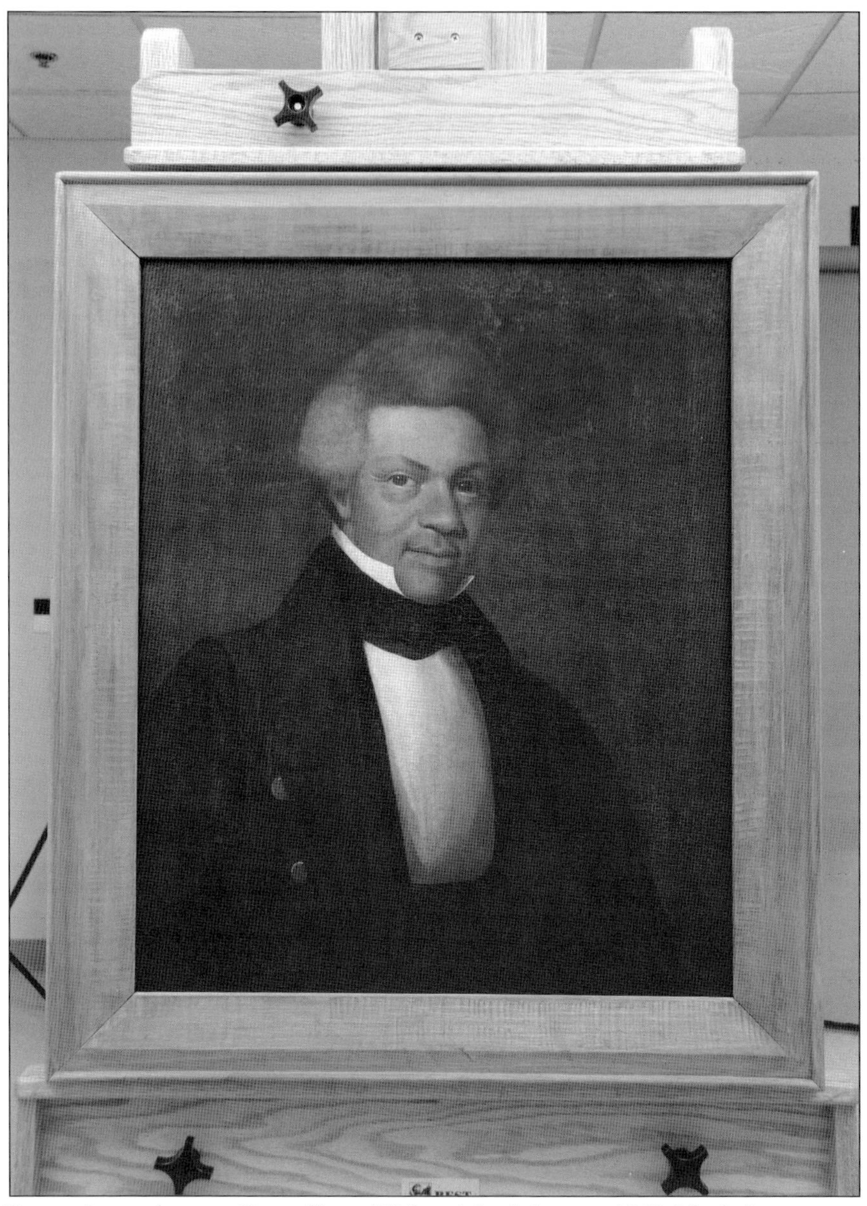

Dennis Doram Jr. was born in Danville in 1796 and died there in 1869. His father was supposedly an American Indian, and his mother, Lydia Barbee, was the daughter of her master, Gen. Thomas Barbee. The Doram family was freed when Dennis was about two months old. Throughout his life, Doram purchased land and, by 1860, owned 300 acres on the Dix River as well as land in Danville, including the brick building on the site where the Kentucky 1792 Constitution was written. He also purchased numerous slaves and then freed them, often giving them land. By 1860, Dennis Doram was the wealthiest African American in Boyle County, worth about $10,800, still only a fraction of the wealth of the wealthiest white man. He married Diademia Taylor in 1830, and their children included Sarah (Doram) Faulkner; Gibson (or Gibeon) Doram, a prominent businessman; Thomas Anderson Doram, a respected farmer; Joshua Doram, 1st Sergeant, 114th US Colored Infantry; and Robert Cassius Clay Doram, a "Buffalo Soldier." (Kentucky Historical Society, 2000.29.1.)

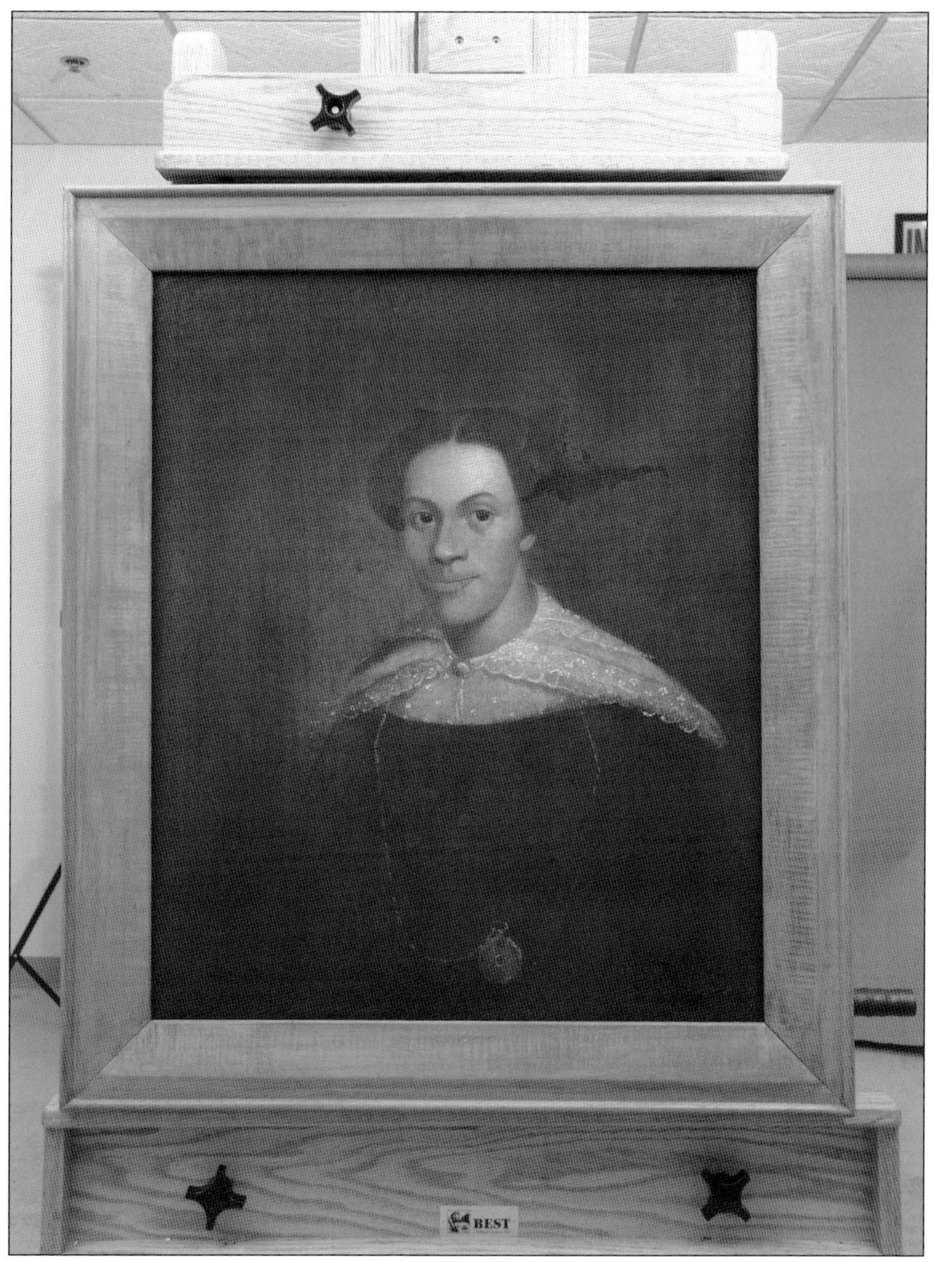

Diademia (Taylor) Doram, born in Harrodsburg in 1810 and died in Danville in 1883, was the wife of Dennis Doram Jr. Her father, Gibson Taylor, a freeman, bought his wife and children from Moses O. Bledsoe of St. Louis, Missouri. At Diademia's death, her daughter Sarah (Doram) Faulkner, purchased the Doram land in downtown Danville at the corner of West Main and South Second Street, now the site of the Governor's Circle in Constitution Square. The portrait shown here, as well as the one of Dennis Doram, was painted by artist, tavern owner, and banker Patrick Henry Davenport in 1839. The portraits were found in a barn in Clifton in the late 1990s in very poor condition. The Kentucky Historical Society purchased them in 2000 and had them restored. They are now on display at the Thomas Clark Center for Kentucky History in Frankfort, Kentucky. (Kentucky Historical Society, 2000.29.2.)

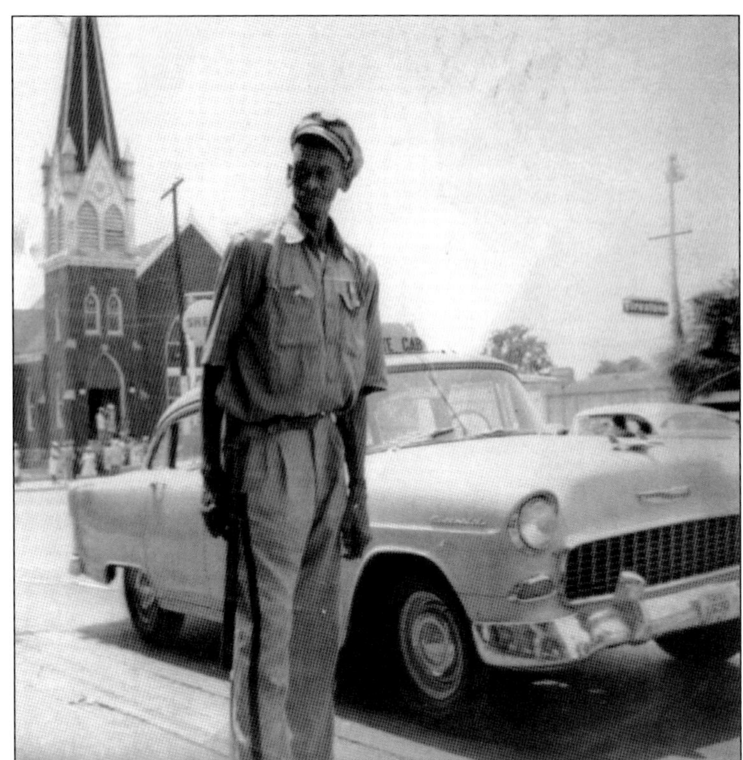

Bronston Hale is pictured on South Second Street in front of the Elite Cab Company. Hale also owned or ran a restaurant on South Second Street. He died in 1961 and is the last recorded burial in the Shelby City African American Cemetery. His height was a result of physical infirmity, as noted on his World War I draft registration form.

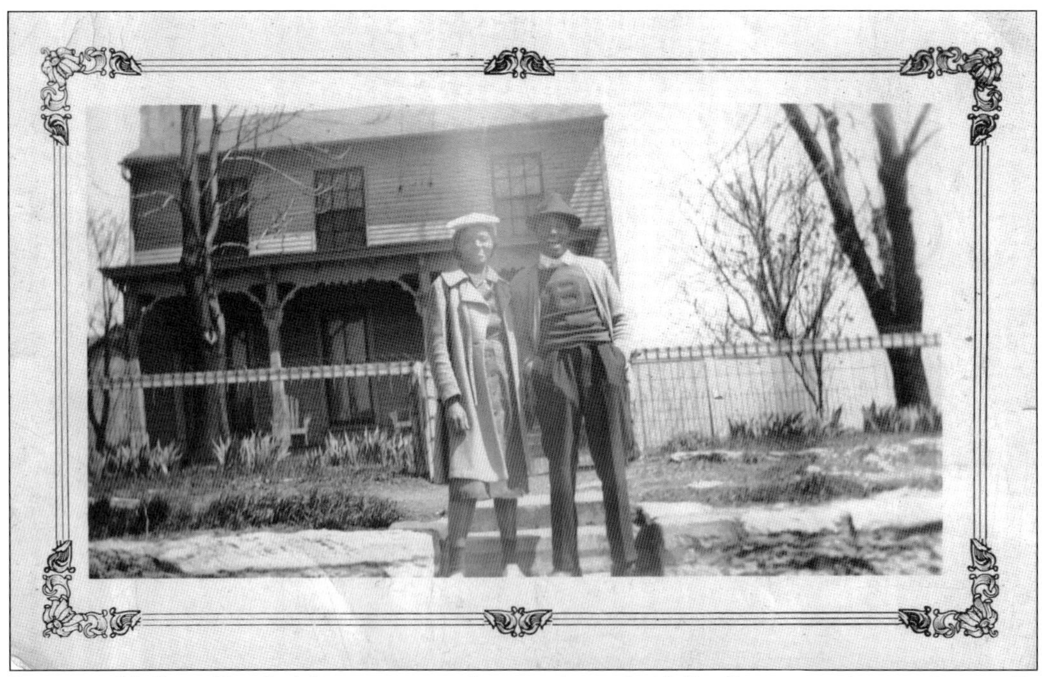

Bunny and Lillian (Beasley) Davis are seen here in the early 1940s. Bunny was born in Perryville in 1917 and died in 2001. He was a star athlete in football, baseball, and basketball and later a businessman in Danville. He was highly respected in both the Black and the White communities and served as an officer of the state legislature in Frankfort.

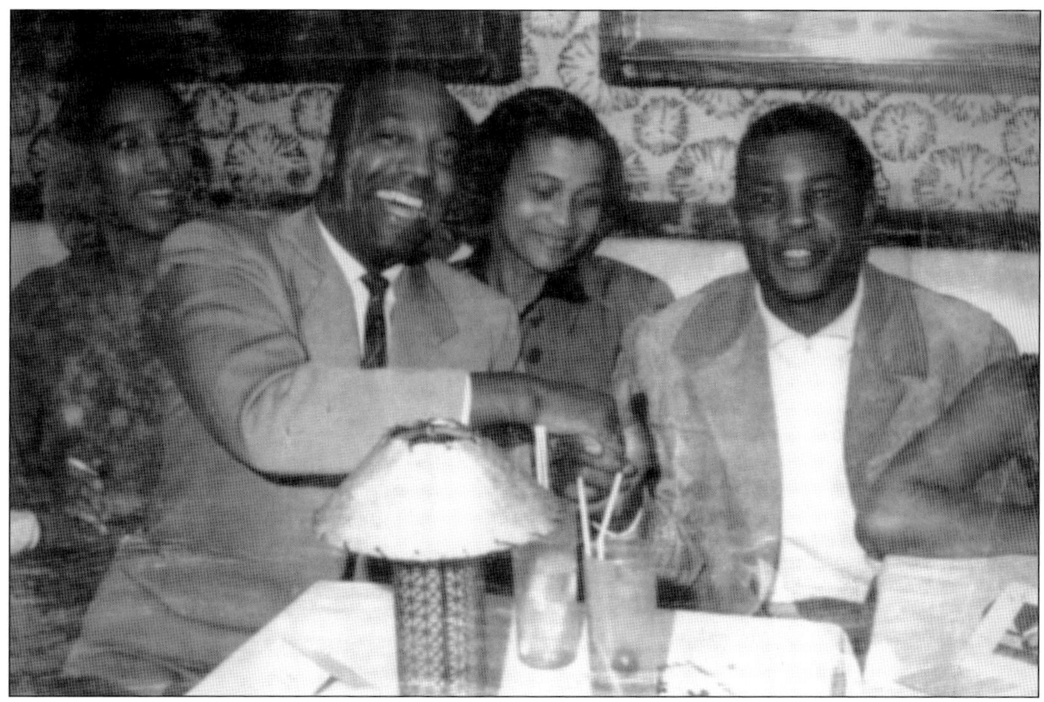

Bunny Davis (left) and baseball great and Hall of Fame member Willie Mays are pictured here. Davis, a longtime member of the Danville Yankees and Lexington Hustlers, played against the best— Jackie Robinson, Satchel Paige, and Mays, who played for the Negro Leagues Birmingham Black Barons, then the New York (later San Francisco) Giants, and the New York Mets from 1951 to 1973.

Donald (left) and Theodore Davis (right) are sitting on Bunny Davis's car across from the Doric Lodge building. Singleton's Super Market is clearly visible on the first floor. Other buildings include the properties of Sarah Perkins, Mary Jones, and V.H. Cheatham. A local landmark, Henson Hotel is the three-story building seen on the far left, where the DBCAAHS is currently located.

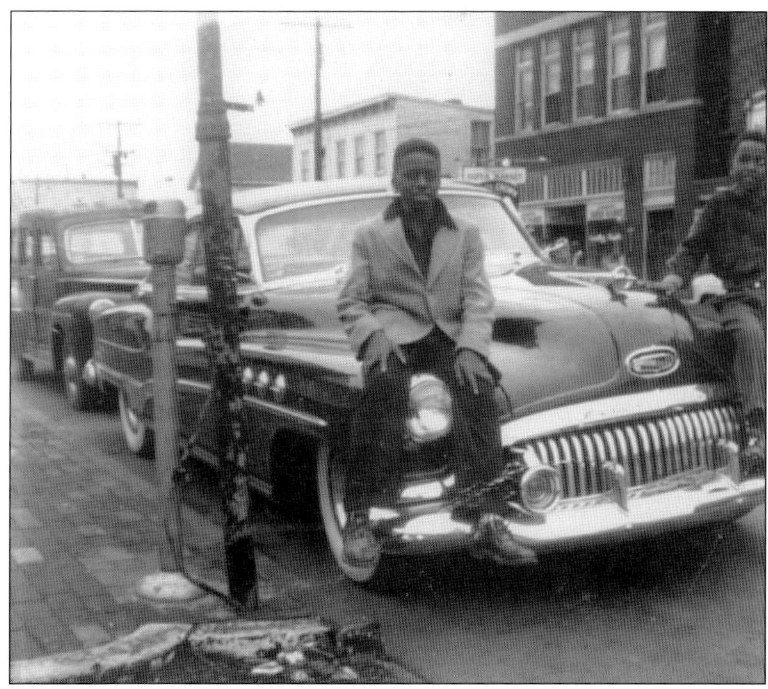

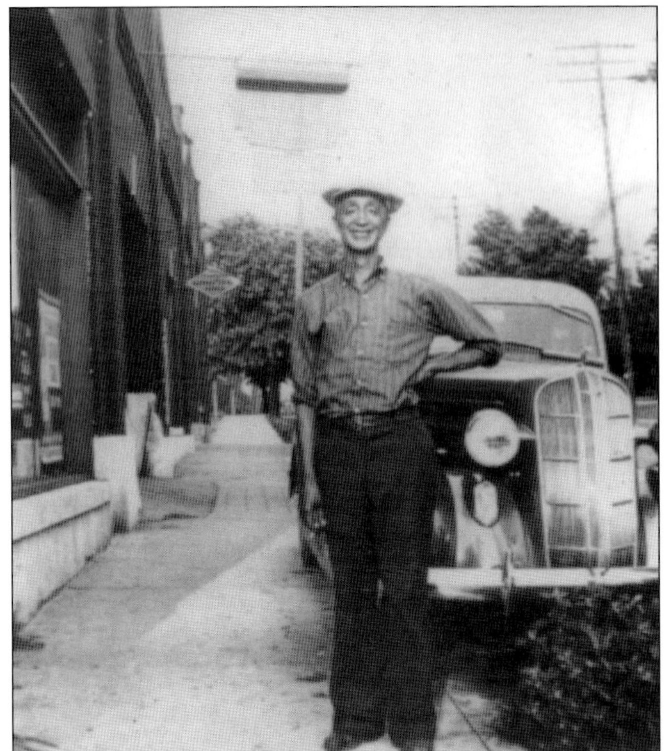

Richard "Turk" Frye is pictured in front of either the Driesler Motor Company, at 206 East Main Street, or Williams Motor Company, at 118 East Main Street. Born in 1892, he was a World War I veteran and a mechanic at Williams Motor Company in 1942. He married Ellen Holmes, and they resided at 127 Rowe Street, according to the 1940 Census.

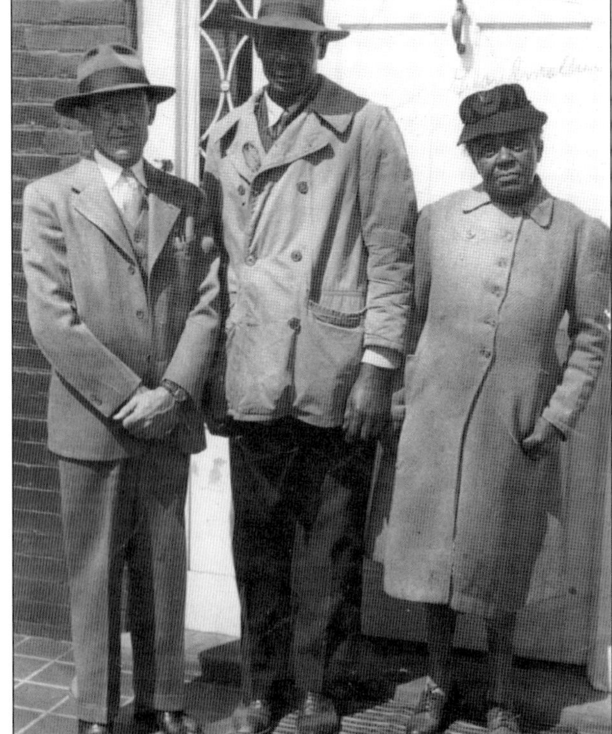

Standing with the Danville City engineer Ralph Wyatt are (left) Tom and Mary (Thomas) Routt. Tom was born in 1885, Mary was born in 1887, and they lived on West Lexington Avenue in 1918. Tom worked for the City of Danville for many years, and it is said he knew the location of every pipe in the city.

These women are gathered in front of the Golden Gate Café on Easter Sunday. In 1948, the Golden Gate was located at 128 South Second Street, which puts it in the Doric Lodge building, where later Singleton's Grocery and Napier's Café were also located. The finery on display on South Second Street was proof that African American women could and did walk proudly in Danville.

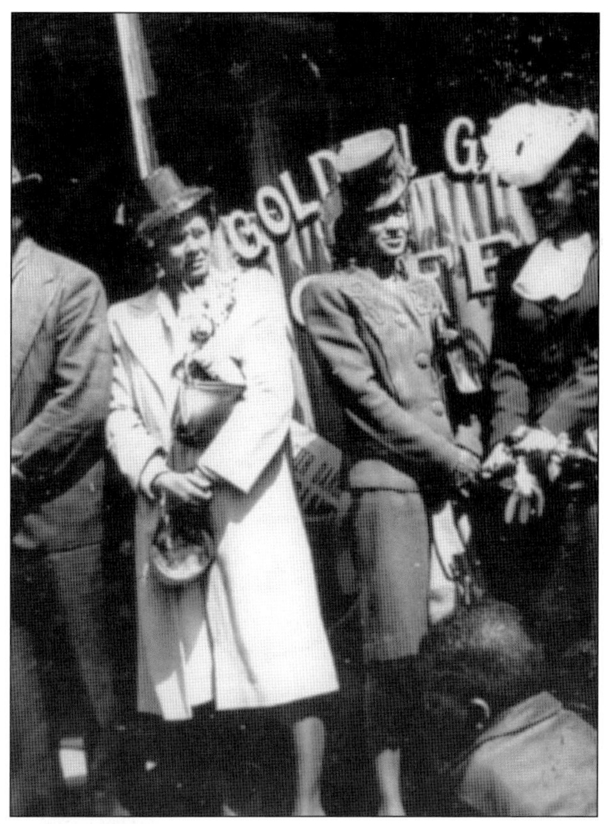

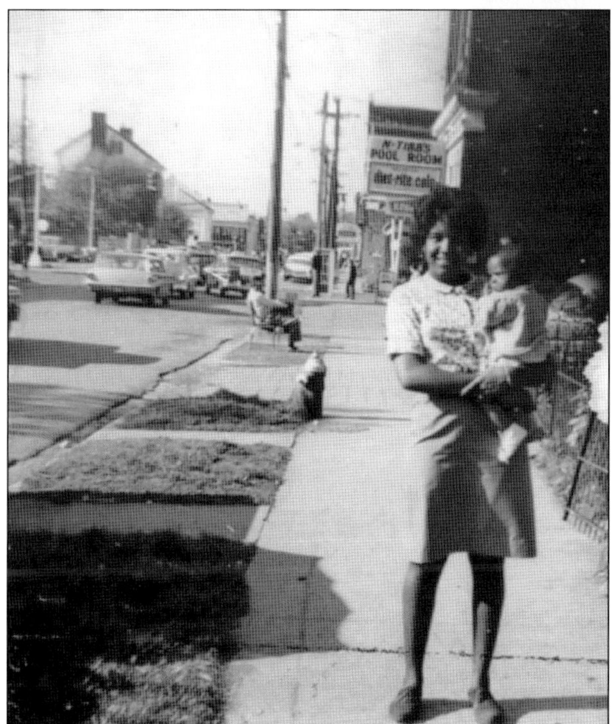

Beverly Jean Jones and her son Doug Jones are on the 200 block of South Second Street, near Tibbs' Pool Hall, probably in the mid-1960s. She was the daughter of Jesse H. and Data May (Clayton) Jones, and her siblings were Beverly, Everett Danny, Denise, Christopher, and Patricia. Also seen here is the McDowell House, and the view reaches all the way down to the State Theater on Main Street.

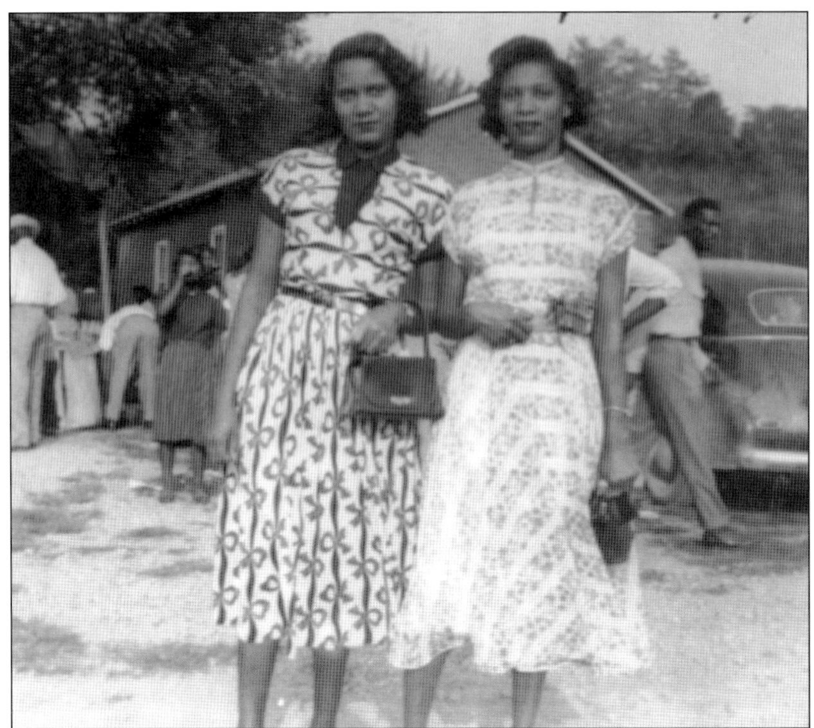

Agnes Riffe, born in Lincoln County in 1926, and her sister Ruby Riffe, born in Lincoln County in 1932, were both teachers, and daughters of James Elbert and Lucille (Tarrence) Riffe of Hustonville. Patsy Riffe was freed before the Civil War and earned enough money to buy her own husband; the two are the ancestors of all the Riffe families in the area.

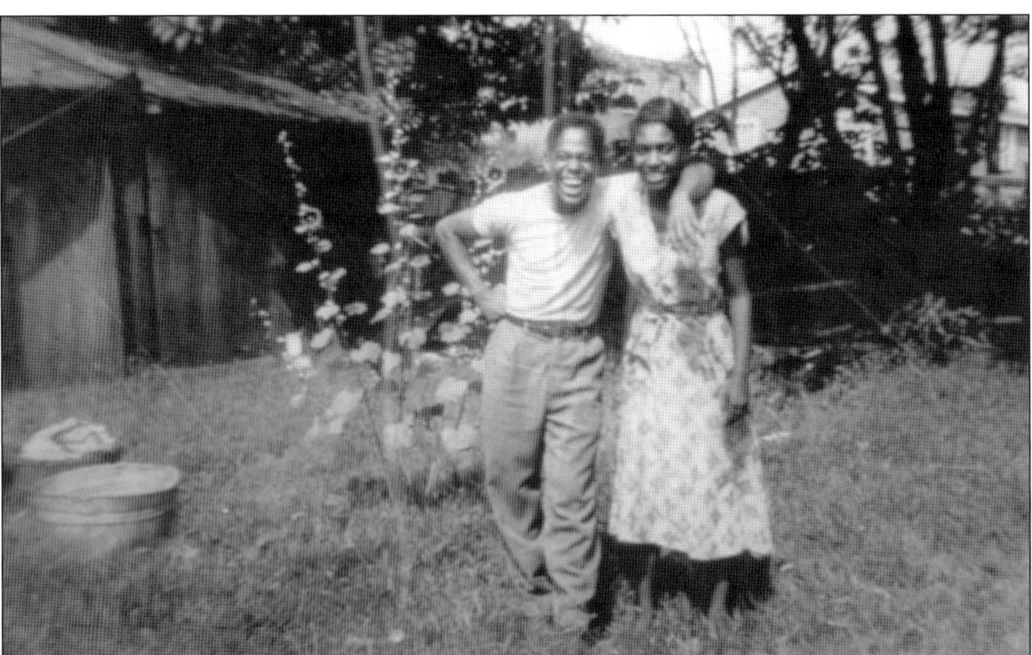

Theo "Bear" and Anna (Adams) Burdette are pictured at their home at 240 East Green Street in 1948. He was an employee of the city waterworks, was born in 1928, died in 2001, and was the son of Ulysses Burdette, a longtime employee of Kentucky School for the Deaf. Although life was difficult for African Americans in those days, Theo's attitude says volumes.

Carl Bailey was born June 23, 1914, and enlisted in the US Army on December 18, 1942. He is listed then as separated with dependents. In late October 1943, he was home visiting his mother Sallie (Wright) Bailey on Russell Street. African Americans in Boyle County certainly did not shirk their military obligation, despite how they were treated both before and after military service.

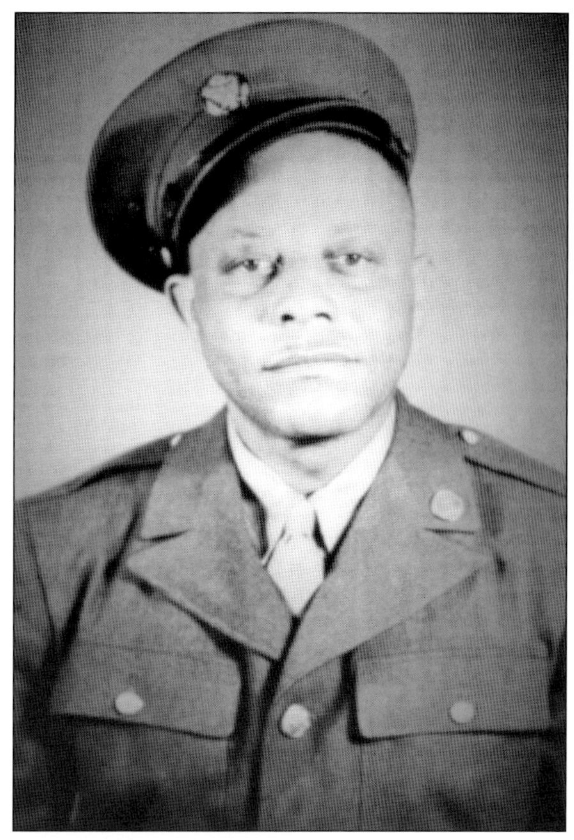

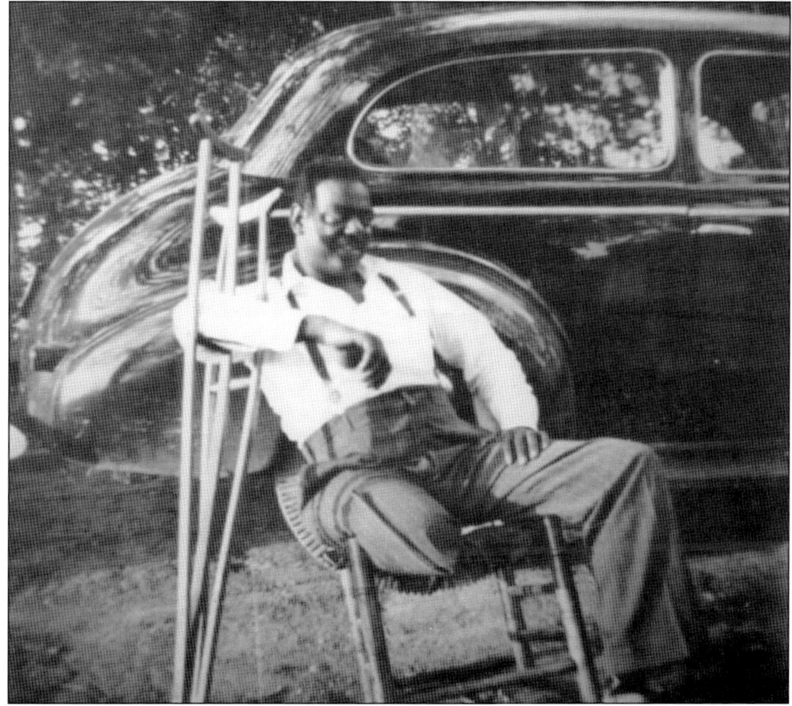

David Lee Burton was born in Lincoln County on October 17, 1914, the son of Joe and Amanda (Smith) Burton. He married first wife Leontine Marshall in 1943, and she married second husband James Baughman in 1955. Burton lost his leg due to complications from diabetes.

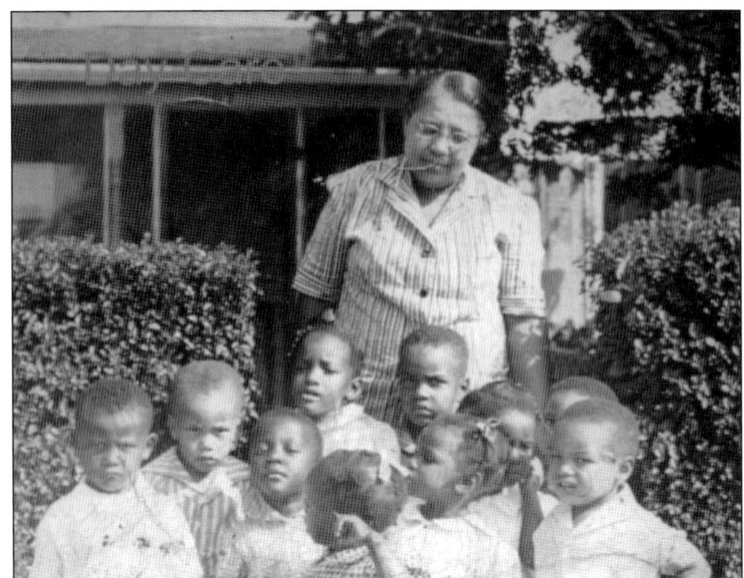

These children were in Georgia Doneghy's daycare. She was a longtime teacher at Bate School and music director at First Baptist Church. Many people owe their musical skills to her. She ran a daycare on East Green Street. The children she is watching this sunny day include Frank Walker, Johnny Whitley (second from left), Minnie Lou Crowdus, Arthur Napier, Eique Bay, and Gene Johnson.

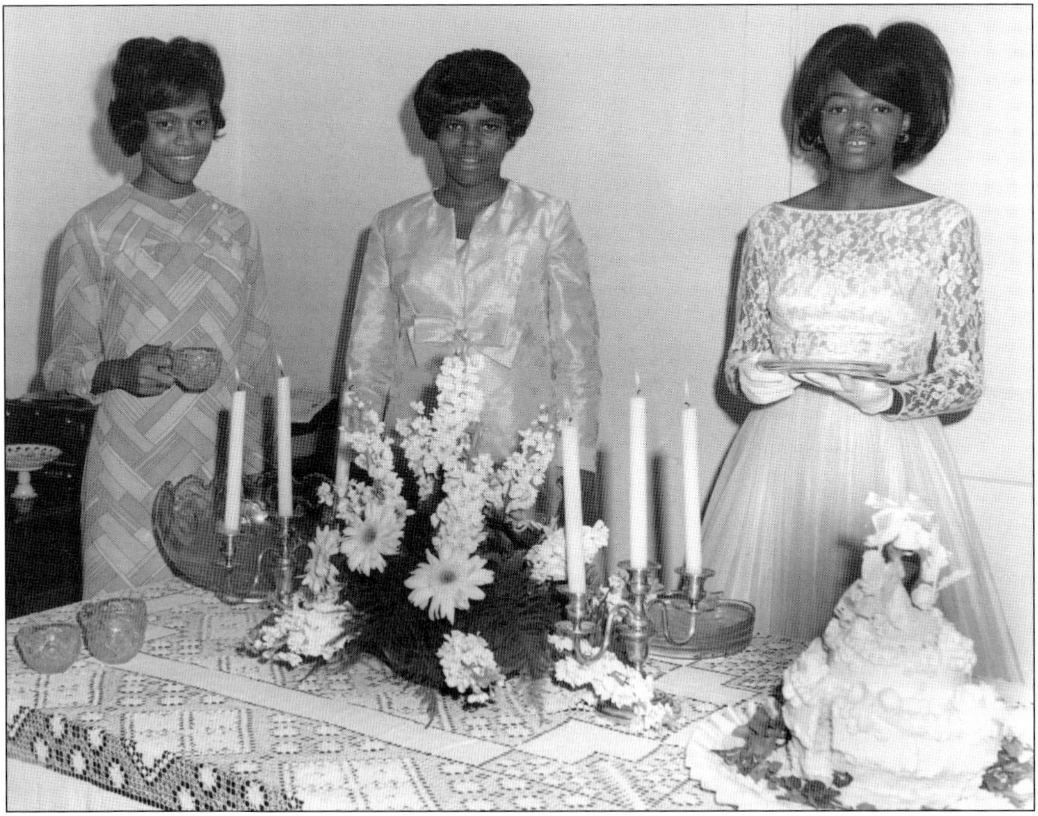

All dressed up for a joyous occasion, pictured from left to right, Joan (Jenkins) Riley, Delores (Penman) Townsend, and Hattie (Ingram) Claybrooks graduated from Danville High School after 1968. Joan married Thomas Riley in 1975. Delores married Thomas Thrash in 1971 and a Townsend, date unknown. Hattie married in Maryland after 1976. The occasion, supposedly in 1967, was at the home of Mr. and Mrs. George Harlan on Green Street in Danville.

Elizabeth Craig (Tarrance) (Overstreet) Boyd was Theora (Tarrance) Coates's sister. Her writing on the back apologizes for the photograph but says they were not allowed to smile. Elizabeth was born in 1921 and died in 2005; she was the daughter of Levi and Ada (Simpson) Tarrance. She graduated Bate High School in 1939, three years after Theora, and married George Overstreet in 1943, followed by Marion Boyd.

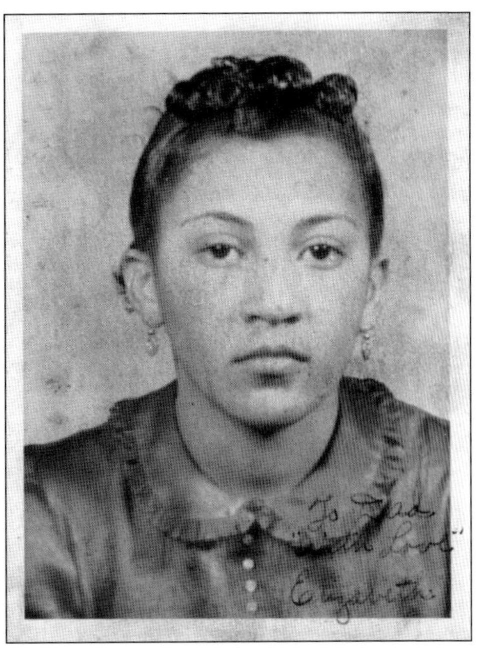

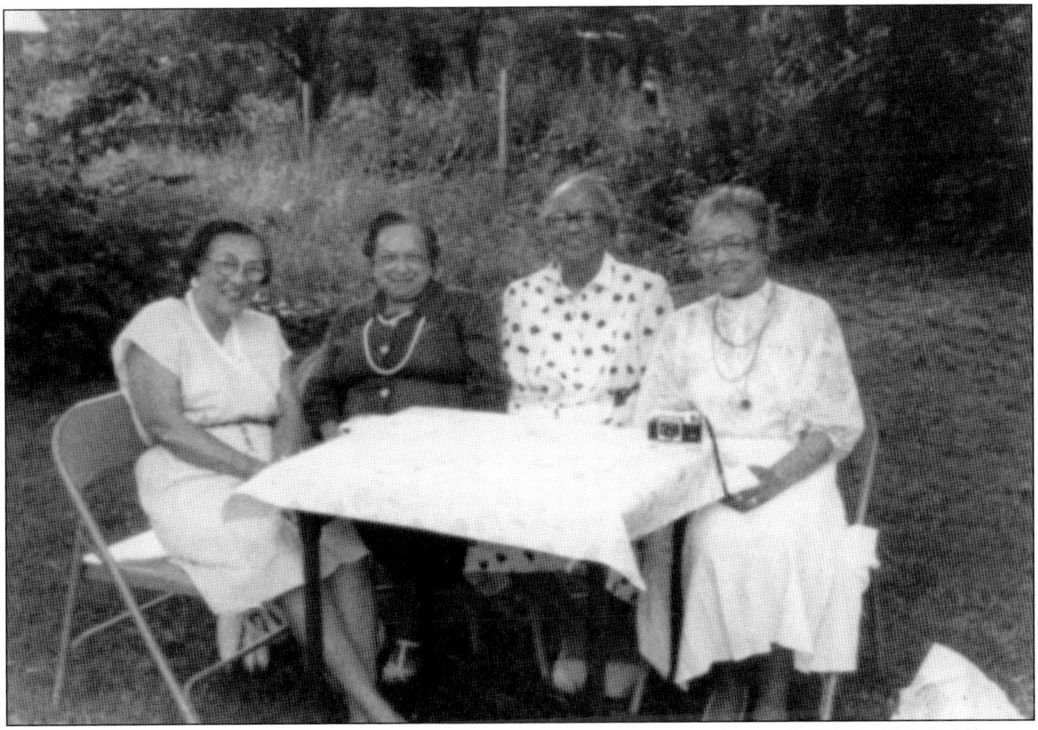

Pictured from left to right are Elizabeth (Tarrance) (Overstreet) Boyd (1921–2005), Theora (Tarrance) Coates (1918–2018), Marzie (Burchett) Durr (1909–1999), and unidentified. Theora married James Coates, a Danville barber, on June 23, 1945. Marzie married Marvin Durr on December 17, 1947. He was among the first group of Black pilots who earned their wings at Tuskegee, Alabama, and formed the segregated 99th Squadron, later the 332nd Fighter Group (Red Tails).

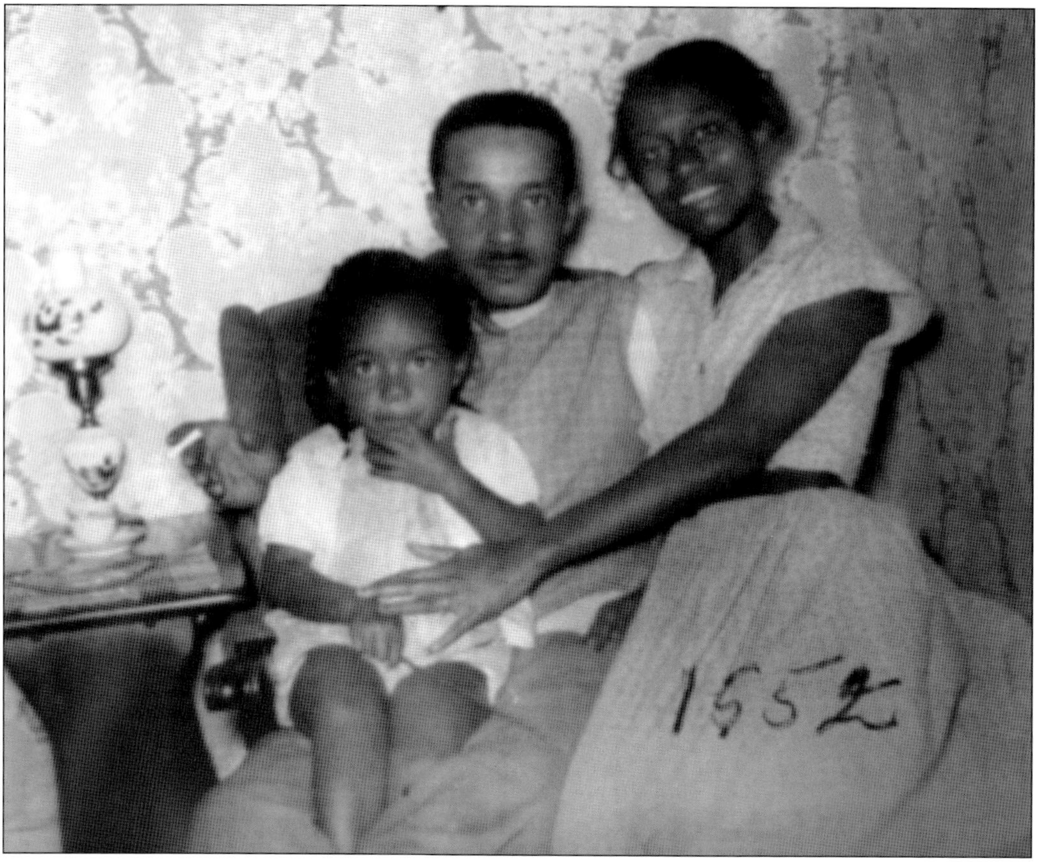

The Jarmon family included Rosalyn Marie, also known as Marie Rosalyn (1948–), William Eugene (born in Hustonville in 1925, died 1995), and Bernice Ophelia (Garr) Harlan (born in Mt. Salem, Lincoln County in 1925, died 1999. William held numerous offices in the Second Street Christian Church, the Kentucky Club, Doric Lodge No. 18, Royal Arch Masons, and Willis Russell Historical Society, among others. The couple married on January 26, 1948. They later had a child named Rita Gail (1963–).

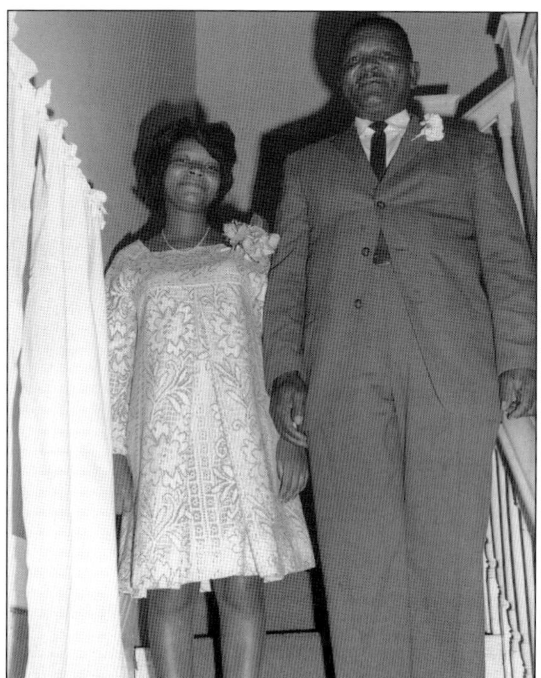

Patricia Harlan and her father, George Lee Harlan, are at a function at the Bate School. She was the daughter of George and Margaret Louise (Young) Harlan. He was the son of Joseph and Alma (Grimes) Harlan, born in 1917. Patricia was born in 1950. Bate had all the same functions that white schools did, including homecoming, proms, and other activities.

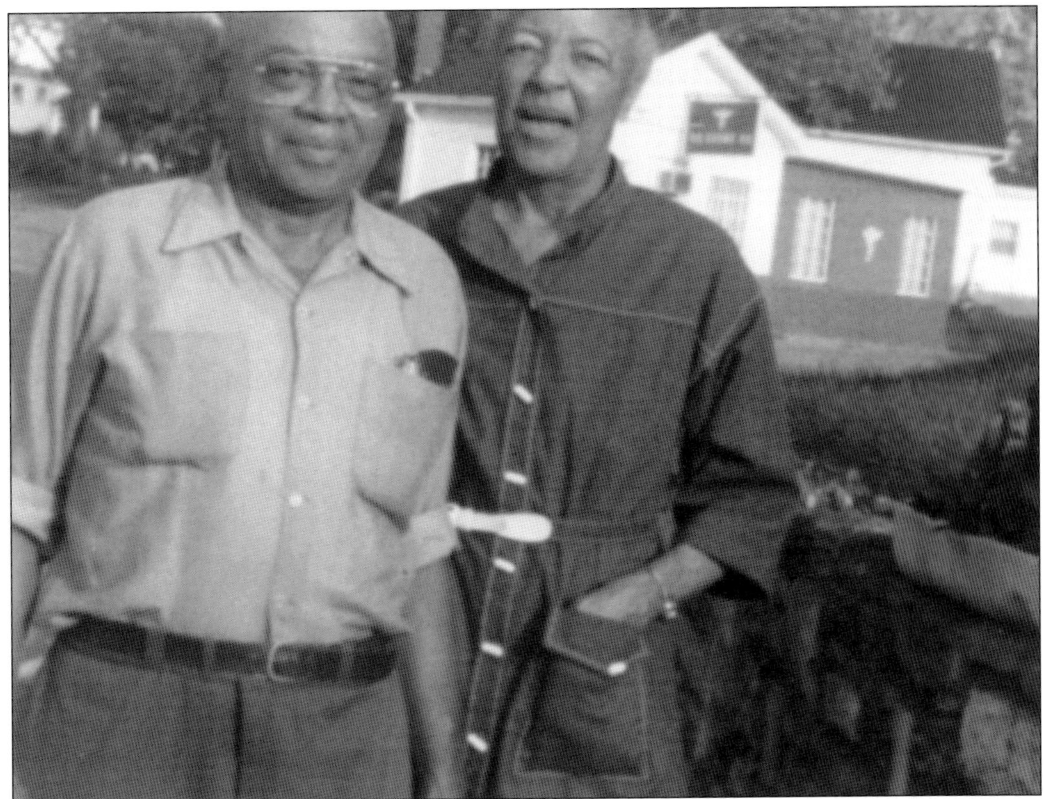

Marvin and Marzie (Burchett) Durr are seen in their later years. By May 22, 1942, Marvin was among the first group of Black pilots who earned their wings at Tuskegee, Alabama, and formed the segregated 99th Squadron, later the 332nd Fighter Group, which flew 1,578 missions over Europe, destroyed 409 enemy planes, and earned the reputation of never losing a single escorted American bomber.

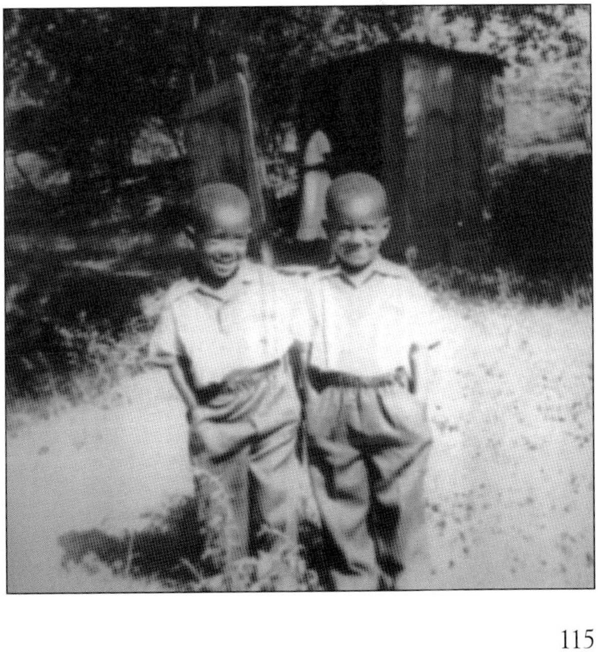

These two boys are enjoying a day at the ballpark. Baseball became one of the favorite pastimes within the African American community, and Boyle County was fortunate to have had two semiprofessional teams—the Yankees and the Cubs—as well as two ball fields for residents to enjoy. Sunday afternoon in the summertime was baseball time.

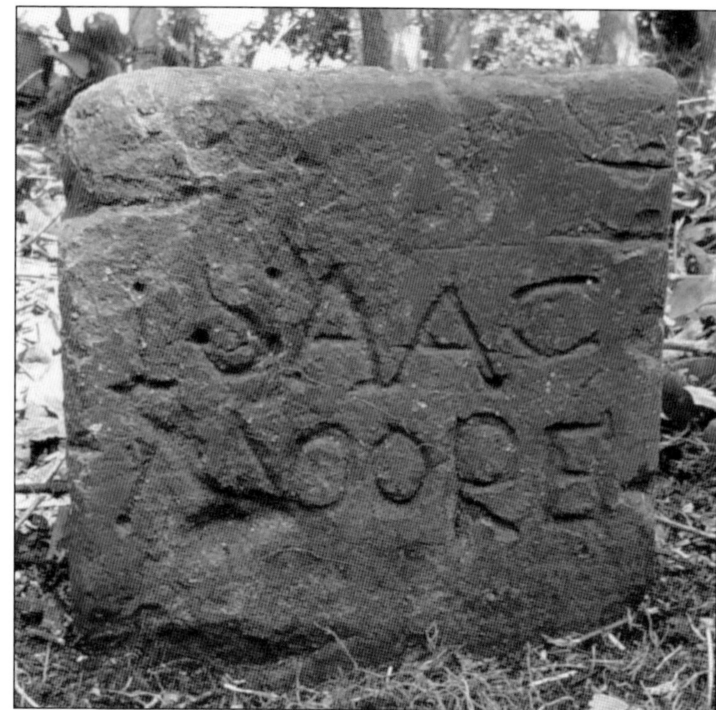

Isaac Moore's hand-made gravestone is located in the Meadow Lane African American Cemetery. Isaac was born in 1860, enslaved to Charles Moore, and lived his entire life and died within a few hundred feet from where he was born. After many years of neglect, this cemetery is now owned and maintained by the City of Danville. (Michael Denis.)

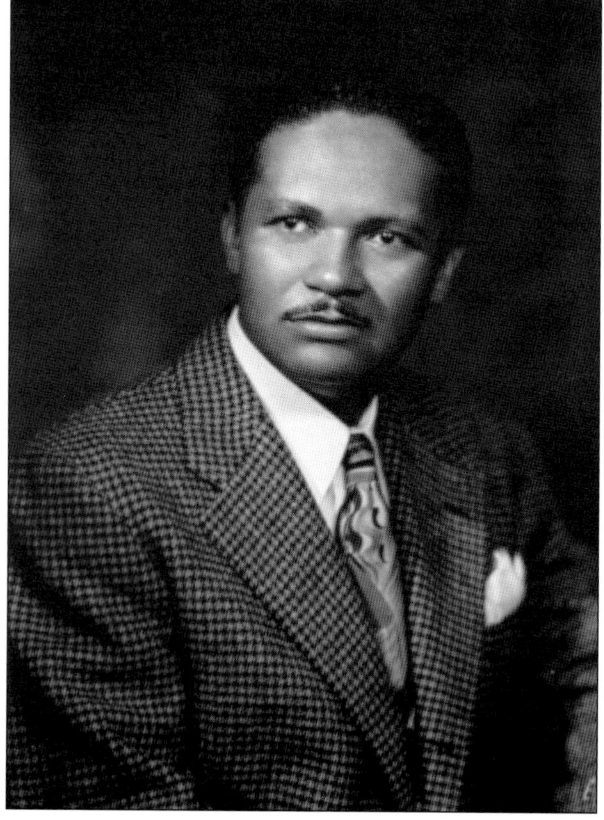

Robert Todd Duncan, who was born in Danville in 1903 and died in Washington, DC, in 1998, originated the role of Porgy in *Porgy and Bess*. He was a champion of integration. In 1955, Duncan was the first to record "Unchained Melody" for the soundtrack of the obscure prison film *Unchained*. The song went on to become one of the most recorded songs of the 20th century. (National Museum of American History)

Dr. Thomas Madison Doram, the grandson of Dennis and Diademia (Taylor) Doram, was the first African American veterinarian in the United States, though some sources continue to dispute this. In 1892, he entered Eckstein Norton University at Cane Spring, Kentucky. While there, the building was destroyed by fire. Dr. Doram then helped to rebuild the college building. In 1896, he entered the McKillip Veterinary College in Chicago, Illinois. (Tai Doram.)

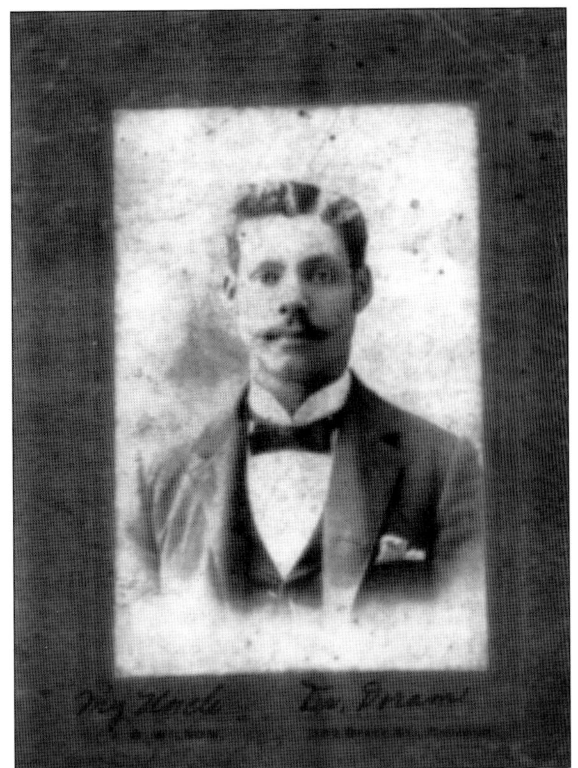

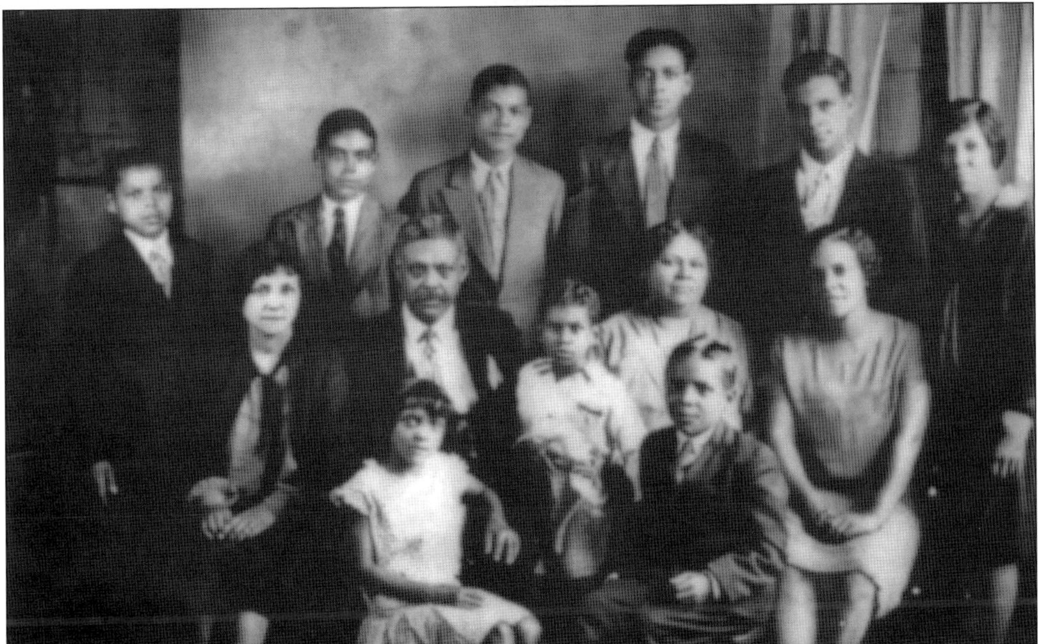

The family of Dr. Thomas Madison and Bertha (Hancock) Doram is pictured here, including children (from oldest to youngest), Dorothy, Ruth, Loretta, Hugh, Arthur, Thomas Madison, James Evans, Roscoe McDonald, Ralph, Glenna C., and Roy B. Dr. Doram was born in 1871 and died in 1941; his wife, Bertha, was born 1880 and died in 1948. (Tai Doram.)

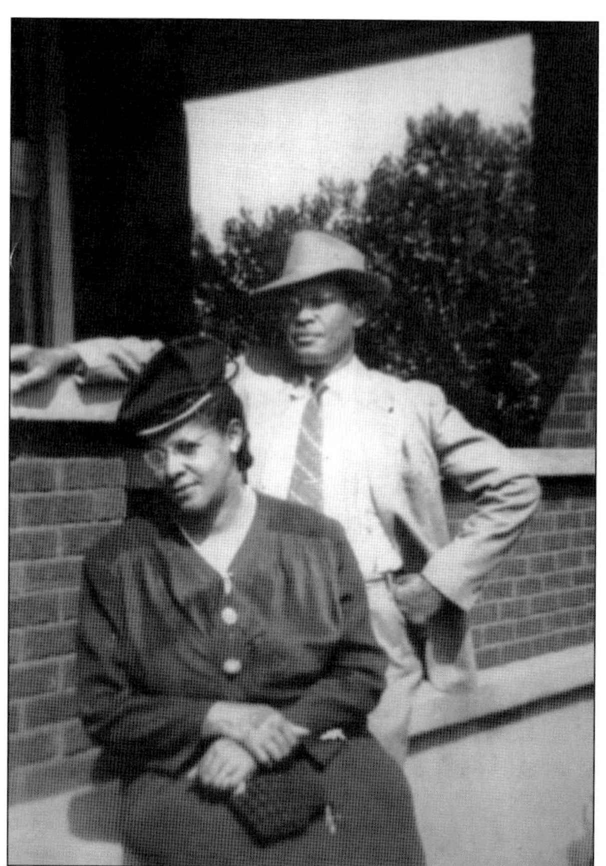

Agnes and Montague Adams are pictured here. He graduated from Knoxville College, was supervisor of buildings for several years, and taught school in Boyle County for 12 years, being principal of Junction City's colored school in 1924. He was an excellent cook, a barber, and a master furniture refinisher as well. He is buried in Hilldale Cemetery with his second wife, Agnes Louisa (Higgins) Adams.

Albert Dudley Doneghy (left) was born in 1894 and died in 1962. He was the athletic trainer and equipment manager beginning in the 1920s and at the famous Centre-Harvard football game. Eugene Harlan Jr. was born in Danville about 1925 and died in 1997. He married first wife Louvenia Baughman, followed by second wife Opal (Sleet) Grey.

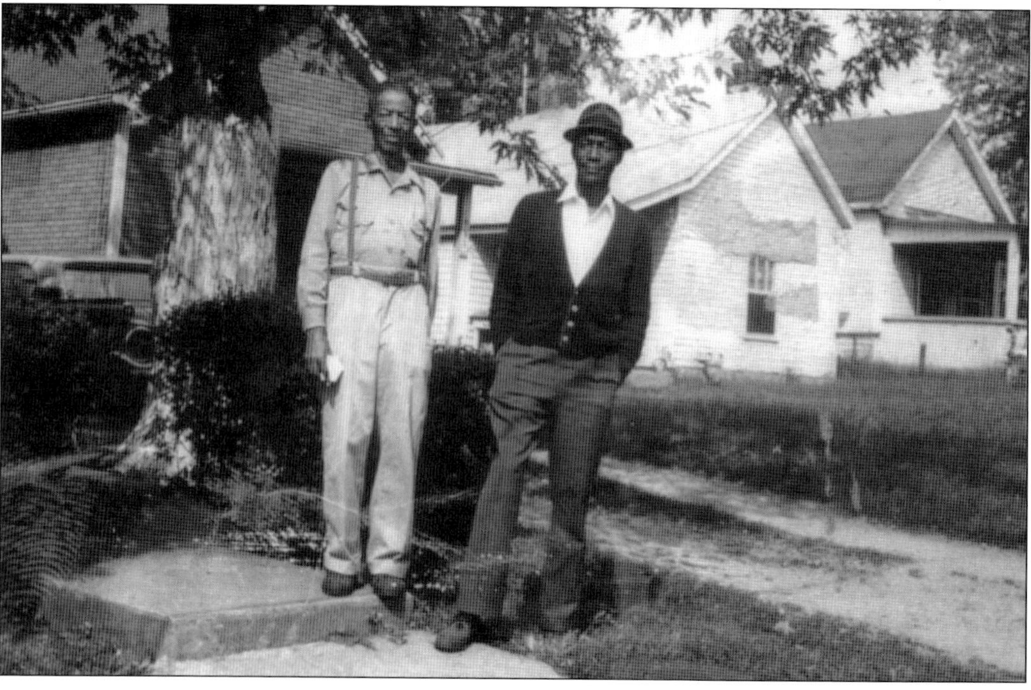

The Andrew(s) sisters, named by age, are Alta Andrew (1913– 2001), married Frank Shobe in 1937); Essie Andrews (1915– 2006, married James Cunningham in 1939); Talitha Malvenia Andrew (1926–2014, married George Kinley in 1948); and June Alice Andrew (1931–2001). They were the daughters of William and Oshia Lee (Bertram) Andrews. Some of the 12 children went by "Andrews," while others went by "Andrew."

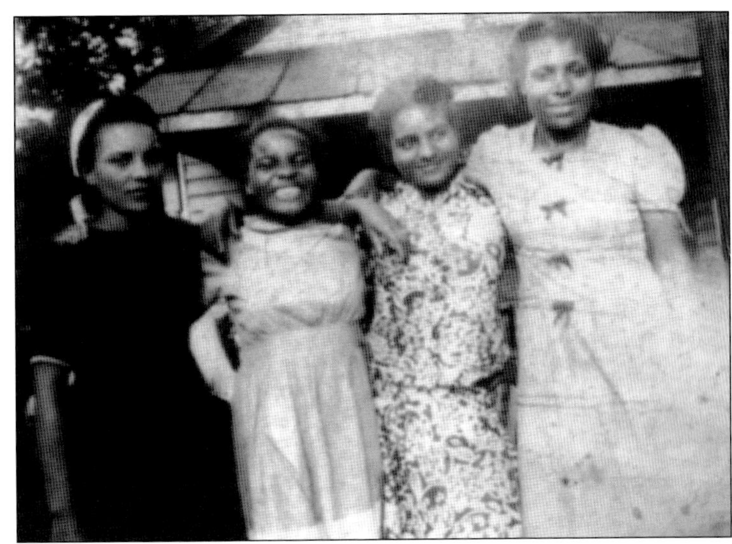

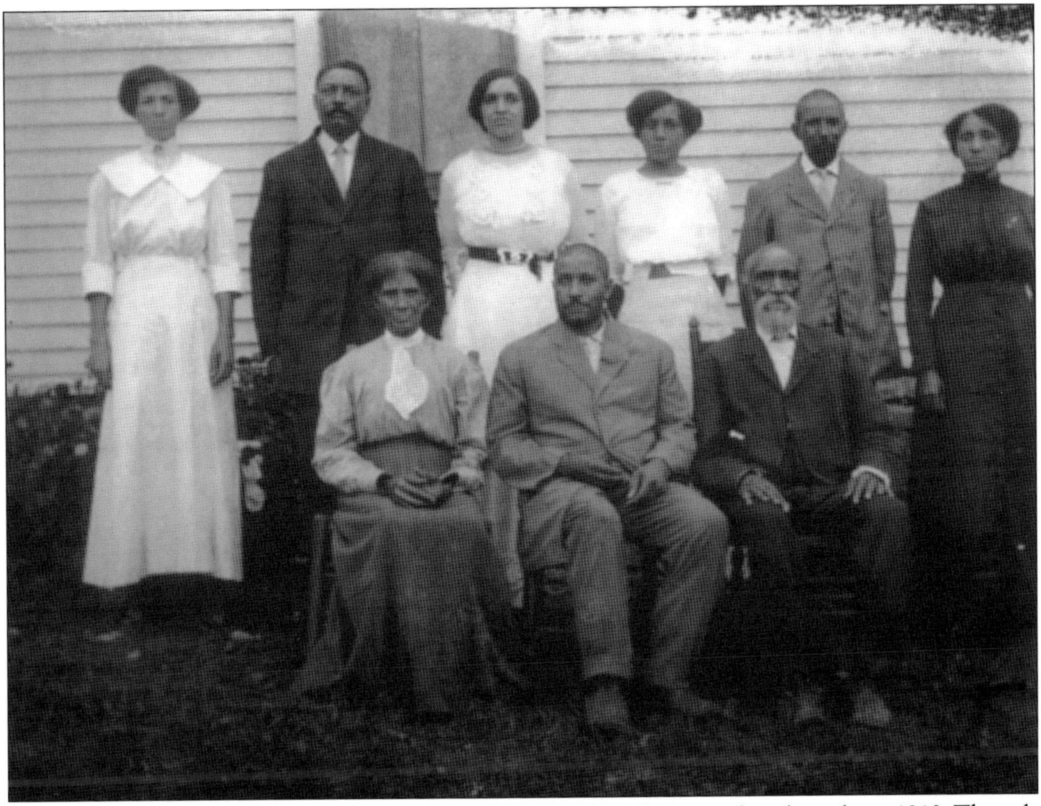

Members of the Sleet family of Perryville are shown in this photograph, taken about 1910. Though few if any of the people can be identified nowadays, the Sleet family was, and still is, an important part of the history of Perryville in western Boyle County. Sleettown, in fact, was an early Black community, settled after the Civil War.

John "Papa Skeets" Brown (1895–1973) is buried in the Lebanon National Cemetery. He served in World War I in some of the most famous battles and regaled youngsters on South Second Street with his war stories. He was noted for saying, "I'm just talking about what I'm talking about," meaning he saw those things and related them as he remembered them. (Charles D. Grey.)

Frank X. Walker, a native of Danville, is the first Black writer to be named Kentucky poet laureate. Walker has published 11 collections of poetry, including *Masked Man, Black: Pandemic & Protest Poems*, and *Isaac Murphy: I Dedicate This Ride*. Walker coined the term "Affrilachia." He is a professor of English and African American and Africana studies at the University of Kentucky in Lexington. (Frank X. Walker.)

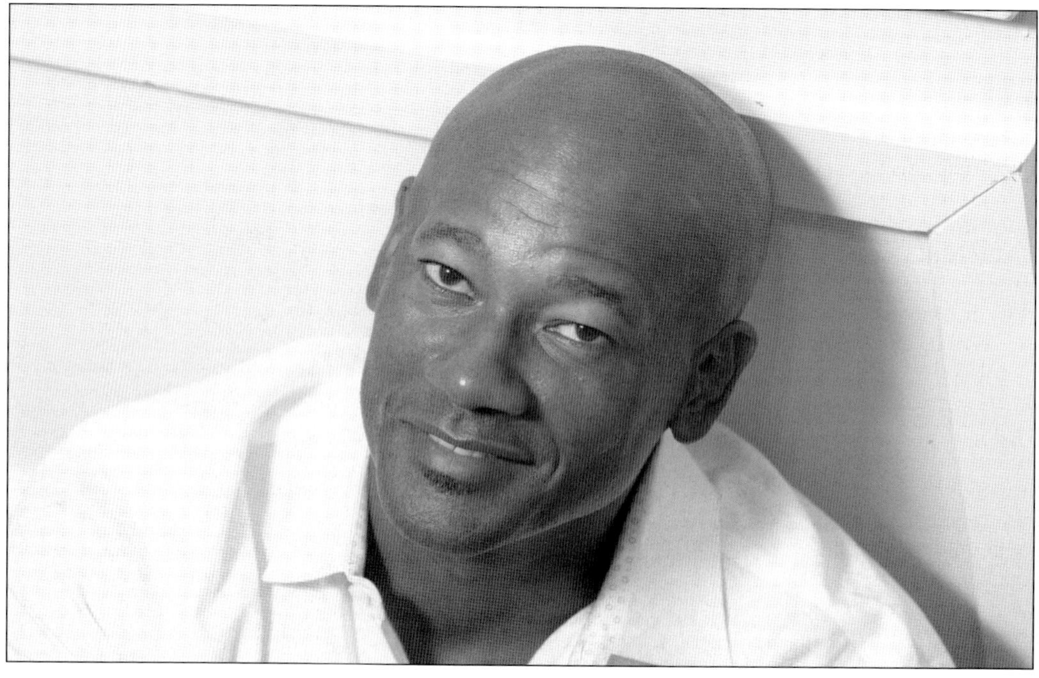

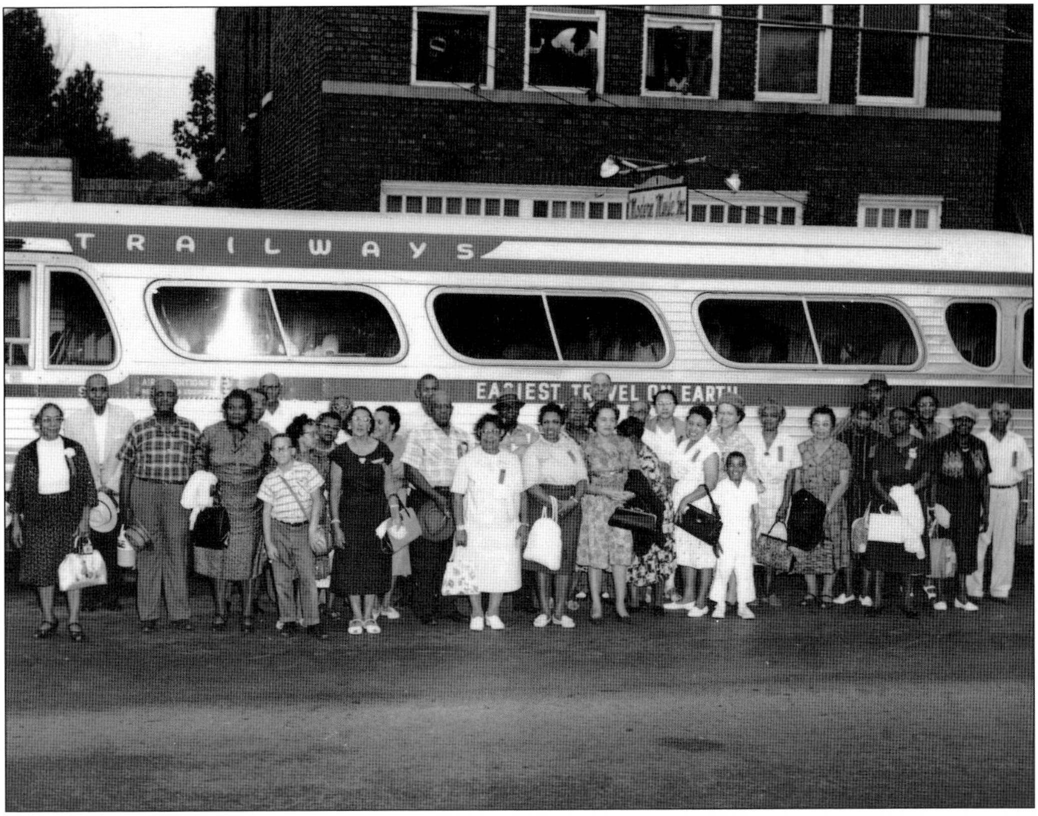

This is probably a photograph of the Kentucky Club on a trip. People in the image include DeRoy Kincaid, Craig Toliver, Tommy Coates, Theora (Tarrance) Coates, Elizabeth (Tarrance) Overstreet Boyd, William Summers, Ricky Jenkins, Madison Tarrance, Madeline Summers, Levi Tarrance, Jimmy Tarrance, Ben Jenkins, and Mabel Tarrance.

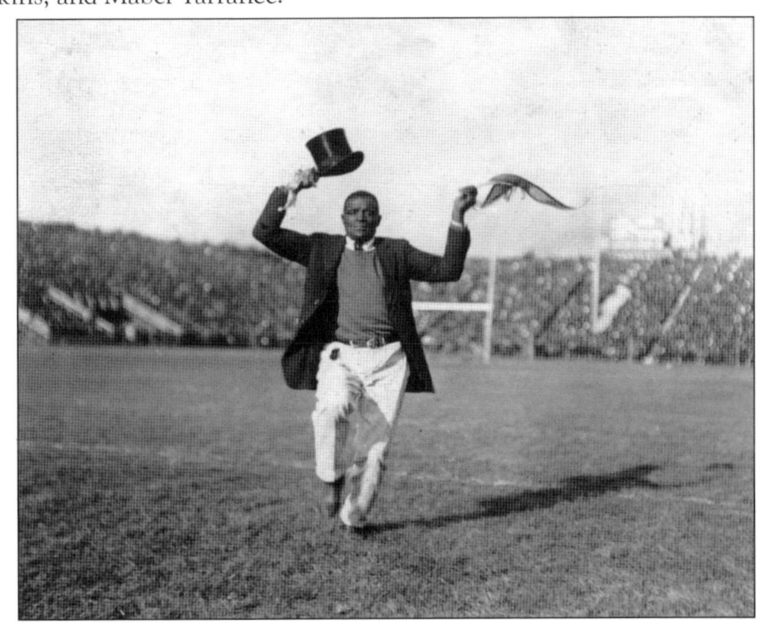

Roscoe Conklin Brumfield, also known as Roscoe Arbuckle Conklin Breckinridge, famously did a cakewalk after the Centre-Harvard football game in October 1921. The October 31, 1921, issue of the *Harvard Crimson* wrote "just about three shades darker than any other colored man in Greater Boston, he looked like a Kentucky tobacco ad. His nimbleness in getting off and on the gridiron belied his years."

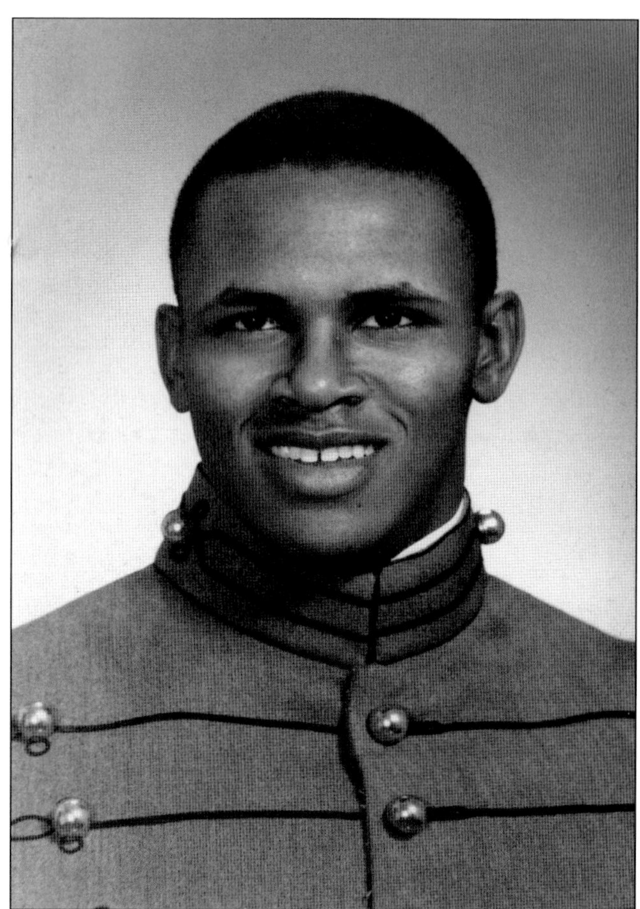

Dwayne Anthony "Tony" Walker was born in Boyle County on April 17, 1963. Tony was raised, along with his three older sisters, by a single mother. He graduated from Danville High School in 1981, where he played both football and baseball, then graduated from the US Military Academy as the first African American from Boyle County to do so. His mother's passing caused him to look instead to motivational speaking.

Vernille L. Tarrance, seen here with a 1959 model automobile, was born August 29, 1944, the son of John Thomas and Amanda Lorraine (Mayfield) Tarrance. He married Glenda Jean ? and was living in Dayton, Ohio, in 2015, at the death of his brother Jerry Tyrone Tarrance.

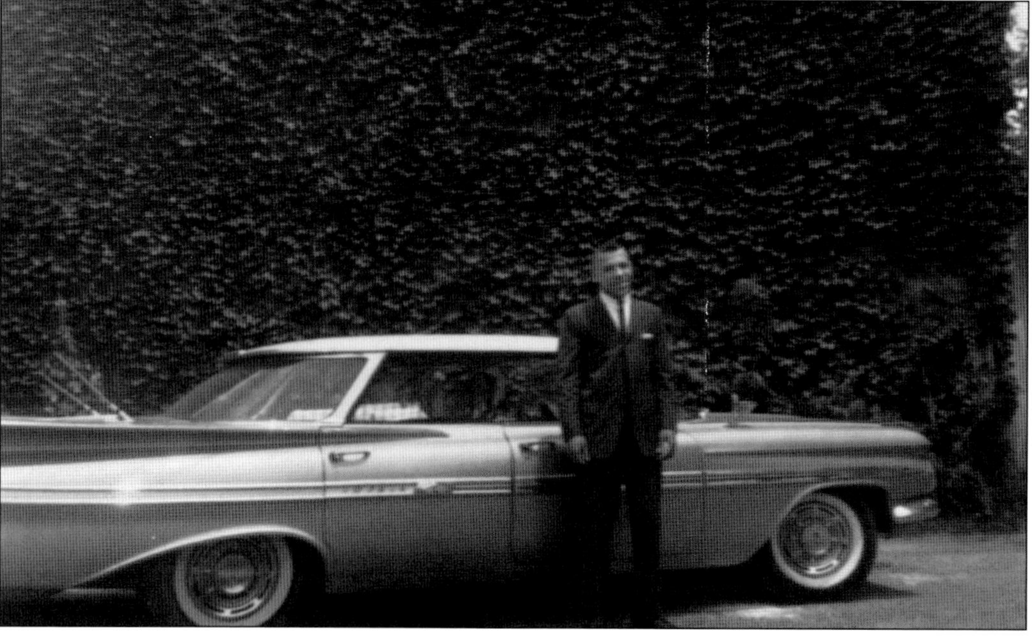

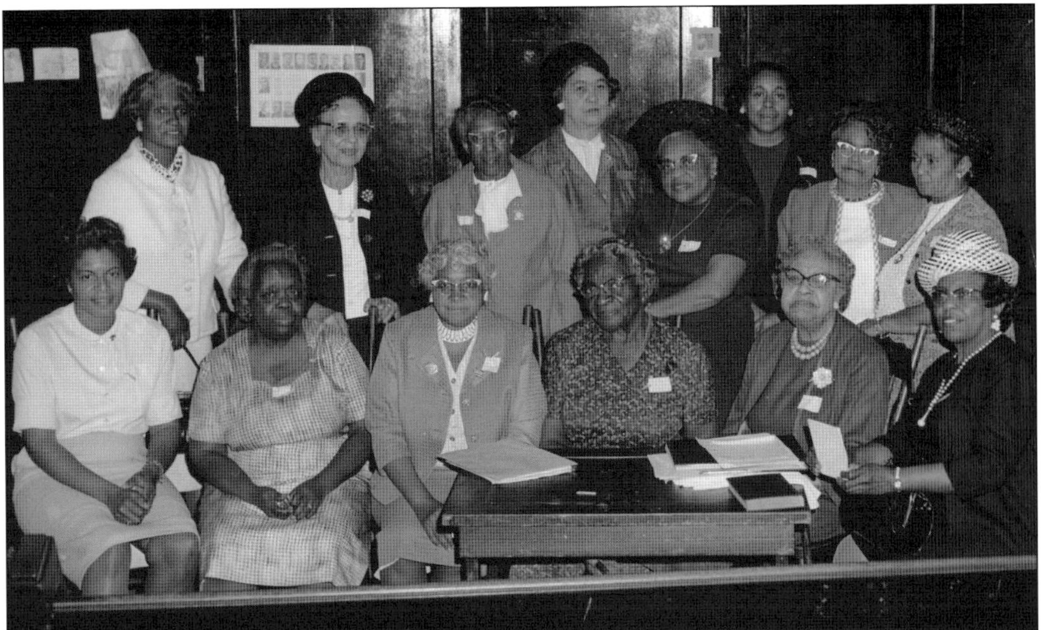

This is a group of ladies at St. James AME Church. It is not known what the occasion is, who the women are, nor even what the organization was. This photograph is one reason why it is so important to preserve what is known about Black history in Boyle County.

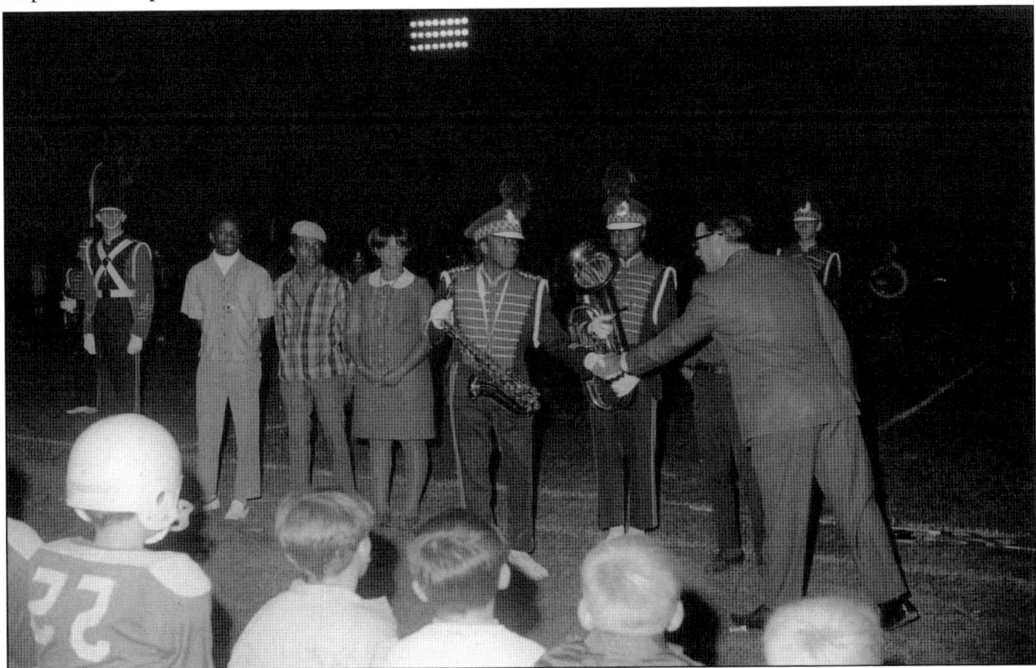

The winner of Louisville television station WHAS's "Crusade For Children" for 1968 was Meadowlark and the Mystics of Danville. From left to right are unidentified, Michael Hughes, Ben Kinley, Deborah Kay (McCowan) Stevenson, James Simpson (in uniform), Charles Chenault (in uniform), and Danville school superintendent James Purdom. Tommy Coates was also a member of the combo.

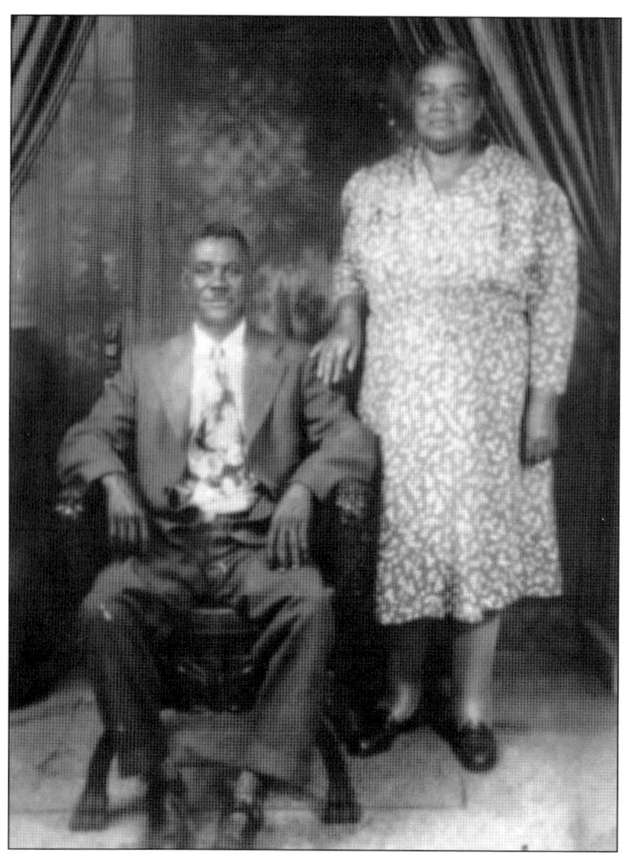

James Walker and Emma Eliza (Jones) Bright, who lived in Danville from 1889 to 1957, are pictured around 1935. He was the brother of mortician Joseph Sampson Bright, one of two Black morticians in Danville. He was born in Lincoln County on February 2, 1886, died in Danville on January 2, 1938, and married Emma Eliza Jones (1889–1957) on April 27, 1909. (Mary Bright-Jewell.)

James "Burrhead" Owsley, the son of Frank and Edna (Patton) Owsley, was born in Lincoln County in 1936 and died in 2010. He was known for his "Jimmy Church Band" on weekends, his gardening, and the fried chicken his wife, Shirley (Logan) Owsley, served at the Club Ponderosa.

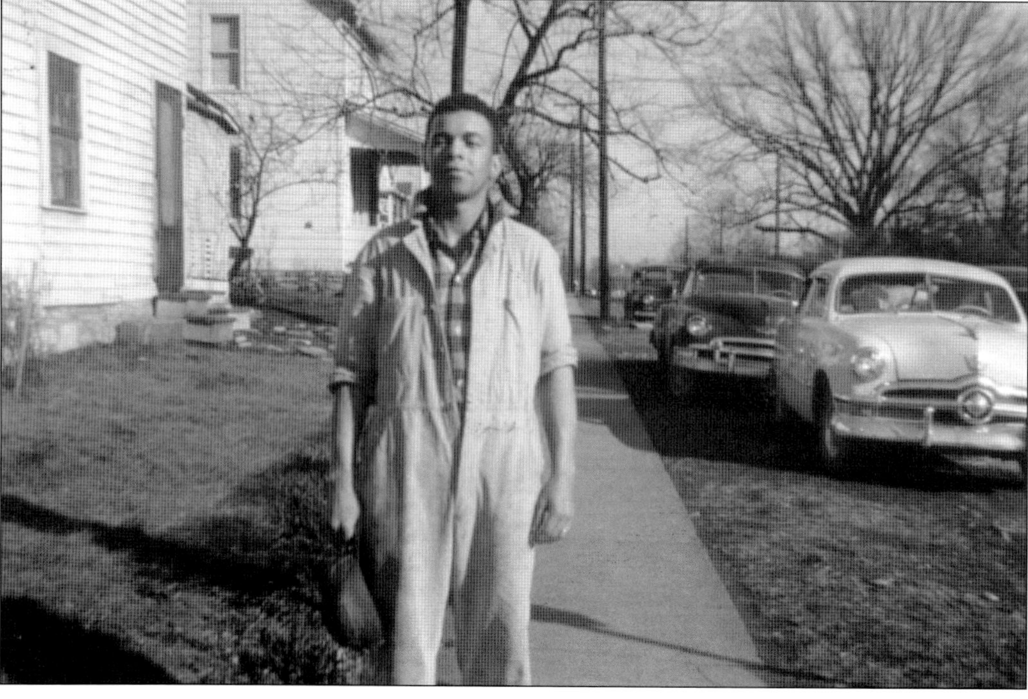

Written on the back of this real-photo postcard is "To Theora from Charles." It was in the Theora Coates collection, so it is assumed that "Charles" was a friend of hers. William Rensler's photography studio at 527 Central Avenue is mentioned in the Cincinnati newspapers many times from 1936, when he opened the studio at that address, to his death in 1946. Rensler originated the real-photo postcard many years before.

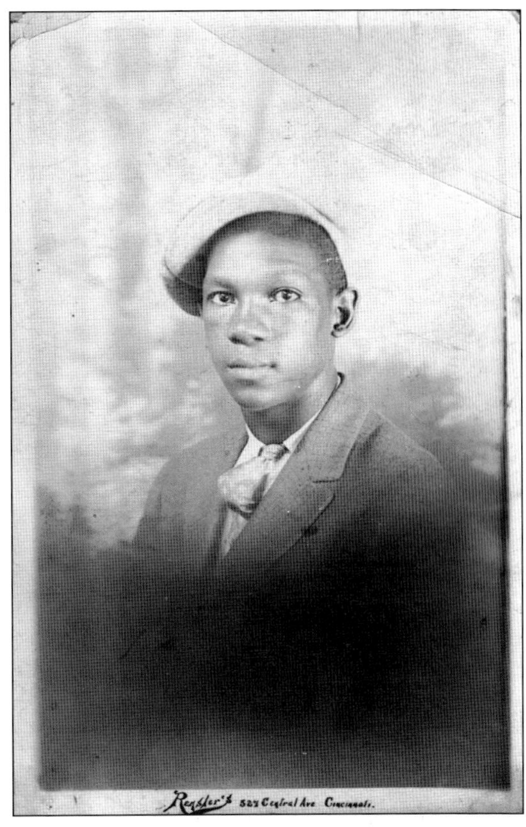

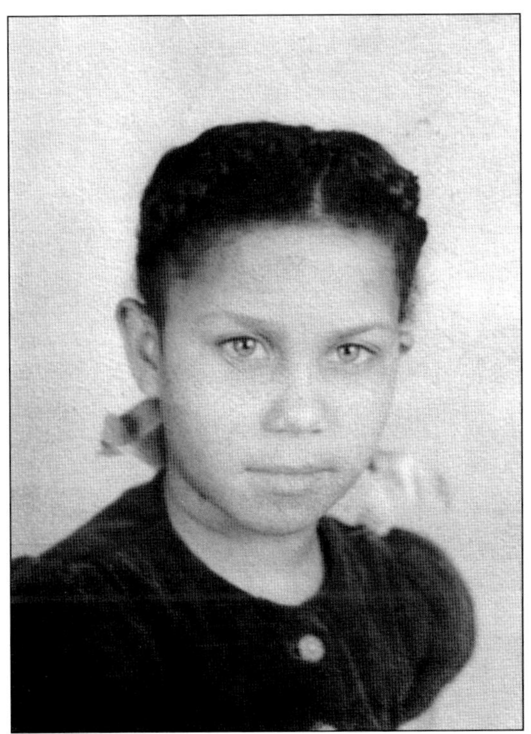

Mary Odell(e) (Bradshaw) Pittman was born in Boyle County on February 15, 1939, the fourth child and third daughter of Herman and Sadie (1910–1974) Bradshaw. Herman was born in Mercer County between 1906 and 1910 and died in 1960. In 1968, she married William Harrison Pittman Jr. (1935–1997), a chef at Springs Inn, a landmark in Lexington, Kentucky.

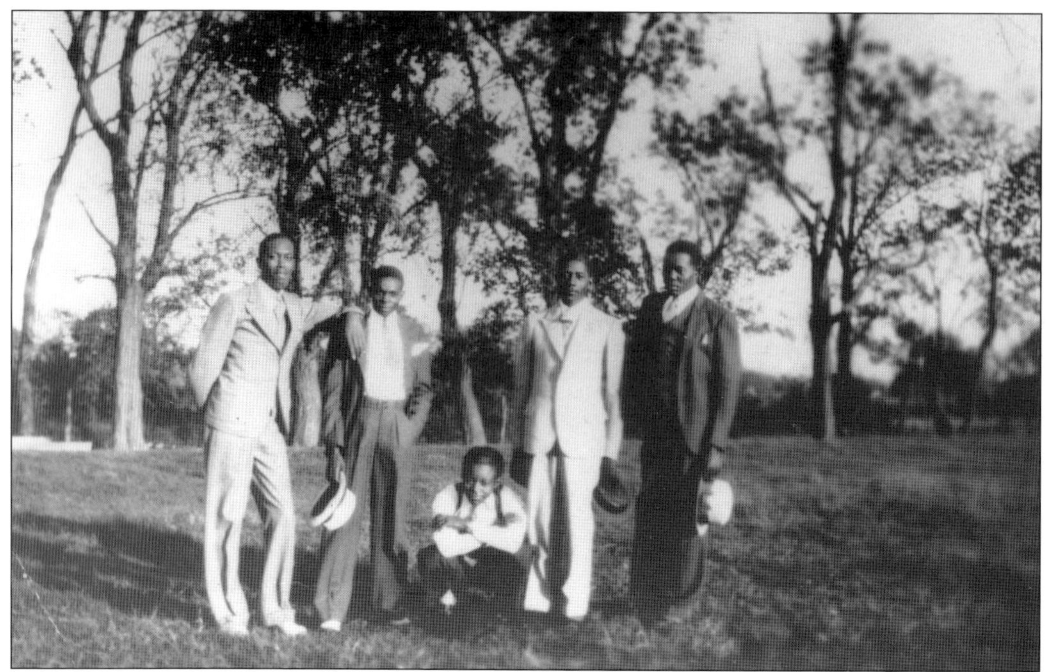

Second from the left, all dressed up in Wilsonville, is Felbert (or Filbert) Logan Marshall (1904–1984), son of John Henry and Florence (Hughes) Marshall and brother of Ella Mae Marshall. Like his father, he was a retired railroad employee. He married Mary Eliza McKitric, who survived him. The others in the picture are unidentified.

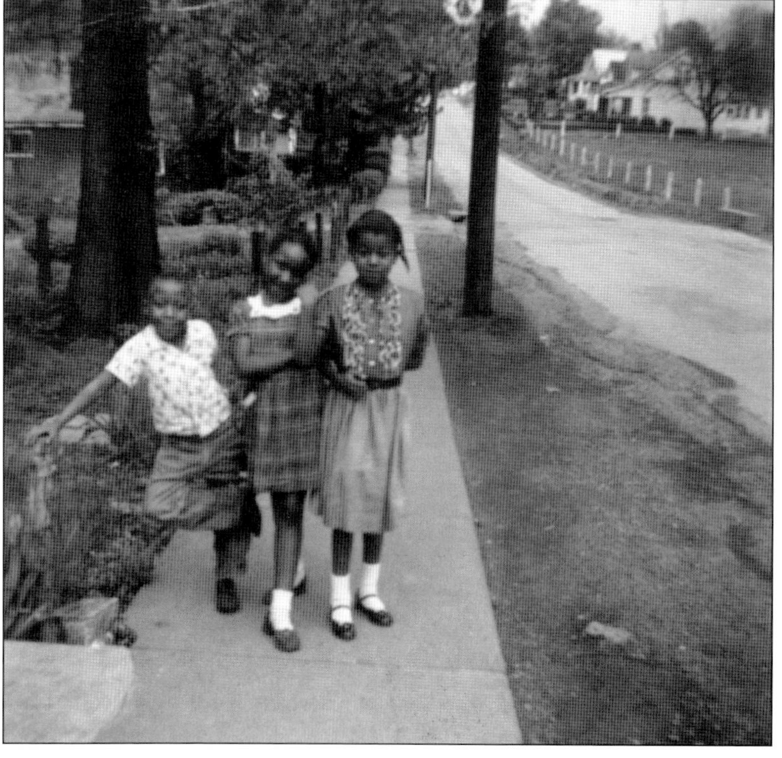

On Green Street (now MLK Jr. Boulevard) are Paul D. Lewis, Amelia (Lewis) Ball, and Betty L. (Caldwell) White in about 1961–1962. Paul Lewis was born in 1952 and married Gloria Raines. Amelia Lewis was born in 1949, and married ? Ball; The Lewises were children of Jeannette Lewis. Betty Caldwell was born in 1949, daughter of Rose M. Caldwell, and married the late Howard Chris White of Detroit, Michigan.

About the Danville Boyle County African American Historical Society, Inc.

The Danville Boyle County African American Historical Society Inc. is one of only a very few African American historical societies in Kentucky, having been organized in December 2013. The society has produced the award-winning Soul of Second Street Festival for several years, temporarily paused due to COVID-19. The first festival attracted thousands of guests from all over the eastern United States—many from Boyle County, but others with roots in Boyle County now living elsewhere.

During the COVID-19 pandemic, the DBCAAHS actually opened a public history center. In 2021, the society was the focus of a Kentucky Historical Society video on the topic of "Legacy." Since 2013, the DBCAAHS and its members have collected memorabilia, artifacts, family stories, and other items reflective of Black history in the county. Members have researched family genealogies, pored over tens of thousands of newspaper articles, and collected over 5,000 photographs.

Its library of Kentucky and African American history is growing almost daily, and many groups, ranging from elementary school children to high school age, have visited the history center.

Classes from Centre College have visited and learned about the deep, rich Black heritage of the city in which they attend college, and a strong working relationship is being created with Centre, in part to make up for past injustices.

The DBCAAHS has obviously had great support from all segments of the Boyle County community, and as the organization moves into the future, many more stories and much more history will come to light to be shared with everyone in the region.

Consistent with our mission to preserve history on a local level, this book was printed in South Carolina on American-made paper and manufactured entirely in the United States. Products carrying the accredited Forest Stewardship Council (FSC) label are printed on 100 percent FSC-certified paper.

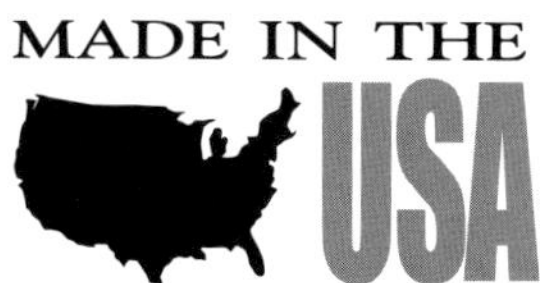